D1120355

Progressivism
and the
New Democracy

A Volume in the Series

Political Development of the American Nation:
Studies in Politics and History

Edited by   Sidney M. Milkis and
Jerome M. Mileur

Progressivism and the New Democracy

Edited by
Sidney M. Milkis
and
Jerome M. Mileur

University of Massachusetts Press
Amherst

Copyright © 1999 by
The University of Massachusetts Press
All rights reserved
Printed in the United States of America
LC 99-19459
ISBN 1-55849-192-9 (cloth); 193-7 (pbk.)
Designed by Dennis Anderson
Set in Galliard
Printed and bound by BookCrafters, Inc.

Library of Congress Cataloging-in-Publication Data
Progressivism and the new democracy / edited by Sidney M. Milkis and
   Jerome M. Mileur.
        p.   cm. — (Political development of the American nation)
     Includes bibliographical references.
      ISBN 1-55849-192-9 (alk. paper). —
   ISBN 1-55849-193-7 (pbk. : alk. paper)
      1. United States — Politics and government — 1901–1909.   2. United
   States — Politics and government — 1909–1913.   3. United States —
   Politics and government — 1913–1921.   4. Progressivism (United
   States politics)   5. Democracy — United States — History — 20th
   century.   I. Milkis, Sidney M.   II. Mileur, Jerome M.   III. Series.
   E756.P77   1999
   320.973'09'041 — dc21   99-19459
                                                                     CIP

British Library Cataloguing in Publication data are available.

Contents

Progressivism and the New Democracy

Introduction

Progressivism, Then and Now

Sidney M. Milkis

This volume takes as its task a reexamination of the Progressive Era and the progressive tradition in American political history.[1] Just as the Progressive Era brought profound changes to the country's ideas, institutions, and policies during the first two decades of the twentieth century, so it gave rise to a progressive tradition that has had an enduring influence on politics and government in the United States.

As the chapters of this volume make clear, interest in the meaning and legacy of progressivism has intensified as we have approached a new century. Indeed, progressivism is not only of interest to scholars but also to prominent journalists and political activists. In a recent spate of books and articles, both liberals and conservatives — and even some who call themselves "Progressives" — have invoked progressive ideas in setting forth principles and programs to guide the United States into the twenty-first century.[2] The contemporary interest in the Progressive Era signifies its profoundly important legacy for American political life. Just as surely, the different interpretations that these inquiries offer about progressivism reveal the rich possibilities and competing programs that animated the reformism of this critical period in American political history. Born at the turn of the twentieth century, the Progressive Era has widely come to be viewed as a historical period that can teach us something important about ourselves and the possibilities of our own political time.

This volume seeks a better understanding of the Progressive Era and its legacy for contemporary political developments with attention to three major lines of inquiry. We ask how the challenges of our own political time resemble those of a century ago. We consider whether the Progressive Era gave rise to a regime that shapes contemporary politics and government in the United States. And we consider whether there are roads that were not traveled during the Progressive Era that might now be revisited beneficially as we search for solutions to the most pressing challenges of late twentieth-century America.

Progressivism and Realignment

First, most obviously, we ask whether there are parallels between the turn of the twentieth century and our time, as we move toward the twenty-first century. The essays in this volume consider whether the similarities go deeper than simple chronology. Just as the end of the nineteenth century marked a profound transformation of American political life, so too a seismic shift—economic and political—is occurring in the twilight years of the twentieth century. To be sure, the desultory 1996 presidential election between Bill Clinton and Robert Dole hardly brought to mind the dramatic contest between William McKinley and the Great Commoner, William Jennings Bryan, a century earlier. But the profound changes in the political economy, the public's yearning for a different kind of politics, and the fundamental differences that divide Democrats and Republicans on the role of government in the economy and society present us with momentous choices similar to those at the end of the nineteenth century.

In truth, we are likely to miss the unsettled character of things in American political life if we focus obsessively on particular elections and parties. Samuel Huntington is correct to characterize the Progressive Era as a realigning era, even though it did not result in a full-scale partisan transformation.[3] Arguably, as Eldon Eisenach's essay suggests, the so-called critical election of 1896 did not consolidate the Republican party's hold on the electorate and government but rather marked the beginning of a major historical change in representation that "emancipated" American politics and government from political parties and the traditional pattern of realignments they produced. The study of partisan realignments has made an unquestionable contribution to our understanding of the rhythms of political history in the United States. At the same time, it has deflected attention from long-term secular changes that have weakened the influence of parties in the electorate and rendered the concept of partisan realignment far less relevant to contemporary political developments.[4]

From this broader perspective, the 1912 election was more critical than the 1896 contest in sanctioning the major transformation of the ideas, institutions, and policies that shaped political life in the United States at the turn of the century. "In several respects, the election of 1912 was the first modern presidential contest in American history," Arthur Link and Richard McCormick argue. "The use of direct primaries, the challenge to traditional party loyalties, the candidates' issue orientation, and the prevalence of interest-group political activists all make the election of 1912 look more like that of 1980 than 1896."[5] Four political parties presented presidential candidates in 1912: the Socialists named Eugene Debs, the labor leader from Indiana; the Republicans offered William Howard Taft, the incumbent president; the Democrats nominated Woodrow Wilson, the governor of New Jersey; and the Progressives selected former president Theodore Roosevelt. As Francis L. Broderick observes, all four candidates recognized that fundamental changes were occurring in the American political system, and each attempted to "answer . . . the questions raised by the new industrial order that had grown up within the American constitutional system."[6]

The Progressive Party campaign of that year, especially, was a barometer of fundamental changes taking place in American politics. With the popular former president — indeed the most recognized statesman of his era — Theodore Roosevelt, as its standard bearer, the Progressive Party advanced the political fortunes of the new social movements and of candidate-centered campaigns, and thus went far to legitimate the plebiscitary form of governance that has evolved over the course of the twentieth century and appears, for better or worse, to have come into its own in recent elections.

Considering how the 1912 election advanced a shift from localized party politics to mass democracy suggests how a study of the Progressive Era helps us probe the deep historical roots of contemporary developments in the United States. Equally significant, this transformation occurred amid a great contest of opinion about the future direction of the country. As the important Progressive thinker and editor, Herbert Croly, wrote in the wake of the 1912 election, "the really salutary aspect of the present situation is the awakening of American public opinion to the necessity of scrutinizing the national ideal and of working over the guiding principles of its associated life. The American democracy is becoming aroused to take a searching look at its own meaning and responsibilities."[7]

So contemporary politics, for all its inertial tendencies, has the feel of everything being up for grabs. The recent struggles over the Clinton administration's health care plan and the Republican Party's program to reform welfare entitlements went deeper than the petty, mean-spirited quarrels portrayed by the mass media. Indeed, the conflicts were so raw and disruptive precisely because they mattered so much, because they were symptoms of our own search for the meaning and responsibilities of "the American Democracy."

As was the case during the Progressive Era, this search reflects not merely a conflict over principles and policies but also a widespread concern that public debate and the resolution of public questions have become disassociated from the American people, that a crisis of citizenship is at hand. As Alonzo Hamby says in his essay, "Above all, progressives saw themselves as fighters for democracy ('the people') locked in combat with 'the interests' (primarily concentrated corporate and financial power), as crusaders with a moral mission, and as battlers for social justice in relations between the classes." Most sought to rescue American politics from special business interests who appeared to control and corrupt elections and government for their own profit.

The country's present discontents are also partly a response to major changes in the political economy and the unsavory role that money appears to have in elections and government. The controversy over how presidential campaigns were financed during the 1996 election shows that most voters at least sense, Wilson Carey McWilliams observes, that "mass politics, while democratic in form, is more and more oligarchic in content."[8] But as was the case during the Progressive Era, the current corruption of the electoral process has often been attributed to deeper symptoms, to an atomistic individualism — the perversion of America's rights-based culture — that scorns the most limited standards of public life.[9]

In their disdain for America's narcissism, contemporary critics reveal an affinity for early twentieth-century reformers.[10] Theodore Roosevelt, who more than any other single leader embodied the progressive cause, excoriated the "malefactors of great wealth." Even more, he challenged the country to temper its celebration of rights with a proper sense of responsibility. "We can just as little afford to follow the doctrinaires of an extreme individualism as the doctrinaires of an extreme socialism," he declared in a 1910 address. "Individual initiative, so far from being discouraged, should be stimulated; and yet we should remember that, as society develops and grows more complex, we continually find that things which once it was desirable to leave to individual initiative can, under the changed conditions, be performed with better results by common effort."[11]

The current search for order frequently has sought inspiration from TR's quest for a common sense of destiny in the country. To be sure, as one commentator offers, "ours is not an era in which Roosevelt would have felt at home, with its gentle focus-group politics, its rituals of self-exposure, and its soft gender-gap issues."[12] Nevertheless, Roosevelt's unabashed nationalism still resonates with public intellectuals and political leaders who decry contemporary rights-based politics. This yearning for national community has transcended partisanship. While the liberal pundit Michael Lind criticizes multiculturalists for degrading the progressive commitment to a nationalism that transcends sectional or personal advantage, the conservative journalist David Brooks derides Republicans for playing to narrow self-interest and to the instinctive desire of the American people to get government off their backs. This is a shallow conservatism, Brooks scolds, that abandons TR's "nationalist impulse and with it the mystic chords of national memory that play in people's hearts."[13]

Progressives sought to sustain a sense of national identity in the face of the profound changes brought by the rise of the corporation and the expansion of immigration. Committed to strengthening the national government to prepare the country to address the growing complexity and diversity of political life in the United States, progressives faced the daunting challenge of allying democracy and centralized administrative power. In one sense, this was a novel problem, though it was surely a task inherent in the nature of the American political system. As Martha Derthick and John Dinan tell us, the Progressive Era is of interest because its political thinkers and statesmen "grappled with the central question of the American political experiment: whether it is possible to realize self-government on a grand scale."

The essays of this volume make clear that the political dilemmas of the late twentieth century demand no less from its political leaders and thinkers. Just as contemporary intellectuals and statesmen identify the challenges posed by the rise of the global economy and the demands of multiculturalism to sustaining a common national destiny, so they must explore the deep philosophical and historical dimensions of these tasks. Like TR, contemporary statesmen and thinkers must have the wit and wisdom to speak persuasively about a national destiny, to pull the chatter of an estranged and self-absorbed public in the direction of civic dialogue. In the final analysis, the cultivation of *public* philosophy is the principal ingredient of a political realignment.

Progressivism as a Regime

A second concern of this volume is how progressive democracy relates to our own soul searching. As many authors indicate, the Progressive era is relevant not simply as an episode of fundamental reform, but also as a period that brought secular changes that are still with us, indeed, that shape contemporary politics and government in the United States.

Progressivism as it emerged during the first two decades of the twentieth century had three major objectives, which, although not fully realized, went far enough to initiate such a major restructuring of American politics. Most significant, Progressives sought to dissolve the concentration of wealth, specifically the power of giant trusts, which, according to reformers, constituted uncontrolled and irresponsible units of power in American society. These industrial combinations created the perception that opportunity had become less equal in the United States and that growing corporate power threatened the freedom of individuals to earn a living. This threat, in turn, focused attention on the decentralized polity of the nineteenth century, as reformers came to believe that the great business interests, represented by newly formed associations such as the National Civic Federation, had captured and corrupted state legislatures and local officials for their own profit. Party leaders — Democrats and Republicans alike — were viewed as irresponsible "bosses" who did the bidding of these "special interests."

In addition, progressives sought to close the space between the cup of power and the lips of the people, championing government *of* the People directly *by* the People. Indeed, in their attack on intermediary associations such as political parties and interest groups, reformers in the early twentieth century issued a battle cry that enlisted popular support not only for woman's suffrage and direct election of senators, but also for methods of "pure democracy"—direct primaries, as well as direct initiative, referendum, and recall. To be sure, progressives did want to strengthen certain social institutions that might buttress the new form of politics they championed. In defending institutions such as labor unions, moral and political reform movements, settlement houses, and universities, progressive reformers envisioned a new form of citizenship that would be practiced outside of localized parties and that might circumvent the constraints of limited constitutional government. But these "parastates," as Eisenach calls them, represented in thought and practice institutions that were expected to prepare individual men and women to have a direct effect on government. Combined with the advent of new forms of political communication, such as independent magazines and newspapers, Croly argued, these institutions would enable "the mass of people to assume some immediate control of their political destinies."[14]

Especially controversial was the Progressive program to subject constitutional questions to direct popular control, including proposals for an easier method to amend the Constitution and referenda on laws that the state courts declared unconstitutional. This commitment to direct democracy became the centerpiece of the Progressive Party's campaign, which was sanctified as a "covenant with the people," as a deep and abiding pledge to make the people the "masters of their constitution." Like the Populist Party of the late nineteenth century, the Progressives invoked the Preamble of the Constitution to assert their purpose as making effective "We the People," but unlike the Populists, they sought to do this by strengthening the federal government's authority to regulate the society and economy and by hitching the will of the people to this new national administrative power. The Populists were animated by a radical agrarianism that celebrated the Jeffersonian and Jacksonian assault on monopolistic power. The Populist concept of national democracy rested on the hope of arousing the States and the Congress for an assault on the centralizing, unholy alliance between the national parties and the trusts. In contrast, TR and the Progressive Party championed national administration — a "new nationalism" that could not abide the localized democracy of the nineteenth century. For Progressives, public opinion would reach fulfillment with the formation of an independent executive power, freed from the provincial, special, and corrupt influence of political parties and commercial interests.

In condemning reformers for lacking a coherent set of principles, contemporary scholars point to the apparent contradiction between the Progressives' celebration of direct democracy and their hope to achieve more disinterested government, which seemed to demand a powerful and independent national bureaucracy.[15] In truth, the progressive faith in public opinion was far from complete. As Eileen McDonagh's chapter shows, most progressives celebrated an idea of national community that did not include immigrants and African Americans. Moreover, the Progressive commitment to forming an independent executive led to support for technical expertise that insulated government decisions from the vagaries of public opinion and elections.[16]

Without denying that Progressivism was weakened by a tension between reforms that diminished democracy and those that sought to make democracy more direct, its central thrust was an attack on political parties and the creation of a more direct, programmatic link between government and the people. Progressives argued, not without reason, that the expansion of social welfare provisions and "pure democracy" were inextricably linked. Reforms such as the direct primary, as well as the initiative and referendum, were designed to overthrow the localized two-party system in the United States, built on Jeffersonian and Jacksonian principles, which bestowed on the separated institutions of the federal government a certain unity of control while at the same time it restrained programmatic ambition and prevented the development of a stable and energetic administration of social policy. By the same token, the triumph of "progressive" over "pioneer" democracy, as Croly frames it, would put the American people directly in touch with the councils of power, thus strengthening the demand for government support and allowing, indeed requiring, administrative agencies to play their proper role in implementing progressive social welfare policy.

The realization of progressive social welfare policy was the final objective of progressive reform. In the view of Progressives, as TR said in a 1912 New Orleans speech, direct democracy reforms and social justice went hand in hand. "The object must be the same everywhere," he declared, "that is, to give the people real control . . . in a spirit of the broadest sympathy and broadest desire to secure social and industrial justice for every man and woman, so that the lives of all of us may be lived . . . under conditions which will tend to increase the dignity, the worth, and the efficiency of the individual."[17]

With the assistance of social reformers like Jane Addams and Charles McCarthy, Roosevelt made these commitments a principal part of the Progressive Party's platform. Anticipating the New Deal of his distant cousin Franklin, TR added a critical sentence to the platform that dedicated the party to "[t]he protection of home life against the hazards of sickness, irregular employment and old age through a system of social insurance adopted to American use." This commitment to social security was dramatized in TR's famous Confession of Faith speech at the Progressive Party convention, in which he argued that "it was abnormal for any industry to throw back upon the community the human wreckage due to its wear and tear, and the hazards of sickness, accident, invalidism, involuntary unemployment, and old age should be provided for through insurance."[18]

TR and the Progressive party thus played a critical part in transforming the American concept of charity into a public obligation, the seedbed of the contemporary concept of entitlement. Abraham Lincoln had spoken of the government's affirmative responsibility "to afford all, an unfettered start, and a fair chance, in the race of life."[19] Progressives extended this idea of public responsibility to one where the government, in certain circumstances, was viewed as the guarantor of economic security. As TR wrote the Colorado progressive Benjamin Lindsey with regard to the mothers' pension program, the precursor to the New Deal's Aid to Families with Dependent Children: "This law represents aid given not as charity but as a right, as justice due mothers whose work in rearing their children is a work for the State as much as that of the soldier who gives his services on the battlefield. It is the recognition, for the first time, that the State must make itself responsible for the plight of the mother who through no fault of her own is left unable without assistance to provide for the children she has borne."[20]

These three elements of the Progressive movement — a concern with the power of business, a commitment to "pure democracy," and the dedication to new rights as a bulwark against the uncertainties and injustices of the marketplace — advanced a new understanding of the rela-

tionship between the individual and the government. A century later
these progressive commitments remain both a source of inspiration and
a target: contemporary liberals, centrists, and conservatives view them as
representing the "established regime." Calling for a revival of "liberal
nationalism" in the face of conservatives' devotion to property rights and
the Left's infatuation with entitlements, Lind beholds a revitalization of
the central government as the guarantor of economic opportunity and
political equality.[21] Similarly, E. J. Dionne, a columnist for the *Washington Post*, finds solace in the "radical" assault on the welfare state that
followed from the 1994 elections and their aftermath, in which the
Republicans assumed control of both houses of Congress for the first
time since 1954. "The Republican attack on Progressivism," he predicted, "will lead to its revival by forcing its advocates to an open defense
of first principles and to a modernization of their program."[22]

In contrast to the hopes of Lind and Dionne for the renewal of collectivism, self-styled "New Democrats," or, as they sometimes call themselves, "New Progressives," argue that liberal nationalism, though enormously successful in its time, offers false hope for the future. The cause of
new democracy is rooted in the rediscovery of "liberalism's lost tradition," the New Freedom of Woodrow Wilson and Louis Brandeis, that
emphasized democratic participation over statism. Invoking what they
take to be the New Freedom's commitment to the dignity of the democratic individual, New Democrats such as Will Marshall and Fred Siegel
call on us to embrace the obligations of citizenship.[23] Contemporary
progressives, they argue, should be defending compulsory national service and public work projects rather than entitlements. "The old welfare
system always slighted the fact that citizens have a duty and a right to
contribute to national life," Carey McWilliams writes, "and defending
that moral imperative" could realize some of the unfulfilled promise of
progressivism.[24]

Whereas contemporary progressives look to reform traditions of the
early part of the century for guidance in meeting the political demands of
the new fin de siècle, modern conservatives return to the dawn of the
progressive era to expose the original sin of twentieth-century politics
and government. Although often respectful of the New Democrats' dedication to individual responsibility, conservatives view their dalliance
with the New Freedom strand of progressivism as a sign of irresolution,

as the false hope that liberalism can be saved by resorting to non-bureaucratic and decentralized forms of government activism. Just as the New Nationalists prevailed over their more circumspect brethren, conservatives warn, so New Democrats will be dominated by more orthodox liberals who offer more tangible forms of succor to a citizenry that has grown all too dependent on the bounties of the progressive state. Conservative hopes rest in a more radical rejection of progressivism, one that promises to dismantle, rather than "reinvent," the liberal state. Only then, conservatives claim, can a new civic life be built that will rededicate the country to individual responsibility and self-government.[25]

Thus, while liberals hope to renew this reform progressivism, and moderate activists, such as the self-styled "New Democrats" of the Democratic Leadership Council, want to correct its deficiencies, conservatives seek to remove progressive institutions and politics from the political landscape root and branch. And yet each ideological camp appears to operate in a political milieu shaped by America's restructuring at the turn of the century.

The pervasive influence of progressivism on contemporary politics and government cries out for a reconsideration of the underlying principles that gave rise to it. Scholars such as Bruce Ackerman and, more recently, Walter Dean Burnham talk of important episodes in our history, such as the Civil War and the New Deal, as "constitutional moments" — as surrogate constitutional conventions — when first principles and attendant governing arrangements are redefined.[26] The authors of this volume disagree about whether the Progressive Era was such a constitutional episode; yet all acknowledge that something very important was taking place during the first two decades of the twentieth century. Indeed, the essays of Alonzo Hamby, Martha Derthick and John Dinan, Morton Keller, and Eileen McDonagh suggest that the New Deal might best be understood within the stream of progressivism, as a movement that consolidated fundamental changes that have their origin in the Progressive Era.

The constitutional legacy of the Progressive Era, I would argue, was determined in important ways by the Progressive Party campaign; indeed, the robust debate it aroused about the future course of constitutional government is what defines the 1912 election as a critical episode in American political development. The Progressive program seemed to challenge the very foundation of republican democracy: the idea under-lying the U.S. Constitution that space created by institutional devices such as the separation of powers and federalism allowed representatives to govern competently and fairly. Likewise, the Progressive vision of de-mocracy rejected party politics, at least as they had traditionally worked in the United States. Forged on the anvil of Jeffersonian principles, political parties in the United States were welded to constitutional prin-ciples that impeded the expansion of national administrative power in the name of the people's economic welfare. The origins and organizing principles of the American party system established it as a force against the creation of the "modern state." The Progressive reformers' commit-ment to building such a state — that is, to the creation of a national political power with expansive programmatic responsibilities — meant that the party system either had to be weakened or reconstructed. As Barry Karl notes, the Progressive campaign of 1912 "was as much an attack on the whole concept of political parties as it was an effort to create a single party whose doctrinal clarity and moral purity would represent the true interest of the nation as a whole."[27]

The Progressive Party's vision of democracy, which TR made the centerpiece of his reform program, created a campaign, George Mowry writes, that "was one of the most radical ever made by a major American political figure."[28] Not surprisingly, this campaign aroused strong op-position. Standpat Republicans and large industrial interests who long had appreciated TR's disdain for radical economic and political remedies rapidly abandoned the former president.[29] But the opposition to "pure democracy" went far beyond the embattled "standpatters" of the Repub-lican Party. TR's challenge to representative institutions also led moder-ate progressives, such as Taft, Elihu Root, and Henry Cabot Lodge, to fashion a new understanding of Republican conservatism, one rooted less in a militant defense of property rights and business, one that harked back to the Whig's defense of ordered liberty.

During the 1912 campaign, the burden of this fight fell most heavily on Taft. The incumbent president had supported the pragmatic progres-sive program TR had pursued while in office when he cooperated with Republican Party regulars to pass specific policies such as the Hepburn Act. Now Taft found his efforts to carry on that pragmatic tradition of reform the object of scorn and derision, the target of TR's celebration of "pure democracy." "The initiative, the referendum, and the recall, together with a complete adoption of the direct primary as a means of selecting nominees and an entire destruction of the convention system are now all made the sine qua non of a real reformer," Taft lamented. "Everyone who hesitates to follow all of these or any of them is regarded with suspicion and is denounced as an enemy of popular government and of the people."[30]

Yet, this very "hesitation" enabled Taft to find honor in the charge of conservatism leveled against him. Taft could now "stand pat" in defense of the Constitution and argue that the Progressive idea of democracy would destroy it.

> With the effort to make the selection of candidates, the enactment of legislation, and the decision of the courts to depend on the momentary passions of the people necessarily indifferently informed as to the issues presented, and without the opportunity to them for time and study and that deliberation that gives security and common sense to the government of the people, such extremists would hurry us into a condition which would find no parallel except in the French revolution, or in that bubbling anarchy that once characterized the South American Republics [the president warned his fellow Republicans at a Lincoln Day celebration in 1912]. Such extremists are not progressives—they are political emotionalists or neurotics—who have lost that sense of proportion, that clear and candid consideration of their own weakness as a whole, and that clear perception of the necessity for checks upon hasty popular action which made our people who fought the Revolution and who drafted the Federal Constitution, the greatest self-governing people the world ever knew.

Support for "pure democracy," Taft charged, tended to encourage the very same "factional spirit" that Madison warned against in his famous discussion of republican government in *Federalist* 10, an unruly majority that would "sacrifice to its ruling passion or interest both the public good and the rights of other citizens."[31]

In resisting this temptation to flatter the whims and passions of the majority, the most sacred duty of true conservatives was to uphold the courts. As Taft told an audience in Boston, Massachusetts, TR's defense of direct democracy "sent a thrill of alarm through all the members of the community who understood our constitutional principles and who feared the effect of the proposed changes upon the permanence of government."[32] It was unthinkable to the great majority of leaders in Congress and the states, and to the great mass of people as well, Taft argued, that Roosevelt should seriously propose to have a plebiscite upon questions involving the construction of the Constitution. TR's audacity drew most clearly the fundamental issue that divided Republicans and Progressives:

> The Republican party . . . , respecting as it does the constitution . . . , the care with which the judicial clauses of that fundamental instrument were drawn to secure the independence of the judiciary, will never consent to an abatement of that independence to the slightest degree, and will stand with its face like flint against any constitutional changes in it to take away from the high priests upon which to administer to justice the independence that they must enjoy of influence of powerful individuals or of powerful majorities.[33]

In response to such criticisms, Progressives insisted that the political reforms championed by the new party's platform were not a radical rejection of the American constitutional tradition, but an effort to restore it. State and local machines, they argued, had perverted the original design of the Constitution, which was dedicated to the emancipation of the American people from provincial and special interests, embodied by the Articles of Confederation. Whereas the Articles of Confederation read "We the undersigned delegates of the States," the Preamble to the Constitution of 1787 was declared by "We the People." The change to "We the People," claimed Theodore Gilman at a Progressive Party rally in Yonkers, New York, "was made at the Federal Convention with the full understanding of the meaning and effect of the new form of words," signifying that the new Constitution represented the aspirations of one sovereign people to create a "more perfect union."[34] Political parties had preempted this original design, shifting power to states and localities in the service of "local self-government." Jeffersonian and Jacksonian reforms were necessary in the nineteenth century to thwart the "aristocratic" pretensions of the Federalists, but the problems thrown up by the industrial revolution demanded that progressives revisit the potential for national democracy in the original constitution. As Croly put it, "the nationalism of Hamilton with all its aristocratic leaning, was more democratic, because more constructively social, than the indiscriminate individualism of Jefferson."[35] Just as the original theory of the electoral college had been abandoned after the "Revolution of 1800," closing the space between presidential politics and popular choice, so Gilman claimed, "the people now propose to come into closer touch with their representatives by the abolition of the machine, and the substitution thereafter of the direct primary, the initiative, referendum, and recall. This is all one logical and irresistible movement in one direction, having as its object the restoration of our form of government to its original purity and ideal perfection, as a government under the control of 'We, the people,' who formed it."[36]

Gilman's defense of progressivism against the charge of radicalism received indirect support from socialists, who were no less hostile to the progressive idea of democracy than were conservatives. Eugene Debs attacked the Progressive Party as "a reactionary protest of the middle classes, built largely upon the personality of one man and not destined for permanence."[37] The Progressives' transience stemmed not just from TR's notoriety, Debs argued, but also from the flimsy doctrine that underlay it. Although supportive of political reform, Debs had long considered devices such as the referendum a very small part of the Socialist Party program. "You will never be able, in my opinion, to organize any formidable movement upon [the referendum] or any other single issue," he wrote in 1898. "The battle is narrowing down to capitalism and socialism, and there can be no compromise or halfway ground. . . . Not until the workingman comprehends the trend of . . . economic development and is conscious of his class interests will he be fit to properly use the referendum, and when he has reached that point he will be a Socialist."[38]

Given his view of progressivism, Debs was chagrined that TR "stole the red flag of socialism" to symbolize his fight for the rule of the people. That Roosevelt selected the crimson bandanna handkerchief as the symbol for the Progressive Party did not make socialism, which he had long denounced as anarchy, respectable. Rather, this fight for the rule of the people deflected attention from the injustices of capitalism, Debs complained, which were truly the cause of the people's discontent.[39]

In truth, the Progressive Party's celebration of direct rule of the people was not reactionary; yet it beheld a program of reform that sought to preserve the dignity of the democratic individual. Emphasizing the candidate instead of the party, the Progressives deflected attention from class conflict. Seeking to build a welfare state within unified public opinion rather than through a social democratic party, it championed individual political action. The primary, referendum, and recall, after all, were devices that asked citizens to vote their individual consciences. Progressives were disdainful of collective organizations, such as the

Democratic and Republican Parties, formed on personal, family, or community attachments. Similarly, they found repugnant the idea of sectarian partisanship where "enlightened" voting decisions were submerged in class or racial conflicts.

To the extent that Progressive democracy was radical, it represented a sui generis American form of radicalism—one conceived to rescue American individualism from an emotive attachment to the Constitution, especially the designated "high priests" of the Constitution. "[I]t is difficult for Englishmen to understand the extreme conservatism of my proposition as to the referendum to the people of certain judicial questions," TR wrote to a friend abroad; "and this difficulty arises from the fact that in England no human being dreams of permitting the court to decide such questions! In England no court can declare any legislative act unconstitutional." In actuality, TR claimed, he sought to avoid the delegation of policy to an unchecked legislature that might truly embody the sort of factionalism that plagued France and England and had so worried the architects of the Constitution. Recognizing that factionalism was abetted by militant partisanship in government, he wrote: "I do not propose to make the legislature supreme over the court; I propose *merely* to allow the people . . . to decide whether to follow the legislature or the court."[40]

The Progressive Party's "compromise" with public opinion in the United States points to its legacy for American politics and government. The old saw of the historical literature on the Progressive Era is that the Progressive Party of 1912 was essentially a personal vehicle for Theodore Roosevelt, an organization relegated to serving his own political ambitions. TR's bolt from the Republican convention in 1912, the argument goes, was born of his party's rejection of his designs to return to power after a brief retirement from politics. Accordingly, the Progressive Party was not invested with a collective mission and organization that could survive his return to the fold in 1916. Arguably, the failure of the 1912 experiment and the Progressive Party's demise underscore the incoherence of the progressive movement.

Nevertheless, the Progressive Party advanced the fortunes of a movement of public opinion that affected the prestige and fortunes of all political leaders. It was neither the Democrats nor the Republicans (or Socialists) but the Progressives who set the tone of the 1912 campaign. Since 1912 its program of political and social reform has been an enduring feature of American political discourse and electoral struggle. The form of politics progressives championed involved more than a shift in partisan alignments; indeed, the ascendance of progressivism signaled a fundamental change in the concepts of representation and citizenship, as well as a redefinition of the social contract. Taking account of this reordering of the nation's constitution sheds light on progressivism's enduring and widespread legacy, on a transformation of the political landscape in the United States so pervasive that thereafter even many conservative office holders and activists would be tempted to practice politics according to the progressive idea of democracy.

The Progressive Era: Roads Not Traveled

Although the authors of this volume disagree about how much change actually occurred in the Progressive Era, they agree that it was a time of remarkable intellectual ferment, of incredibly rich debate about the future course of American constitutional democracy. This debate sheds light on roads not taken as well as those that were. In setting the tone of the 1912 election, the Progressive Party established a path of reform that obviated both conservatism and socialism. Similarly, the importance of TR's leadership in advancing progressive doctrine and practices tended to subordinate the movement's support for "grassroots" democracy to the plebiscitary schemes in the platform, such as the initiative, referendum, and recall, that exalted mass opinion. The need to explore these lost traditions of the Progressive Era represent the third important aspect of our inquiries into the link between the progressivism then and now.

Progressivism's Communal Tradition

The communal strain of progressivism, embodied in the New Freedom of Wilson and Brandeis, is identified by some contemporary reformers as a place worthy of reexamination. In the wake of the New Deal revolution, "New" Democrats lament, the New Freedom strain of progressivism has either been ignored or scorned as a conservatism masquerading as liberalism. The task of contemporary progressives, Marshall and Siegel of the Progressive Policy Institute argue, is to uncover the New Freedom's "radical" potential, revealing its dedication to reforms that would rely less on centralized administration and more on citizen and community initiative. Like the great Democratic reformers of the nineteenth century — the Jeffersonians and Jacksonians — New Freedom progressives defended local liberties and political participation; they appealed to the better angels of our nature, calling on us to embrace the obligations of citizenship, or as Marshall and Siegel put it, our "reciprocal responsibility" to society.[41]

As the essays by Derthick and Dinan, and Ethington, suggest, the communal strain of progressivism had strong support during the early part of the twentieth century. Indeed, the Progressive Party crusade was badly crippled by fundamental disagreements among its supporters over issues that betrayed an acute sensitivity, if not attachment, to the idea of local self-government. The party was deeply divided over civil rights, resulting in bitter struggles at the Progressive Party convention over delegate selection rules and the platform that turned on whether the party should confront the shame of Jim Crow. In the end, it did not, accepting instead the right of the states and localities to resolve the matter of race relations. Moreover, Progressive delegates waged an enervating struggle at the party convention over whether an interstate trade commission with considerable administrative discretion or militant antitrust policy was the appropriate method to tame the Trusts. New Nationalists, led by Roosevelt, prevailed, pledging the party to regulate, rather than attempt to dismantle, corporate power; however, this disagreement carried over to the general election. The Democratic Party, under the tutelage of their candidate for president, Wilson, and his advisor Brandeis, embraced an alternative version of progressivism, which prescribed antitrust measures and state regulations rather than the expansion of national administrative power.

The split between New Nationalism and New Freedom progressives threatened the modern state. As Croly acknowledged, the progressive program presupposed national standards and regulatory powers that "foreshadowed administrative aggrandizement." Yet, progressives could not agree on how administrative power should be used. Indeed, the conflict between New Nationalism and New Freedom progressives revealed that many reformers shared the profound uneasiness of their populist forbears about the very prospect of expanding national administrative power. This anxiety was not hastily contrived in reaction to the administrative ambitions of New Nationalism; rather, it was allied to a celebration of local self-government that was deeply rooted in American political culture. Wilson expressed reverence for provincial liberties in a series of lectures he delivered at Columbia University in 1907:

> Moral and social questions originally left to the several states for settlement can be drawn into the field of federal authority only at the expense of the self-dependence and efficiency of the several communities of which our complex body politic is made up. Paternal morals, morals enforced by judgement and choices of central authority at Washington, do not and cannot create vital moral habits or methods of life unless sustained by local opinion and purpose, local prejudice and convenience, — unless supported by local convenience and interest; and only communities capable of taking care of themselves will, taken together, constitute a nation capable of vital action and control.[42]

The reluctance of many progressive reformers to embrace centralized administration did not mean that they championed the localized democracy of the nineteenth century. The "complex republic," as James Madison called it, was shaped in the nineteenth century by party organizations and legal doctrines that formed a wall of separation between government and society. New Freedom progressives wanted to expand the responsibilities of the national government but hoped to find nonbureaucratic and noncentralized solutions for the ills that plagued the political economy. For them, reconciling government centralization and administrative decentralization involved, in part, building on measures such as the Sherman Act of 1890 that would rely on competition and law to curb the abuses of big business, rather than on administrative tribunals. Equally important, New Freedom progressives hoped to cultivate local forums of public discussion and debate that would "buttress the foundations of democracy." Wilson and Brandeis, for example, were active in the social centers movement that sought to make use of school buildings for neighborhood forums on the leading issues of the day. This movement, which began early in the twentieth century in cities like Rochester, New York, emerged as a national association by the eve of the 1912 election. Its ambition, as George M. Forbes, president of Rochester's Board of Education, announced at the National Conference on Civic and Social Center Development, was to form local institutions through which the people in the community could gain an understanding of civic obligation:

> [W]e are now intensely occupied in forging the tools of democracy, the direct primary, the initiative, the referendum, the recall, the short ballot,

commission government. But in our enthusiasm we do not seem to be aware that these tools will be worthless unless they are used by those who are aflame with the sense of brotherhood. If action of a democracy is to be but the resultant of a clash of selfish interests, it is hardly worth battling for. . . . The idea [of the social centers movement is] to establish in each community an institution having a direct and vital relation to the welfare of the neighborhood, ward, or district, and also to the city as a whole. . . . [This] means that our public school buildings, consecrated to education, may become the instruments of that deepest and most fundamental education upon which the very existence of democracy depends.[43]

The movement for neighborhood organization was not entirely new, of course. The tradition of local self-government in the United States went well beyond the legal division between national and state governments and left considerable discretion to counties and townships. As Alexis de Tocqueville observed in the 1830s, the vitality of townships and counties depended on the well-founded idea in the United States that "each man [was] the best judge of his own interest and best able to satisfy his private needs." The practice of leaving townships and counties in charge of their "special interests" in turn cultivated civic attachments by giving each individual "the same feeling for his country as one has for one's family." Happily, Tocqueville concluded, "a sort of selfishness makes [the individual] care for the state."[44]

The more populist progressives wanted to extend the "municipal spirit" that Tocqueville so admired into twentieth-century urban America. At the same time, they hoped to reconstruct the primary unit of political life as a more cosmopolitan sphere, as a place that could more easily dovetail with the nation and, indeed, the international community. As Mary Parker Follett put it, "The relation of neighbors one to another must be integrated into the substance of the [national] state. Politics must take democracy from its external expression of representation to the expression of that inner meaning hidden in the intermingling of all men."[45] This rather cryptic, idealistic aspiration found more concrete expression in the progressive hope for the neighborhood school, which according to social centers activists, was the only "nonexclusive institution" in the United States. As George Forbes wrote:

The truth is that we have developed every kind of institution and every form of education except the one fundamental kind of institution and form of education upon which the very existence of democracy depends. Every institution within the state, except the public school, is more or less exclusive. The family, the church, the political party, the social classes, the endless social groupings and organizations, commercial, industrial, fraternal, purely social — all are exclusive and have exclusive interests. They can never develop the ethical spirit as a community spirit, a spirit that transcends all such bounds and feels that its supreme membership is in the whole community and that the greatest good is that which may be shared by every human being in the community.[46]

Thus, as Derthick and Dinan argue, progressives were not merely state-builders, determined centralizers looking to overrun the localized polity of the nineteenth century. Rather, "the communitarians among them . . . rested their theories explicitly on respect for small-scale societies, leaving an important legacy in defense of the local." At the same time, these modern defenders of community and neighborhood advanced a new way of thinking about localism that rested on ideology rather than constitutional forms and political associations. Ultimately, the progressive hope of strengthening self-government in the United States depended on transmuting local self-government into direct rule of the people, who would not have to suffer the interference of decentralizing associations and institutions. Only then could individuals participate in a national movement of public opinion that might cultivate a "more perfect union." "Truly, the voice of the people is the voice of God," wrote a progressive journalist early in the twentieth century, adding the qualification "but that means the voice of the *whole* people."[47]

The celebration of direct popular rule was not limited to the more populist progressives. New Nationalist reformers, no less than New Freedom progressives, championed institutions and practices that would nurture a well-digested, direct system of popular rule on a national scale. Just as surely as the Progressive movement's wrenching conflicts over how to reform the political economy betrayed fundamental disagreements in its ranks, so too its commitment to "pure democracy" elicited a shared sense of endeavor. Indeed, during the 1912 campaign, TR joined Wilson in celebrating the use of schoolhouses as neighborhood headquarters for political discussion. Declaring his enthusiastic approval for the maxim, "Public buildings for public uses," Roosevelt proposed that the neighborhood school be turned into a "senate of the people," where they could discuss the issues of the hour.[48] Even the unreconstructed nationalist, Herbert Croly, was careful to differentiate between nationalization and lifeless centralization, subordinating the objective of strengthening national administrative power to the will of the people. "A prevailing public opinion after the lapse of a sufficient time for deliberation," he insists, "must obtain the power to accomplish any program demanded by the national interest." By the same token, the cultivation of the national interest, properly understood, "frequently required administrative and legislative decentralization."[49]

Unlike modern liberals, then, who disdain federalism and local self-government, Progressive Era reformers combined a desire to strengthen the national character of American democracy with a concern to preserve the virtues of decentralization and provincialism. Just as New Democrats lament the passing of progressivism's lost communal tradition, so Derthick and Dinan regret that contemporary political science has failed to appreciate the imaginative engagement of Progressive Era thinkers with the dilemma of scale in a democracy.

Progressivism and Social Democracy

For Eldon Eisenach, the reluctance of progressives to mount a full-scale attack on localism was unfortunate; he laments that the triumph of New Nationalism was shallow, fraught with compromises. The real "lost promise" of progressivism, Eisenach suggests, is that it sacrificed the chance to build a real state on the alter of "localism" and "coalitional games." Whereas Derthick and Dinan are intrigued by Josiah Royce's argument for preserving "provincialism" as an ingredient of national community, Eisenach scorns such concessions to local self-government as a "major subversion of progressive ideals."

To be sure, the ideal of "pure democracy," championed by New Nationalism and New Freedom reformers alike, marked them as diffident state-builders. It is significant in this regard that some of Roosevelt's political allies, who wanted the Progressive party to flower into a European-style social democratic party, were hardly less contemptuous than was Debs of the former president's obsession with "pure democracy." "I am weary to death of the Rule of the People and a millennium created by constant elections and never-ending suspicion of authority," Learned Hand wrote in the wake of the storm created by TR's democratic platform. "When will the day come that some courageous men will stand sponsors for a real programme of 'social justice' in the words of our leader?" Gazing enviously across the Atlantic at the progress of social democrats in England, Hand asked Felix Frankfurter plaintively, "Can you see a single man who would really dare to commit himself to any plan like the Fabians? Why have we nowhere any Fabians? Why aren't all of us Fabians?"[50]

That questions like this were asked so passionately by a prominent jurist reveals how rich the debate over the future course of the country was during the Progressive Era, how open-ended the possibilities seemed. More to the point, Hand's bitter lament highlights the warning of Eisenach's essay that progressivism should not try to reinvent itself as communitarianism. Still, there is much to be learned from the progressives' reluctance to sacrifice the dignity of the democratic individual on the altar of a national state. "Telling Americans to improve democracy by sinking comfortably into a community, by losing themselves in a collective life, is calling into the wind," Robert Wiebe has written. "There has never been an American democracy without its powerful strand of individualism, and nothing suggests there will be."[51]

To defenders of "direct democracy," the collectivist prescriptions of Debs and Hand, however well intended, were doomed to fail. As Croly argues in *Progressive Democracy,* such reformers attached too much importance to the accomplishment and maintenance of specific results and not enough to the permanent moral welfare of democracy: "An authoritative representative government, particularly one which is associated with inherited leadership and a strong party system, carries with it an enormous prestige. It is frequently in a position either to ignore, to circumvent or to wear down popular opposition. But a social program purchased at such a price is not worth what it costs."[52]

Progressives dedicated themselves to the welfare state. At the same time, they stood for the proposition that any program of social control, social insurance, or a standardization of industry could not be adopted unless supported by public opinion. There was no prospect in the United States, where centralized administration was a cardinal vice, that the people would confer legitimacy on a welfare state that was not attuned to the preferences, even biases, of public opinion. The popularity of the direct primary in the United States, Croly noted, revealed how centralized and disciplined parties went against the looser genius of American politics. To the extent that government became committed to a democratic program that was essentially social in character, the American people would find intolerable a two-party system that stood between popular will and the machinery of government. As Jane Addams noted in

1914, a fundamental principle of the Progressive Party was that a welfare state could not be created in the United States "unless the power of direct legislation is placed in the hands of the people, in order that these changes may come, not as centralized government [has] given them, from above down, but may come from the people up; that the people shall be the directing and controlling factors in the legislation."[53] As such, the American people would only support a national reform party, like the Progressives, that presented itself as a way station on the road to direct rule by the people, a pause on the path to a constitutional order dominated by the Rights of the People.

In this sense, the death of the Progressive Party is attributable not to the cult of TR's personality, nor to disagreements over race or trusts that divided its leaders, but to the almost hopeless task in the United States of attempting to reconcile loyalty to the progressive ideal with loyalty to a particular organization. "The logic of the progressive democratic principle" was self-destructive, Croly predicted. "Just in so far as a progressive political program is carried out, progressive social democracy will cease to need a national political party as an instrument."[54]

The essays in this volume reveal that Croly's observation speaks tellingly of the strengths and weaknesses of the Progressive idea of democracy. Alonzo Hamby shows that the progressive movement never clearly existed as a recognizable organization with common goals, but, rather, is better understood as a movement of public opinion that has been aroused episodically to our own time by powerful issues, domestic and international crises, and charismatic leaders.

Given this history, it is not surprising that for the past quarter century, the scholarly effort to define progressivism or identify its principles and organizational forms has been under full-scale attack.[55] Indeed, as Morton Keller reveals, the surges of progressivism sometimes brought policies that appeared reactionary. Emancipated from the "wheelwork" of the two-party system, public policy came to betray more centrally the mores and biases of public opinion. Thus, woman's suffrage, a principal cause of the Progressive Party, triumphed, but so did immigration restriction and Prohibition, which many if not a majority of progressives supported in the 1920s. More to the point, in their rejection of traditional constitutional remedies and their indifference to political associations, reformers risked the manipulation of progressive means for ends that badly fractured the Progressive movement, ends that some reformers abhorred. The mere fact that immigration restriction and prohibition "were potentially or actively regressive does not mean that they were not progressive," Arthur Link argues. "On the contrary," he continues, "they superbly illustrated the repressive tendencies that inhered in progressivism precisely because it was grounded so much upon majoritarian principles."[56]

Constitutional Conservatism

This dedication to majoritarian principles suggests an especially prescient lost tradition of the Progressive Era, albeit heretical today, namely: William Howard Taft's opposition to direct popular rule. As progressivism became defined by a commitment to direct popular rule, so too conservatism sought terra firma in a defense of the Constitution. Yet as their infatuation with Theodore Roosevelt suggests, many influential conservatives now choose to draw on progressive solutions, even as they profess the desire to "relimit government." The strand of conservatism that arose in opposition to the Progressive movement, represented by Taft's support for constitutional forms like the separation of powers and federalism, embraced a settled, standing body of law, upheld the right of property, and resisted popular and populist solutions to political and social discontents. This whiggish defense of traditional institutions and values has been largely eclipsed by a new form of conservatism that prescribes a less "defensive" strategy in the war against the progressive state. A large number of contemporary conservatives have concluded that government — even the federal government — has the responsibility to shape proper habits and behavior. Such a view permeates conservative proposals to restrict abortion, require work for welfare, enforce child support, and supervise unwed teen mothers.[57] "Today's task," writes one leading conservative intellectual, "is radical rather than conservative, proactive rather than defensive: it is to foster a sociology of virtue rather than merely stemming further erosion of virtue's moral capitol. That erosion has today gone too far for a merely 'conservative' approach."[58] Put simply, these modern conservatives glimpse the possibility of success in a reverse progressivism, in "a thinking through of the ways in which social institutions can be reinvented, restructured, or reformed to promote virtue and foster sound character."[59]

Not all conservatives, of course, agree. Indeed, some scorn the sociology of virtue as apostasy, as confirmation of progressivism's triumph at the hands of the very prophets who presume to call it to account.[60] But these voices of restraint might be lost amid the populist uprising against progressivism, abetted as it is by activists who rest their hopes for change in the possibility that progressive institutions and politics can be reinvented as agents of conservatism. Indeed, many, if not most contemporary conservatives express little faith in upholding constitutional space between government and public opinion; like progressives, they promote populist schemes that seek to overcome the distance between government and the people.[61] Witness many conservatives' support for term limits; indeed, one leading conservative thinker, frustrated by the courts' failure to roll back liberal constitutional doctrines, proposes "to implement term limits for federal judges."[62]

There is a real sense, then, in which contemporary conservatism has become the mirror image of progressivism. The faith that William Howard Taft expressed in limited constitutional government has given way to support for ambitious programmatic initiatives that are pursued through political methods that corrode political and government institutions. As Chester Finn argues, Croly's vision of the Constitution has trumped Taft's. Contemporary politics and government, he writes, is shaped by "the Crolyesque tendency, shared by many on the political left and now by some on the right, to perceive government as the primary engine of change and progress — and to construe that progress in terms of their own vision of the good society."[63]

Thus we are left with the question, "Can there still be a meaningful exploration of the rich political terrain of the Progressive Era?" Or is such an inquiry rendered moot by the emergence of a political culture that no longer questions itself? The very pervasiveness of the progressive tradition calls for a reconsideration of its moral foundation.

The Moral Basis of Progressive Democracy

Many of the essays that follow portray a tragic flaw in progressive democracy. Born of moral, indeed religious convictions, it ultimately corrupted political life in the United States. Progressives' faith in the *whole* people betrayed them, McWilliams argues, for they ignored or slighted the implication that "we all begin in a world of particulars, from which the human spirit ascends, on any account only slowly and with difficulty."

It was precisely on these grounds that the antifederalists had warned that the Constitution would fail to create self-government on a grand scale. "Enlarge the circle of political life as far as conceived by the Constitution," Cato warned, and "we lose the ties of acquaintance, habits, and fortune, and thus, by degrees, we lessen in our attachments, till, at length, we no more than acknowledge a sameness of species."[64] The persistence of local self-government and decentralized political associations through the end of the nineteenth century postponed the question of whether the founders' concept of "We the People" was viable. But as Derthick and Dinan observe, with the Civil War, its aftermath, and the rise of industrial capitalism, constitutional government in the United States entered a new phase. It fell to the Progressives to confront the question of whether it was possible to reconcile democracy with an economy of greatly enlarged institutions and a society of growing diversity.

The test of this proposition in the Progressive Era appeared to validate the Antifederalist fears. "The long-term danger of Progressivism," McWilliams concludes, "points in the direction of the 'tyranny of the majority' and the sort of happy nihilism that is apt to be celebrated in our time." As Tocqueville might have expected, this popular despotism is a soft one, based not on mob rule but on bureaucratic torpor and endemic apathy. As it sucked the meaning from elections and party competition, Philip Ethington laments, "pure democracy" proved to be fool's gold; so-called direct democracy, he argues, has "left the political process open to massive colonization by the logic of the marketplace and the influence of the money power."

In the final analysis, then, the failings of progressivism shed light on the limitations of the American constitutional order. Like the Antifederalists, progressives rejected the Federalist view that institutional arrangements could be substituted for virtue. But progressives were unwilling to subordinate their vision of the nation's destiny to provincial liberties, even as many of them acknowledged the importance of localism. With John Dewey, progressives fell back on the hope that locality could be allied to larger loyalties by "freeing and perfecting the processes of inquiry and of dissemination of their conclusions." The dignity of the democratic individual, progressives held, had to shift from the emotive grounds of local ties to "the cumulative and transmitted intellectual wealth of the community." As Dewey put it optimistically, "the Great Community, in the sense of free and full intercommunication," would do "its final work in ordering the relations and enriching the experience of local associations."[65]

Dewey believed that progressivism could have a profound effect on the American polity insofar as it could be transformed into a new liberal tradition — one that did not celebrate a rugged individualism that abhorred state interference with private property, but instead emphasized a new concept of individualism that viewed the state as a guarantor of social and economic welfare. In his influential *Liberalism and Social Action*, which was dedicated to Jane Addams, Dewey wrote, "these new liberals fostered the idea that the state has the responsibility for creating institutions under which individuals can effectively realize the potentialities that are theirs."[66] Although the hope of many social reformers that the Progressive Party would serve as an instrument for unifying disparate advocacy groups came unraveled, Dewey's celebration of a new conception of liberalism underscores the important ties between the Progressive Era and the New Deal's programmatic and institutional aspirations.

Indeed, the New Deal realignment marks the consolidation of changes begun by the Progressive campaign of 1912. The so-called purge campaign and other partisan practices during the New Deal period suggest a commitment to forming a national programmatic two-party system. The system of party responsibility, Franklin Roosevelt argued, "required that one of its parties be the liberal party and the other be the conservative party."[67] Ultimately, however, Roosevelt and his New Deal allies, some of whom were erstwhile Bull Moosers, took actions and pursued procedural reforms that would extend the personal and nonpartisan responsibility of the president to the detriment of collective and partisan responsibility. Like his cousin, FDR conceived of a party program as an assault on party politics, but he presided over a full-scale partisan realignment, the first in American history to place an independent executive at the heart of its approach to politics and government. Understood in the context of the progressive tradition, the New Deal is appropriately viewed as the completion of a realignment that makes future *partisan* realignments unnecessary. As the important Brownlow Committee report put it, "Our national will must be expressed not merely in a brief, exultant moment of electoral decision, but in persistent, determined, competent administration of what the nation has decided to do."[68]

Yet Eisenach argues that the expansion of national administrative power that followed the New Deal realignment did not result in the kind of national state for which progressive reformers like Croly and Dewey had hoped, one that established regulation and social welfare policy as expressions of national unity and commitment. Eisenach suggests that this failure followed from the New Deal's compromise with the natural rights tradition in American politics. FDR's economic constitutional order — the economic bill of rights he championed — perverted Dewey's idea of new individualism, subordinating enlightened administration to group entitlements. Whereas Dewey had expressed support for reformed local communities as forums of educated political inquiry, the New Deal defended new rights that undermined the progressive ambition for national community. Particular programs such as social security and medicare achieved popular support, but programmatic liberalism was never defined and defended in a form that could withstand the rights-claims of favored constituencies. As Martha Derthick has written about the social security program, its architects "sought to foreclose the options of future generations by committing them irrevocably to a program that promises benefits by rights as well as those particular benefits that have been incorporated in an ever expanding law. In that sense they designed social security to be uncontrollable."[69]

Indeed, the hallmark of administrative politics in the United States is the virtual absence of a state that can impose its will on the economy and society. The limits of administrative centralization in the American context were revealed clearly by the fact that strong opposition to the growth of the central government continued to be a force in American politics, especially during times of frenetic government activism. The Great Society, which represented an effort to expand and radicalize the New Deal, as well as the culmination of the progressive assault on the two-party system, was widely perceived as "excessive statism," giving rise to a movement that would pose hard challenges to liberal reforms. With Ronald Reagan's ascent to the White House, government was no longer "the solution to our problems; government was the problem."[70]

The Reagan "revolution," however, did not mark a revival of traditional natural rights liberalism. The Reagan administration became committed to programmatic innovations in defense and foreign policy that required expanding, rather than rolling back, the national government's responsibilities. Equally important, Reagan championed the causes of social conservatives who disdain the sober conservatism of Taft, who are animated by a missionary zeal that seems to want to abolish, rather than restore, the distinction between state and society. As the cultural wars of the 1980s and 1990s confirmed, many conservatives do not want to dismantle the progressive state; instead, they desire to put it to new uses — fighting enemies abroad, protecting the domestic economy, and preserving "family values."

Notwithstanding the continuing expansion of national administrative power, our current politics does not confidently presume the existence of a national state. As Barry Karl has argued, Americans continue to abhor, even as they embrace, national administrative power.[71] The Republican victories in the 1994 off-year elections, in which they achieved majority control of the House and Senate for the first time in forty years, testified to growing public concern with "big government" and its cumbersome regulatory structures. The Republicans, significantly, achieved this dramatic victory after running a national, ideological campaign, which promised to fulfill the failed promise of the Reagan revolution — to get government off the backs of the American people.[72] Even so, the public's persistent commitment to middle-class entitlements, such as social security and medicare, and its strong support for regulatory initiatives dedicated to environmental and consumer protection, makes unlikely the revival of limited government.[73]

Americans have a love-hate relationship with the national state, a profound ambivalence that seeks refuge in progressive democracy — the *direct* form of democracy Americans have adopted to ease their anxiety about the expansion of national administrative power. Unwilling to embrace or reject the state, we have increasingly sought to give the "people" more control over it. Consequently, "pure" democracy has evolved, or degenerated, into a plebiscitary form of politics that mocks the progressive concept of "enlightened administration" and exposes citizens to the sort of public figures who will exploit their impatience with the difficult tasks involved in sustaining a healthy democracy. As the shifting fortunes of Bill Clinton's two terms as president have illustrated dramatically, progressive democracy has freed the executive office from party politics, only to enslave it to a demanding and fractious public.

The displacement of localized parties by progressive democracy has not meant the end of party conflict. The erosion of old-style partisan politics has produced a more national and issue-oriented party system, one that is more compatible with the "nationalized" electorate created by progressive reforms and the mass media. But this more centralized party system, while strengthening national party organizations and allowing for more partisan discipline in Congress, has weakened even more the partisan loyalties of the electorate. More and more, parties seem to be "centralized bureaucracies," writes McWilliams, "less mediators *between* rulers and ruled than a *part* of the government tier."[74]

The insurgency of H. Ross Perot in the 1992 presidential campaign, the most significant assault on the two-party system since TR's Bull Moose campaign, revealed at once the triumph and disappointment of progressive democracy. TR's campaign foretold not only of the emergence of an active and expansive national government but also of presidential campaigns conducted less by parties than by individual candidates. Perot's campaign suggested just how far presidential politics had been emancipated from the constraints of party. Disdaining the importunities of those interested in party renewal that he form a third party, Perot launched his campaign without the formality of a nominating convention — his supporters were summoned to Armageddon on *Larry King Live*. Just as significant, the broad appeal of Perot's call for electronic town meetings as a principal vehicle to solve the nation's political and economic problems testifies to the resonance of simple-minded notions of direct democracy — and to the threat this politics of instant gratification poses to constitutional forms. Although Perot's personal popularity had abated four years later, the direct plebiscitary politics he championed did not. Indeed, President Clinton and his Republican challenger, Robert Dole, openly imitated Perot's personalistic politics, even as they diverted funds to their campaigns — "soft money" — that were intended for party building activities. With Perot's politics, if not Perot himself, continuing to have strong support in the nation as the millennium approaches, the Progressive idea of "direct government" might be destined to play an even larger, yet more frivolous, part in American political life.[75]

For much of American history, the dangers of administrative aggrandizement were checked by localized parties. Born of the Jeffersonian and Jacksonian support of local self-government, traditional party organizations and newspapers rectified the Constitution's insufficient attention to the cultivation of an active and competent citizenry. By the same token, the progressive assault on political parties has exposed the fragile sense of citizenship in American political life. To be sure, progressive reformers were mindful of the possibility that dismantling the parties would breed an apathetic public that was susceptible to plebiscitary appeals; it was in this very respect that TR's dominant presence posed the greatest challenge to progressive ideals. But they believed that this risk had to be taken, lest government remain impotent in the face of the major changes taking place in the economy and society. The democratic principle, the Progressive Miles Poindexter wrote in 1912,

> has been kept warm and vigorous in the hearts of the people, but in both the Democratic and Republican organizations it has become so encumbered with party machinery and loaded with the ball and chain of obsolete governmental dogmas that it has ceased to find expression in the Government through either of these organizations. . . . Both parties [Poindexter continues] are verbose in declaring for a government by the people, but the power of the people is so diluted through an indirect choice of officials, a division of powers of government under the Constitution, and an irresponsible party government wholly outside the Constitution, that it largely disappears before it is applied to the actual making and administration of the laws.[76]

In the event that the people failed to participate in progressive democracy, some reformers suggested, they should be, so to speak, forced to be free. "The people will *not* go to the primaries; that is settled," declared an editorial in the progressive journal, *The Arena*. "If they will not do it voluntarily they should be compelled by law to do it and deposit there a ballot, and also at the general election, even though a blank, under the penalty of disenfranchisement and fine."[77] There was no prospect, however, that the American people, dedicated above all to individualism, could be forced to be free. As Tocqueville recognized, civic attachments in modern commercial republics would have to rely largely on associations and practices that encouraged long-term self-interest — "self-interest, rightly understood."[78]

Progressive reformers understood that the development of a more purposeful national government meant loosening the hold of traditional parties on the loyalties and voting habits of citizens. But they failed to appreciate the purpose these parties served as effective channels for democratic participation.[79] Political parties, which embodied the principle of local self-government, were critical agents in counteracting the tendency of citizens to shut themselves up in a limited circle of domestic concerns out of reach of broader public causes. By enticing Americans into neighborhood organizations and patronage practices that were beyond their tiny private orbits, traditional party organizations helped to show individuals the connection between their private interests and public concerns. Similarly, highly decentralized party structures insured that national campaigns and controversies focused on the partisan activities of townships, wards, and cities, thus cultivating a delicate balance between local and national community.[80] Drawn into political associations by the promise of social, economic, and political advantage, Americans might also learn the art of cooperation and form attachments to government institutions. As Tocqueville put it in a nice turn of phrase, "Public spirit in the Union is . . . only a summing up of provincial patriotism."[81]

Still, we must not allow the present discontents of the American people to blind us to the shortcomings of the nineteenth-century polity. It was no "golden age" of parties. Progressive reformers had good reasons to view political parties and the provincial liberties they upheld as an obstacle to economic, racial, and political justice. To be sure, as Eileen McDonagh shows, not all progressives were enthusiastic about challenging these injustices; and in some cases, progressives displayed appalling indifference to the rightful claims of women, ethnic groups, and, especially, African Americans. Still, the resurrection of Hamilton nationalism they favored, which required the weakening of political parties, yielded a stronger executive that became the principal agent for undertaking domestic and international responsibilities that must be assumed by all decent commercial republics. The nobility of the modern presidency comes from, as Woodrow Wilson observes, its "extraordinary isolation," which provides great opportunity for presidents to leave their mark on the nation, even as it subjects them to a volatile mass democracy that makes popular and enduring achievement unlikely.[82]

This volume's examination of progressivism, then, leaves us with a dilemma as old as the republic: its legacy is a more active and better-equipped national state — the national resolve to tackle problems such as forced segregation at home and communism abroad — but one without adequate means of common deliberation and public judgement, the very practices that nurture a civic culture.

Notes

1. This project began with a conference, "Progressivism: Then and Now," held at Brandeis University in October 1996. Most of the essays were presented at the conference, although they were revised for this volume.

2. See Will Marshall, ed., *Building the Bridge: Ten Big Ideas to Transform America* (Lanham, Md.: Rowman and Littlefield, 1997); Michael Lind, *The Next American Nation: The New Nationalism and the Fourth American Revolution* (New York: Free Press, 1995); E. J. Dionne, *They Only Look Dead: Why Progressives Will Dominate the Next Political Era* (New York: Simon and Schuster, 1996); and Lamar Alexander and Chester Finn Jr., eds., *The New Promise of American Life* (Indianapolis: Hudson Institute, 1995).

3. Samuel P. Huntington, *American Politics: The Promise of Disharmony* (Cambridge: Harvard University Press, 1981), chap. 5.

4. On the Progressive Era as a period of fundamental secular change, see Sidney M. Milkis and Daniel J. Tichenor, "'Direct Democracy' and Social Justice: The Progressive Party Campaign of 1912," *Studies in American Political Development* (Fall 1994): 282–340. See also Joel H. Silbey, "Foundation Stones of Present Discontents: The American Political Nation, 1776–1945," in *Present Discontents: American Politics in the Very Late Twentieth Century* (Chatham, N.J.: Chatham, 1997), 1–29.

5. Arthur S. Link and Richard L. McCormick, *Progressivism* (Arlington Heights, Ill.: Harlan Davidson, 1983), 43–44.

6. Francis L. Broderick, *Progressivism at Risk: Electing a President in 1912* (Westport, Conn.: Greenwood, 1983), 4–5.

7. Herbert Croly, *Progressive Democracy* (New York: Macmillan, 1914), 27.

8. Wilson Carey McWilliams, "Conclusion: The Meaning of the Election," in *The Election of 1996: Reports and Interpretations,* ed. Gerald M. Pomper (Chatham, N.J.: Chatham, 1997), 255.

9. See Michael Sandel, *Democracy's Discontent: America in Search of a Public Philosophy* (Cambridge: Harvard University Press, 1996).

10. For the most ambitious attempt to revisit Progressivism as a critical standard to better understand our present discontents, see Eldon J. Eisenach, *The Lost Promise of Progressivism* (Lawrence: University Press of Kansas, 1994).

11. Theodore Roosevelt, "Citizenship in a Republic," Address delivered at the Sorbonne, Paris, 23 April 1910 (New York: Review of Books, 1910), 2204.

12. David Brooks, "Bully For America: What Teddy Roosevelt Teaches," *Weekly Standard,* 23 June 1997, 14.

13. Ibid., and Michael Lind, *The Next American Nation.*

14. "While it is more impossible than ever before for the citizens of a modern industrial and agricultural state actually to assemble after the manner of a New England town meeting, it is no longer necessary for them to assemble," Croly wrote. "They have abundant opportunities of communication and consultation without actually meeting at one time and place. They are kept in constant touch with one another by means of complicated agencies of publicity and intercourse

which are afforded by the magazines, the press, and the like. The active citizenship of the country meets every morning and evening and discusses the affairs of the nation with the newspaper as an impersonal interlocutor. Public opinion has a thousand methods of seeking information and obtaining definite and effective expression which it did not have four generations ago." Croly, *Progressive Democracy,* 264.

15. See Daniel T. Rodgers, "In Search of Progressivism," *Reviews of American History* 10 (December 1982): 114–23.

16. Martin Shefter, *Political Parties and the State* (Princeton: Princeton University Press, 1994), 77.

17. Theodore Roosevelt, "Who Is A Progressive," *Outlook* 13 April 1912, 809.

18. "Draft Platform" with handwritten changes by TR; "A Contract With the People," Platform of the Progressive Party, adopted at its First National Convention, 7 August 1912, both in the Theodore Roosevelt Collection, Harvard University, Cambridge, Mass. Theodore Roosevelt, "A Confession of Faith," Address before the National Convention of the Progressive Party, 6 August 1912, *The Works of Theodore Roosevelt,* vol. 17 (New York: Charles Scribner's, 1926), 269.

19. Abraham Lincoln, "Message to Special Congress," 4 July 1861, *The Political Thought of Abraham Lincoln,* ed. Richard N. Current (Indianapolis: Bobbs-Merrill, 1967), 187–88.

20. Theodore Roosevelt to Benjamin B. Lindsey, 26 February 1913, Benjamin B. Lindsey Papers, Box 41, Folder: February 1913, Manuscript Division, Library of Congress, Washington, D.C.

21. See Lind, *The Next American Nation,* especially chaps. 8 and 9.

22. E. J. Dionne, *They Only Look Dead,* 12.

23. Fred Siegel and Will Marshall, "Liberalism's Lost Tradition," *The New Democrat* September/October 1995, 8–13.

24. Wilson Carey McWilliams, "The Meaning of the Election," 260.

25. Michael Joyce and William A. Schambra, "A New Citizenship, A New Civic Life," in Alexander and Finn, *The New Promise of American Life,* 139–63.

26. Bruce Ackerman, *We the People: Foundations* (Cambridge: Harvard University Press, 1991); Walter Dean Burnham, "Dialectics of a System of Change in the U.S.A.: The 1990s Crisis as a Case in Point," Paper delivered at the annual meeting of the American Political Science Association, San Francisco, California, 29 August–1 September 1996.

27. Barry Karl, *The Uneasy State: The United States from 1915 to 1945* (Chicago: University of Chicago Press, 1983), 234–35.

28. George Mowry, "The Election of 1912," in *History of American Presidential Elections,* ed. Arthur Schlesinger Jr. and Fred I. Israel (New York: Chelsea, 1971), 2160.

29. George Mowry, *Theodore Roosevelt and the Progressive Movement* (Madison: University of Wisconsin Press, 1947), 217.

30. William Howard Taft, "The Sign of the Times," Address to the Electrical

Manufacturers Club, Hot Springs, Virginia, 6 November 1912, William Howard Taft Papers, Manuscript Division, Library of Congress, Washington, D.C.

31. William Howard Taft, Address to the Republican Club of New York, 12 February 1912. Taft Papers; Alexander Hamilton, James Madison, and John Jay, *The Federalist Papers* (New York: New American Library, 1961), 80.

32. Address of William Howard Taft, 25 April 1912, Senate Document 615 (62–2, vol. 38, 2), 3–4.

33. William Howard Taft, Address to Republican Club, 12 February 1912. Taft Papers.

34. Theodore Gilman, "The Progressive Party Comes Not to Destroy, But to Fulfill the Constitution," Address delivered at a public rally in Yonkers, New York, 27 September 1912, Progressive Party Publications, 1912–16, Theodore Roosevelt Collection, 4.

35. Croly, *Progressive Democracy,* 54–55.

36. Gilman, "The Progressive Party," 5–6.

37. Eugene V. Debs, cited in "The New Party Gets Itself Born," *Current Literature,* September 1912, 256.

38. Letter to the Editor, *Milwaukee Social Democratic Herald* (19 November 1898), Eugene V. Debs Papers, Indiana State University, Terre Haute, Ind.

39. Eugene V. Debs, "The Greatest Political Campaign in American History," St. Louis Campaign Opening Speech, 6 July 1912, Debs Papers.

40. Theodore Roosevelt to Sydney Brooks, 4 June 1912, *The Letters of Theodore Roosevelt,* ed. Elting Morrison, vol. 7 (Cambridge: Harvard University Press, 1952), 552–53 (my emphasis).

41. Siegel and Marshall, "Liberalism's Lost Tradition," 8.

42. Woodrow Wilson, "Constitutional Government in the United States," *The Papers of Woodrow Wilson,* ed. Arthur S. Link, vol. 18 (Princeton: Princeton University Press, 1974), 197–98.

43. George M. Forbes, "Buttressing the *Foundations* of Democracy," *The Survey* 18 November 1911, 1231–35.

44. Alexis de Tocqueville, *Democracy in America,* ed. J. P. Mayer (Garden City, N.Y.: Doubleday, 1969), 68, 82, 95.

45. Mary Parker Follett, *The New State: Group Organization of Popular Government* (1918; reprint, Gloucester, Mass.: Peter Smith, 1965).

46. Forbes, "Buttressing the Foundations of Democracy," 1232.

47. William Helmstreet, "Theory and Practice of the New Primary Law," *The Arena* 28, 6 (December 1902): 592 (emphasis in original).

48. TR cited in Editorial, "The Political Use of School Buildings," *The Outlook,* 14 September 1912.

49. Croly, *Progressive Democracy,* 241–43.

50. Learned Hand to Felix Frankfurter, 4 April 1912, Learned Hand Papers, Harvard University Law School, Cambridge, Mass.

51. Robert H. Wiebe, *Self-Rule: A Cultural History of American Democracy* (Chicago: University of Chicago Press, 1995), 264.

52. Croly, *Progressive Democracy,* 281–82.

53. Jane Addams, "Social Justice through National Action," Speech to the Second Annual Lincoln Day Dinner of the Progressive Party, New York City, 12 February 1914, Jane Addams Papers, Swarthmore College, Swarthmore, Pa., File 136, Reel #42.

54. Croly, *Progressive Democracy,* 336.

55. See Peter G. Filene, "An Obituary for the Progressive Movement," *American Quarterly* 22 (1970): 20–34; and Daniel T. Rogers, "In Search of Progressivism."

56. Arthur S. Link, "What Happened to the Progressive Movement in the 1920s," *American Historical Review* 64, 4 (July 1959): 848.

57. See Paul Starobin, "The Daddy State," *National Journal,* 28 March 1998.

58. William Kristol, "The Politics of Liberty, the Sociology of Virtue," in Alexander and Finn, *The New Promise of American Life,* 124.

59. Ibid.

60. See David Frum, *Dead Right* (New York: Basic Books, 1994).

61. Harvey C. Mansfield, "Newt, Take Note: Populism Poses Its Own Dangers," *Wall Street Journal,* 1 November 1994.

62. William Kristol, "The Judiciary: Conservatism's Lost Branch," *Harvard Journal of Law and Public Policy* 17, 1 (Winter 1994): 131–36.

63. Chester Finn Jr., "Herbert Croly and the Cult of Governmentalism," in Alexander and Finn, *The New Promise of American Life,* 38.

64. "Letters to Cato," in *The Complete Anti-Federalism,* ed. Herbert Storing, vol. 2 (Chicago: Chicago University Press, 1981), 112.

65. John Dewey, *The Public and Its Problems* (New York: Henry Holt, 1927), 208, 211.

66. John Dewey, *Liberalism and Social Action* (New York: G. P. Putnam, 1935), 26.

67. Franklin D. Roosevelt, *Public Papers and Addresses,* ed. Samuel I. Rosenman, vol. 7 (New York: Random House, 1938–1950), xxviii–xxxii.

68. *Report of the President's Committee on Administrative Management* (Washington, D.C.: Government Printing Office, 1937), 53. The President's Committee on Administrative Management, headed by Louis Brownlow, played a central role in the planning and politics of New Deal institutions. Charles Merriam, an influential advisor to Theodore Roosevelt in 1912, was an important member of this committee. I am not taking issue here with Otis Graham's argument that many Progressives opposed the New Deal. See Otis Graham, *An Encore for Reform: The Old Progressives and the New Deal* (New York: Oxford, 1967). It is, however, the case that the New Deal political program was very much inspired by TR's Bull Moose campaign of 1912. On the link between Progressivism and the New Deal, see Sidney Milkis, *The President and the Parties,* especially chap. 2.

69. Martha Derthick, *Policy Making for Social Security* (Washington, D.C.: Brookings Institution, 1983), 417.

70. Alonzo Hamby, *Liberalism and Its Challengers: FDR to Reagan* (New York: Oxford University Press, 1985), especially chap. 6, epilogue.

71. Karl, *The Uneasy State,* 225–39.

72. David Shribman, "Contract on the New Deal," *Boston Globe,* 1 October 1995, A35.

73. In fact, conservative Republicans remain profoundly ambivalent about whether the appropriate path to reform is "devolution" or a national conservative policy. With respect to reforming Aid to Families with Dependent Children, for example, the party's campaign document, the so-called Republican Contract with America, proposed to expand the flexibility of the states, allowing them to design their own work programs and to determine who participated in these work programs. As Melissa Buis has shown, however, the Personal Responsibility and Work Opportunity Reconciliation Act of 1996, although giving states more discretion to tailor their individual welfare programs, imposes important new national standards to determine eligibility, to attack illegitimacy and teen pregnancy, and to establish work requirements. See C. Melissa Buis, "Devolution Then and Now: Refining the Federal Role in Welfare Policy," Paper presented to the Northeastern Political Science Association Annual Meeting, Boston, Mass., 1996.

74. Wilson Carey McWilliams, "Two-Tier Politics and the Problem of Public Policy," in *The New Politics of Public Policy,* ed. Marc K. Landy and Martin A. Levin (Baltimore: Johns Hopkins University Press, 1995), 275 (emphasis in original). See also A. James Reichley, "Party Politics in a Federal Polity," in *Challenges to Party Government,* ed. John Kenneth White and Jerome M. Mileur (Carbondale: Southern Illinois University Press, 1992); and Sidney M. Milkis, *The President and the Parties,* chaps. 10–12.

75. Scot Lehigh, "Right Idea, Wrong Leader? Third Party Favored by Many, but Perot Presents a Problem," *Boston Globe,* 1 October 1995, A33. On the cultural and institutional factors that encourage "outsiderism" in contemporary politics, see James W. Ceaser and Andrew Busch, *Losing to Win: The 1996 Elections and American Politics* (Lanham, Md.: Rowan and Littlefield, 1997), especially chap. 6. Perot's promise in 1996 to subordinate his personal ambitions to a collective organization — the Reform Party — was not kept; indeed, as Ceaser and Busch point out, the Reform Party's nomination process "only served to accentuate [Perot's] control and to deepen the split between those who were primarily Perot supporters and those who wanted to depersonalize" the movement he represented. Idem, 112. On the uses and abuses of "soft money," see Anthony Corrado, "Financing the 1996 Elections," in Pomper, *The Election of 1996.*

76. Miles Poindexter, "Why I Am for Roosevelt," *North American Review* 196, no. 683 (October 1912), 473.

77. Helmstreet, "Theory and Practice of the New Primary Law," 589–90 (emphasis in the original).

78. Tocqueville, *Democracy in America,* 525–28.

79. There were some notable exceptions, of course. Jane Addams was highly critical of machine politics in Chicago; at the same time, she warned her fellow reformers that the ward bosses ruled in spite of their vices because they practiced "simple kindness" in the community day in and day out. "[I]f we discover that men of low ideals and corrupt practice are forming popular political standards

simply because such men stand by and for and with the people, then nothing remains but to obtain a like sense of identification before we can modify ethical standards." Jane Addams, "Why the Ward Boss Rules," *The Outlook,* April 2, 1898; reprinted in William L. Riordan, *Plunkitt of Tammany Hall,* ed. Terrence J. McDonald (Boston: Bedford Books, 1994), 122. Mary Simkhovitch had similar advice for the New York reformer. "True reform and lasting reform will come about when public opinion will sustain it," she wrote. "When the reformer understands men as well as the politician friend understands them, he too will have his day." "Friendship and Politics," *Political Science Quarterly* 17, 2 (June 1902): 204.

80. See Michael McGerr, *The Decline of Popular Politics: The American North, 1865–1928* (New York: Oxford University Press, 1986), especially chap. 2. McGerr argues that the promise of entertainment, no less than petty favors, drew Americans to local party organizations. Presidential campaigns, in particular, were occasions for "spectacular partisan displays" in communities that made elections highly emotional episodes. Still, McGerr insists, spectacular displays were not simply a matter of entertainment or emotional identification with a party: "[Nineteenth] century campaigns tied parades and fireworks to long expositions of issues on the stump and in the press. In a sense, the excitement of partisan display could lure men into dealing with complex issues such as slavery. Popular politics fused thought and emotion in a single style accessible to all — a rich unity of reason and passion that would be alien to Americans in the twentieth century" (41).

81. Tocqueville, *Democracy in America,* 162. Although Tocqueville criticized political parties in the United States for being relatively indifferent to broad moral questions and dedicated to the personal ambitions of their members, he also suggested that they might be considered valuable political associations, as "great free schools to which all citizens come to be taught the general theory of association" (522); see also 189–95, 509–13, 520–24.

82. Woodrow Wilson describes the "extraordinary isolation" of the president in *Constitutional Government in the United States,* 114–15.

Progressivism

A Century of Change and Rebirth

Alonzo L. Hamby

In the summer of 1900, a sixteen-year-old boy named Harry Truman attended the Democratic National Convention in Kansas City and heard the inspirational voice of the family hero, William Jennings Bryan. Four years later, Truman, by then a young bank clerk, listened to Theodore Roosevelt make a campaign speech not far from the convention hall. By 1912 Truman, now a farmer south of Kansas City and a subscriber to "muckrake magazines," closely followed the contest for the Democratic presidential nomination between Missouri's Champ Clark and New Jersey's Woodrow Wilson. He favored Wilson, the scholarly progressive. In 1917, at the age of thirty-three, "stirred in heart and soul" by Wilson's call for a crusade to make the world safe for democracy, he enlisted in the National Guard and went off to World War I.

Ten years later Truman was the chief executive officer of a metropolitan county, attempting to practice "business progressivism" within a framework of machine politics, promoting honesty and efficiency in public works, and advocating significant administrative reforms. In another ten years he was a U.S. senator, launching withering rhetorical blasts at Wall Street and the nation's leading financial institutions, which he accused of looting and bankrupting the railroads. Preaching the virtues of decentralization, he also advocated massive regulation of the nation's transportation system, and won the plaudits of such old heroes as Louis Brandeis and George W. Norris. Comfortable as a supporter of the New Deal, he felt closest to colleagues who had ties to the reformism of the early twentieth century. He genuinely believed that he represented the interests of ordinary working Americans, whom he defined as any-one who had to work hard for a decent living — industrial workers, farmers, small businessmen. Speaking out on foreign policy, he advocated an American military buildup against new threats to democracy, arguing from an intellectual framework that Theodore Roosevelt could have embraced. In the war that followed, he used Wilsonian rhetoric in support of a new international collective security organization with its own "police force." In 1948, running primarily as the tribune of the common people and secondarily as the protector of Western democracy against a totalitarian challenge, he won election as president of the United States.[1]

Truman's career has a special impact because he reached the White House, but it is only one of many that illustrate the continuity of the progressive impulse in the first half of the twentieth century. Men who matured politically and intellectually in the progressive era retained much of their formative worldview when they achieved national leadership in the thirties and forties. And they transferred much of it to the generation that wielded power in the 1960s.

This essay assumes that "progressivism" can be understood only as a *political movement* that addressed ideas, impulses, and issues stemming from the modernization of American society. Emerging at the end of the nineteenth century, it established much of the tone of American politics throughout the first half of the twentieth. In the process, it evolved into something called "liberalism." Worn thin at the end of this century by the excesses of its ambitions and by cultural upheavals, it nonetheless remains an often powerful presence in American political life.

What Was It? Searching for Common Denominators

Early historians of progressivism were products of the movement's intellectual climate. They instinctively defined it as a movement of the people fighting against special interests (big business) and corrupt political bosses, related in some fashion to the Populist movement of the 1890s and strongest in the Midwest and the West. An outpouring of critical scholarship beginning in the last half of the 1950s left the old consensus in shreds while producing a plethora of alternative views that defied rational synthesis.[2]

Where did progressivism come from? Almost anywhere except Populism. Probably from the anxieties (and conspiratorial fantasies) of the urban middle classes. Maybe also from the overlooked urban working classes. Perhaps even from numerous corrupt machine leaders more attuned to social welfare issues than was previously understood. Progressives were moral absolutists motivated by traditional Christianity and ideals of social reconciliation. They were pragmatists in touch with all the currents of modernity, developing and acting upon new theories of the state and society. They were conspirators in a well-orchestrated pseudo–reform drive meant to preserve the economic and political dominance of big business. They and their movement simply reflected powerful forces of modernity at work throughout the Western world — bureaucratization, professionalization, the inexorable growth of large organizations. And don't forget the women! In search of meaningful career outlets and more oriented than men toward social welfarism, females were key players in building an empire of reform.[3]

What were the central themes that emerged from this cacophony? Democracy or elitism? Social justice or social control? Small entrepreneurship or concentrated capitalism? And what was the impact on American foreign policy? Were the progressives isolationists or interventionists? Imperialists or advocates of national self-determination? And whatever they were, what was their motivation? Moralistic utopianism? Muddled relativistic pragmatism? Hegemonic capitalism?

Not surprisingly many battered scholars began to shout "No mas!" In 1970 Peter Filene declared that the term "progressivism" had become meaningless, and he made an abortive attempt to write its "obituary." Those who continued to write about the progressive movement as a whole found the enterprise increasingly daunting. In 1991 Alan Dawley, one of the best of the young radical historians, offered his own effort at a synthesis. *Struggles for Justice* was written with verve and passion. It brought to the forefront issues of race, gender, and urban culture that had been at the fringe of earlier accounts, and made systematic comparisons to the political, social, and cultural impacts of industrialism in Germany. Critics agreed that Dawley's book was by no means a failure but judged its parts more interesting than their sum; most seemed to believe that the topic defied persuasive synthesis. John Milton Cooper, a premier historian of the early twentieth century, was more prudent. His book, *Pivotal Decades,* had an ostentatiously neutral title and seldom ventured beyond conventional political-diplomatic narrative. It advanced no major new (or old) ideas about progressivism and even refrained from listing the word in the index. Cooper followed what appears to have been a publisher's editorial policy, and perhaps his response to a conceptual tangle was realistic. But neither interpretive chaos nor interpretive self-denial offered much hope in the quest for understanding.[4]

The restoration of meaning to the word "progressivism" has to begin with respect for the understandings of those who applied the term to themselves, then move on to a search for common denominators. Diversity aplenty existed among the progressives, but so did common attitudes and aspirations. These provide the points of unity among antitrusters and regulators, Christian reformers and secular pragmatists, militarists and pacifists, Democrats and Republicans and Bull Moosers. Above all, the progressives saw themselves as fighters for democracy ("the people") locked in combat with "the interests" (primarily concentrated corporate and financial power), as crusaders with a moral mission, and as battlers for social justice in relations between the classes. Most shared a vision of citizenship built around the ideal of a common social interest that transcended the goals of economic interest groups; they wanted a larger role for the state in advancing that common interest. Most saw the new pragmatic social sciences as critical tools in establishing both a rationale and an agenda for reform.

Such a vision was broad enough to encompass a wide variety of means and worldviews. Moreover, as is usually the case in the real world, many progressives embraced apparently contradictory outlooks and agendas. Richard T. Ely, for example, was a relativist and pragmatist in economics; he also was a committed Christian devoted to the "social gospel" and apparently comfortable with its absolutist assumptions. Muckraking journalists were often sophisticated intellectuals with a realistic grasp of the complexity of political power; yet their work frequently took on a conspiratorial aura and focused on exposing evil men.[5] The great progressive political leaders — Robert La Follette, Theodore Roosevelt, and Woodrow Wilson were perhaps paramount — won popular support with a rhetoric that reflected moral earnestness and inflexible convictions. Yet in power they more often than not were opportunists who achieved their ends in the manner of traditional politicians through patronage-jobbing, compromise, coalition-building, and occasional spectacular programmatic U-turns.

In various ways they attempted to come to grips with forces of "modernity" that hit late nineteenth- and early twentieth-century America like a sledgehammer: the emergence of pragmatism and the pragmatic mood in intellectual life, social thought, and public policy; the mushrooming of the large organization, in business and almost every other aspect of material life; the accompanying threat to individual autonomy and entrepreneurship; the development of the professions and professional outlooks; the rapid growth of large cities peopled by mass migrations and governed by corrupt politicians; the social problems presented by hordes of seemingly unassimilable immigrants crowded together into dense pockets of urban poverty.

The movement's critical mass was in the "urban middle classes," interpreting "urban" as did the census bureau to include small towns and cities, not just metropolitan America. The "middle classes" included small business enterprisers of all types, squeezed by enormous corporations, resentful of what they considered railroad rate gouging, insecure about their future livelihoods. They had rural counterparts, commercial farmers with the same resentments, sometimes employing the rhetoric of the populist movement but no longer pursuing inflationary panaceas. The "middle classes" also included rising professionals, university academics, and trained experts eager to impose their values and expertise upon American society, a sizeable proportion of the Protestant clergy attempting to reassert lost authority, and a remarkable politically oriented intelligentsia endeavoring to reformulate traditional concepts of democracy in ways compatible with the changing world of the early twentieth century.

As with any effort to meet the challenge of the new, progressives drew heavily for their inspiration upon tradition: Protestant Christianity, individual entrepreneurship, agrarian fundamentalism, and American democratic mythology. But they did so without rejecting the forces of change. Many of the progressives eagerly embraced modernity, employing its intellectual tools with zest in their bid to refashion America.

The diversity of progressivism's sources was matched by the multiplicity of its major accomplishments.

By crusading for honesty and advocating a common interest that transcended class, occupational, or ethnoreligious divisions, the progressives raised the tone of government in America. They neither ended corruption nor were as truly disinterested as they believed, but they did leave the nation with higher standards and expectations about government at every level.

They "discovered" poverty in America. Convincingly defining it as a social pathology in an age of increasing affluence, they mapped its extent and location, persuasively asserting causes that went beyond character defects. As settlement house workers, they sought to deal with the poor on a humane, face-to-face basis. As administrators and legislators, they addressed such problems as insufficient medical care, unsafe working conditions, and exploitation of women and children. Yet for all their concern with the most vulnerable among the working classes, they rejected a politics of class conflict. Many, surely a majority of those who identified themselves as Republicans, were uncomfortable with labor unions; so were most nonurban Democrats.

Through practical political action and innovative political theory, they reformulated the concept of a liberal state in a way that rejected both traditional liberal minimalism and revolutionary socialism. Between 1901 and 1917 Herbert Croly, Walter Lippmann, Walter Weyl, Louis Brandeis, and Lincoln Steffens published books that reoriented American political thought. Oliver Wendell Holmes, Brandeis, and Roscoe Pound established a tradition of socially conscious jurisprudence. Robert La Follette, Theodore Roosevelt, Woodrow Wilson, and dozens of other reform-minded political leaders attacked the excesses of corporate and financial power while successfully seizing the middle ground in American politics.

A remarkable burst of legislative and administrative action gave meaning to the new ideas. At the local and state levels, mayors and governors attacked graft, reformed tax policies, established regulatory agencies, brought expertise to government, and pursued social service goals, including substantial benefits for the working classes. In national politics, reform was a dominant theme for a decade and a half. Four major acts of Congress established strong regulation of the railroads, the biggest business in the country and hitherto free of meaningful federal oversight. Sherman Antitrust Act prosecutions broke up several large corporate entities. The Federal Trade Commission was established to provide continuing discipline against anticompetitive behavior. The Underwood tariff subjected big domestic manufacturing to foreign competition and initiated the twentieth-century graduated income tax. The Federal Reserve Act gave the federal government more control over the nation's financial system while cutting into the power of the Wall Street "Money Trust." The Pure Food and Drug Act and the Meat Inspection Act reassured apprehensive consumers. Farmers received meaningful federal credit and educational programs. Labor won limited legislation for workplace safety, workmen's compensation, and the eight-hour day. A federal child labor law seemed to achieve a long-cherished goal of social welfarists.

A critical mass of Americans came out of the Progressive Era with a vastly expanded concept of what government was about and what it should try to do. To most who called themselves progressives, the experience was proof that a movement of ordinary middle-class citizens could achieve power and wield it in the interests of all. To the working classes, it was an alternative to socialism. And, just perhaps, to some captains of industry and finance it showed the potential for government stabilization and preservation of a maturing but inherently chaotic capitalist system — although it is a considerable stretch to argue that they captured the movement for their own purposes.

The progressive effort to deal with modernity often had unintended consequences. No question was more vexing than that of how to deal with the massive concentrations of economic power produced by a rapidly maturing corporate capitalism. The giant corporation did not simply threaten high prices for consumers of many goods and services, it also menaced a faith in small entrepreneurship that had been one of the foundations of American culture. The initial progressive impulse, and always the most popular one, was to break up "the trusts" in the interest of farmers and small businessmen. Theodore Roosevelt, Herbert Croly, and a few others, understanding that the organizational drive was inexorable, argued for government refereeing of a trend that could not be reversed. By 1912, the debate was central to one of the most memorable presidential campaigns in American history, Woodrow Wilson's New Freedom affirming antitrustism and the entrepreneurial past, Roosevelt's New Nationalism asserting the ability of a wise and disinterested government to regulate economic concentration in the public interest. Both visions were defective. The fragmentation of large corporations as a general policy was inconsistent with economic modernization and the material benefits that came with it. Government regulators were rarely capable of distancing themselves from the immediate interests they regulated. By 1917 U.S. corporate policy already had become a de facto regulatory effort that largely accepted big economic units and was simply one element in a larger pattern of pluralistic politics. Antitrust rhetoric would continue for decades; antitrust *action* as originally conceived was already pretty much a thing of the past.[6]

Another central theme became a study in irony. The drive to revitalize democracy became an attack on a traditional party politics that, for all its shortcomings, had displayed considerable vitality and mobilized masses. The direct primary, the non-party-line ballot, and the glorification of political independence excited middle-class reformers but had far less resonance with most other elements of the electorate. Here and there, at-large municipal elections and the professionalization of city management had the side effects (and quite possibly the central objectives) of excluding from political participation both principled socialists and spoils-seeking bosses. The new politics was less corrupt, dedicated to ideals of honesty and efficiency, and more prone to the discussion of issues; it was also more cerebral and less exciting than the mass spectacle of the late nineteenth century. Progressive campaigns that emphasized personality at the expense of party were captives to the vividness of the personalities that headed the tickets — at a time when most of the electorate could never see or hear a presidential candidate. The size and enthusiasm of the electorate failed to keep pace with population growth.[7]

Another irony logically followed. A movement hostile to special interests became an example of interest-group politics.

Until 1912 progressivism was primarily a Republican phenomenon. The GOP at the turn of the century was preeminently the party of the old-stock middle class; ethnically and culturally it was relatively homogeneous. Republicanism was still the doctrine of big government. Much of the political vitality of the early progressive movement came from insurgent Republican leaders in the Midwest and the West, waging a vigorous but ultimately unsuccessful struggle against a dominant standpat Northeastern elite. They were, to be sure, advancing the interests of farmers and small enterprisers who felt oppressed and threatened by a corporate establishment, but they likewise represented the sentiments of a large middle class jolted into political awareness by the upheavals of the 1890s. These sentiments, which provided the rhetorical tone of Republican progressivism, were not always readily attributable to simple economic self-interest. They were often expressed in calls for a revival of traditional morality in politics in the form of (to use David Thelen's phrase) a "new citizenship."[8]

The 1912 progressive walkout from the Republican Party and the subsequent failure to establish a viable Progressive Party created a free-floating constituency in search of a new political home. Thereafter, progressivism resided primarily in the much more pluralistic Democratic Party. The Democrats attracted a much higher percentage of the lower orders and the less educated. Ethnically and culturally more diverse, their constituencies—ranging from the immigrant populations of crowded industrial cities to old-stock Southerners of all classes to angry Western neopopulists—possessed numerous conflicting economic interests and worldviews. More by default than by reason, their patron saint was still Thomas Jefferson—the Jefferson of limited government. All this began to change as William Jennings Bryan increasingly espoused a diversified program of state action on behalf of the underprivileged, as farmers moved toward organization in quest of government benefits, as labor unions developed a greater interest in nonsocialist political action, and as Democratic political leaders responded opportunistically to Republican divisions.[9]

This last development gave rise to what has become the most serious dilemma of postprogressive reformism. The drive to restore the ideal of democratic citizenship working for the common interest transmuted into the most fully elaborated system of pluralist coalition politics in American history. The Democratic Party could achieve political power in no other way. No leader could express the progressive ideal so nobly as Woodrow Wilson. No progressive leader was so wily a coalition builder. Look at a Wilson poster from the 1916 campaign:

> Who Broke the Money Trust?
> Who Keeps Us Out of War?
> Who Stands for the Eight-Hour Day?
> Who Extended the Parcel Post?
> Who Gave the Farmer Rural Credits?[10]

To that list, one could add lowering the tariff on traditional Democratic free-trading assumptions, then establishing a tariff commission to make "scientific" recommendations for "adjustments"; protection for merchant seamen; federal workmen's compensation; and anti–child labor legislation. To be sure, a vision of the national interest and transcendent social justice lay behind some of these measures, but a number of them were calculatedly targeted at specific interest groups, ranging from regional bankers and businessmen to farmers to industrial workers. Not least among Wilson's targets were the Bull Moosers of 1912, obstinately independent, unwelcome in many state and local Republican organizations, already drifting toward the Democrats, and brought on board by Wilson's remarkable progressive agenda. In 1916 Wilson foreshadowed the Roosevelt coalition of 1936. Then, as later, the question of whether unified purpose could be found in diversity was better finessed than addressed squarely.

Progressivism, American Foreign Policy, and World War I

"Progressivism" was the dynamic force in American politics at the time the United States was emerging as a world power. Naturally enough, it imparted its tone to the diplomacy that accompanied that emergence. It is customary to think of the two major progressive presidents as embodying sharply contrasting visions about America's role in the world: Theodore Roosevelt the hard-eyed, power-oriented realist; Woodrow Wilson the utopian sentimentalist who believed in the force of great ideals. The quasi-pacifist isolationism of William Jennings Bryan and Robert La Follette and the "imperialism" of many Bull Moose Progressives fills out a complex picture. However, here as elsewhere the most rewarding approach is to look first for the common denominator, then move outward for the differences.[11]

Whether isolationist or internationalist, "realist" or idealist, imperialist or self-determinist, almost all progressives saw American foreign policy as a moral enterprise, embodying a sense of American mission that in one fashion or another could be traced back to the seventeenth century. Bryan, a sincere internationalist, resigned as secretary of state after the *Lusitania* crisis in 1915 because of pacifist objections to Wilson's aggressive protests to Germany; he publicly opposed a declaration of war in 1917. La Follette, a sincere isolationist, agreed with Bryan; his much more vehement opposition to World War I sprang from his conviction that it was the work of evil industrialists, bankers, and British imperialists. Theodore Roosevelt, allegedly the cool realpolitiker, leaped to moral judgment and customarily employed rhetoric that leaves considerable confusion about whether his calculation of the national interest preceded his heated condemnations of international malefactors. Woodrow Wilson deployed military power freely in the name of liberal democracy, intervening in the Caribbean, the Mexican revolution, and ultimately World War I.

It is fair to speak of a progressive *style* in twentieth-century American foreign policy, but dangerous to generalize about a progressive platform. The original progressives were split between "isolationism" (or unilateralism) and "internationalism." For two decades after World War I, most were isolationist. Then Franklin D. Roosevelt would establish as dominant an internationalist synthesis of the outlooks of the two presidents who had most influenced him, his cousin TR and his old chief Wilson. It would endure for a quarter century until Vietnam forced another reassessment.

"War," wrote Randolph Bourne, "is the health of the state." It also seemed for a time to be the health of progressivism. Bourne was one of a small number of progressives who continued to criticize World War I after it had been declared; a somewhat larger group gave it only perfunctory support. Most, however, backed it enthusiastically, mainly because they found Wilson's invocation of a "crusade" to make the world safe for democracy powerfully appealing. In addition, the fact of war created opportunities — for moral reformation, for social welfarism, for national economic organization — that seemed to point toward the fulfillment of progressivism.[12]

Moral reformism was the most problematic aspect of the progressive experience in the war. Intellectually progressivism was heavily based on a belief that the causes of social ills were environmental rather than individual, that (to take the two issues of individual morality that most disturbed the progressives) most often men became alcoholics and women prostitutes because of social conditions rather than because of personal weakness or innate bad character. In this, progressives were unlike many of the crusaders against alcohol or prostitution, but all of them were caught up in the logic of mass mobilization. Thus, prostitution near military installations endangered servicemen and threatened the war effort. So did alcohol; moreover, the diversion of grain to brewing or distilling took needed foodstuffs away from the allies. Under such circumstances, progressives as agents of change and national reformation, could easily find merit in closing down red-light districts and joining the fight for prohibition. To many, these moves were indistinguishable in purpose from such social welfare policies as publicly constructed housing for war workers or the Child Labor Act of 1918. State promotion of social betterment could have many dimensions in the all-or-nothing atmosphere of a modern war.

The logic of mass mobilization was most evident in an organization of the economy along lines inconceivable at the beginning of 1917: a War Industries Board to coordinate defense manufacturing; a War Labor Board to establish wage and hour policies, work with unions, and adjudicate disputes between labor and management; a Food Administration to organize agriculture (even fixing prices of some commodities) and limit public consumption; a Fuel Administration to manage the production and distribution of coal; and, perhaps most astounding, a Railroad Administration that, to all intents and purposes, nationalized the nation's rail transportation system. Most of these agencies dealt with and legitimized organized labor in a fashion unprecedented in American history, facilitating a large growth in union membership and a pattern of generous wage settlements for workers. An important corollary to the new economic management was the financing of the war in part by the most steeply graduated income tax yet in American history and by hefty corporate levies. Mobilization for war allowed mobilization for reform. The health of the state was the health of progressivism. As the war moved toward a triumphant conclusion in the fall of 1918, many progressives must have thought that the future was at hand—and that it worked.

That future consisted of a far larger and more active national state than Americans could have imagined in 1901. A part of its purpose was the promotion of moral betterment as defined by the old-stock Protestant middle classes. It would also pursue social welfarism aimed at protecting vulnerable groups and raising the living standards of the lower classes. Most stunning was the vision of a state-managed economy built around regulation and supervision of large corporations but possibly with some nationalization. Railway union leader Glenn Plumb advocated permanent government control of the railroads, initiating a serious political discussion. His role in the debate demonstrated that organized labor had become a stronger political force than ever and that it was now a significant part of a progressive movement located primarily within the Democratic Party.

That movement was also more clearly than ever a pluralist political coalition that given its professed devotion to civic virtue, required not just a brokering of material interests but a common vision. At the end of World War I, that seemed no problem. Triumphant progressivism at home was accompanied by the triumph of democracy in Europe. Progressivism had not only changed America; it was about to change the world.

Two years later Americans voted for Warren G. Harding and a return to normalcy.

The collapse of the progressive future in 1919–20 merits close analysis for it lays bare significant flaws not simply in early twentieth-century progressivism but in succeeding reform movements — a reliance on pluralist politics, utopianism, and dependence on charismatic leadership.

The "Wilson coalition" of 1916, although anticipatory of Roosevelt's in 1936, was a weak precursor of FDR's juggernaut. Wilson received less than 50 percent of the popular vote and had to govern with razor-thin partisan margins in Congress. The ideological progressive majority on Capitol Hill was equally slim. The war created situations certain to place stress on any coalition. All those for whom peace had been the paramount issue, most of them inclined toward progressivism, were quickly alienated from the administration. So too were civil libertarians, repelled by the repressive aspects of mobilization. Economic issues and rivalries created divisions. Inflation hit middle-class consumers hard. Wheat farmers resented price controls, especially when cotton farmers were not burdened with similar restrictions. The first year-and-a-half of peacetime saw strikes, surging price increases, and revolutionary terrorism. The onset of a serious recession in the last half of 1920 demonstrated that the progressive accomplishment in economic management was at best modest and perhaps simply an illusion.[13]

Wilson's rationale for the war, a moralistic appeal that denied the pragmatic dimension of progressivism, contained within itself the seeds of its own destruction. The president's crusade to make the world safe for democracy justified the mobilization of thought at home — converting intellectuals into propagandists and repressing dissenters ruthlessly — in a fashion that led to an inevitable backlash. His Fourteen

Points established a basis for a just, nonvengeful peace that blithely ignored the reality of what four years of total war had done to the outlook of the other major combatants. His ironclad commitment to a League of Nations with no-escape collective security guarantees willfully ignored 125 years of American history. These utopian war aims were a noble statement of rationalist liberal democratic capitalism — and thus irresistibly appealing to the progressive mind. Numerous progressives opposed the final result of his effort, the Treaty of Versailles and related settlements, but few did so because they disagreed with the sentiments their president had expressed. Rather they revolted against the imperfections of his execution: the punitive burdens placed upon the Central Powers, the failure to implement every single ethnic or national claim, the survival of imperialism among the victors. It was unfair to say that the war had solved nothing, but Wilson had led Americans to expect that it would solve everything. A wave of disillusionment swept over the last year-and-a-half of his administration, disproportionately affecting and alienating many of the progressives who once had supported him.[14]

In an emerging age of personal politics, the discrediting of Wilson meant the discrediting of progressivism. In the absence of a solid, ongoing institutional or ideological basis that would transcend interest groups to provide independent definition and continuity, reform was defined by, and personally identified with, presidents or other strong leaders. Progressivism had roots in the aspirations, anxieties, and material needs of groups too diverse to feel a sense of mutual identification — farmers, urban workers, small businessmen, middle-class professionals, academic experts. It had no umbrella organization, no union, no political party that could unite its membership. Its diversity was a source of strength when circumstances and leaders provided a common vision, but a chronic weakness when they could not.

The 1920s: False Sightings and Real Development

"What happened to the progressive movement in the 1920s?" asked Arthur Link in an influential essay published in 1959. His answer was audacious, albeit appropriately hedged: if "in decline," progressivism was nevertheless alive — not on a life support machine, but on the road to recovery and going about its work. His evidence? The vigorous La Follette Progressive Party campaign of 1924, the long crusade for farm relief built around various incarnations of the McNary-Haugen Plan, the equally long fight for public development of the federal hydroelectric power and nitrate-producing facility at Muscle Shoals. And, most audaciously, the revival of the protective tariff, immigration restriction, and various efforts at moral "social control," including national prohibition and the activities of the Ku Klux Klan.[15]

Link's essay largely initiated scholarly discussion of an important topic, and it possessed considerable merit. The problem was in its spin. It showed that *pieces* of progressivism survived, not progressivism as a coherent movement. The La Follette candidacy of 1924 drew interest mostly in the Midwest and West and appears to have been most attractive to those who admired La Follette's stand against World War I and the Treaty of Versailles. The McNary-Haugen fight was largely the work of a self-defined, nonideological "farm bloc" with little interest in non-agricultural issues. The Muscle Shoals plan, a pathbreaking concept that presaged the Tennessee Valley Authority, was a side issue that failed of adoption and did not establish a basis for a progressive revival. As for the rest of Link's list, it is clear that before World War I, most progressives had favored a low tariff and had opposed the protection of large manufacturing undertaken by Republicans in the 1920s. Immigration restriction, prohibition, and the Klan attracted numerous progressives, but many conservatives were likewise drawn to them.

Actually, Link's article more persuasively described the elements behind progressivism's decline: the eclipse of the Democratic Party; the subsequent failure of progressives to develop a new organizational vehicle for achieving political power; the social and cultural wars of the 1920s, which divided progressives along urban-rural lines; a "paralysis of the progressive mind" manifest in an inability to develop compelling new ideas for a new era; a more general alienation of the intelligentsia from the idea of democracy and anything resembling reform; the non-emergence of a charismatic leader capable of uniting and rejuvenating the old movement.

A different direction in the quest for progressive remnants — now common but unthinkable a generation ago — leads to Herbert Hoover. As head of the Food Administration, Hoover was an important member of Wilson's wartime economic management team. He was so highly esteemed by men who were undeniably progressives in both parties that there was a bipartisan presidential boomlet for him in 1920. As secretary of commerce under Harding and Coolidge, he pursued policies of voluntary industrial cooperation and standardization designed to organize American business and increase its efficiency in the common interest. He articulately urged the reconciliation of traditional American individualism with the organizational imperatives of the modern age. Unlike most Republican leaders, he took a friendly stance toward labor unions. Seeing himself as an engineer, he believed he possessed a broad view of the political economy that transcended the parochial perspectives of narrowly based interest groups. As president, he backed pathbreaking legislation to ameliorate the farm problem before the depression began. Once it was evident that the country was in a serious economic slump, he took unprecedented steps to combat it, laying the groundwork for Franklin Roosevelt's New Deal. Well into the 1930s, many old progressives continued to believe in him.[16]

Still, whatever its theoretical integrity, Hoover's "progressivism," even before the depression, was simply not accepted as such by large numbers of individuals incontestably identified with the progressive movement. George Norris, for example, spoke against Hoover's presidential candidacy in 1928 because of his opposition to McNary-Haugen and development of Muscle Shoals; the greatest surviving progressive in the Senate, Norris endorsed the Democrat Al Smith. Many other traditionally Republican Midwestern progressives, including Henry A. Wallace and Harold Ickes, followed him, either publicly or privately. They believed that progressivism had moved into the Democratic Party to stay and would evolve in the directions that had emerged under Wilson. The trend continued with the depression. By 1932 most Republican progressives were dissatisfied with Hoover, leaning toward the Democrats, and looking for leadership to Franklin D. Roosevelt.[17]

But before Roosevelt, there was Smith. The Democratic Party of Smith continued the drift begun under Wilson of bringing organized labor and its ethnic working-class constituencies into the progressive movement. But none of the leading personnel was capable of organizing a winning coalition in a party that was more pluralistic than ever. Ripped apart by the cultural conflicts of the 1920s, the Democrats produced would-be leaders who were unable to transcend their factional identities: McAdoo for the more rural and provincial wing; Smith for the metropolitan wing. Protestants and Catholics, drys and wets, nativists and ethnics, Klansmen and anti-Klansmen, moral enforcers and libertarians all enjoyed fighting it out with each other too much to look for a common purpose — until the depression gave them a reason to do so.

Progressives outside the Democratic Party fared little better. Fiorello La Guardia — sometime Republican, sometime independent — cut quite a swath in the House of Representatives during the 1920s. But although he deeply admired many of the older insurgent progressives, he found himself at odds with them on the major cultural issues that most agitated Americans in the 1920s. On prohibition and immigration restriction, many of his heroes were either vocal advocates or skilled politicians who knew when to run for cover. They must have enjoyed listening to the brash young New Yorker denounce "the trusts" and big business, but they surely doubted that he (or Al Smith for that matter) had any genuine understanding of the farm problem. Not until the country was deep into the depression could Norris and La Guardia unite on a bill to protect labor unions, one put through Congress by a coalition of urban Democrats and progressive Republicans in 1932.[18]

If the Norris–La Guardia Act was a harbinger of the future, even more so was the presidential candidacy of Franklin D. Roosevelt. In addition to one of the greatest names in American politics, Roosevelt had enormous assets. A leading official in the Wilson administration, Democratic vice-presidential candidate in 1920, Protestant and rural by birth but with close ties to the urban wing of the Democratic Party, governor of the nation's largest electoral state, he was a near-perfect unity candidate — and not just for his party. His goal, clear to perceptive observers in 1932, was a grand progressive coalition that would reshape the Democratic party.

The New Deal

By the time Roosevelt became president, the term "progressive" was being displaced in political discourse by the word "liberal." More than rhetorical, the shift indicated a belief that reformism in the 1930s was in some measure distinct from its precursor. From the mid-1950s into the 1970s, scholars, arguing from mushy and shifting frames of reference, debated whether the New Deal was in fact mostly new and different. In the end the nonempirical nature of the controversy exhausted the discussion. For the past generation, historians usually have assumed discontinuity, but few bother with a rationale.[19] Because it compels analysts to formulate and defend a large view of the course of twentieth-century American reform, the argument is important. But it is not subject to an either/or resolution. The New Deal possesses powerful elements of continuity with progressivism; it also is in many respects a departure. Such a conclusion does not fudge the question; rather it asserts an evolutionary development.

Continuity is most evident in the personnel. Franklin Roosevelt had been an enthusiastic progressive, inspired first by his cousin Theodore, then by Woodrow Wilson. Most of the leading figures in his administration had clear links to progressivism. Secretary of State Cordell Hull had sponsored the income tax provision of the Underwood Tariff. Secretary of the Interior Harold Ickes had been a dedicated follower of Theodore Roosevelt and a prominent Chicago antimachine activist. Secretary of Labor Frances Perkins and relief administrator Harry Hopkins were leaders of the social work establishment that had grown out of the settlement house movement. The "Brains Trust" — Raymond Moley, Adolf Berle, and Rexford Tugwell — was a case study in progressive era intellectual descent. Moley's early political heroes were William Jennings Bryan and Tom Johnson; his intellectual mentor Charles A. Beard. Berle was the son of a prominent social gospel minister; as a young attorney, he resided for two years at the Henry Street settlement house. Tugwell was greatly influenced by leading progressive era economic thinkers Charles Van Hise, John R. Commons, and Simon Patten. Louis Brandeis, appointed to the Supreme Court by Wilson, remained active as a behind-the-scenes advocate. His most important disciple, Felix Frankfurter, himself a prominent progressive, recruited many former students for Roosevelt's government, including David Lilienthal, Benjamin V. Cohen, and Thomas Corcoran. Those who gave the New Deal its intellectual capital and developed its programs were, with few exceptions, products of the progressive movement. The same appears true of leading New Deal supporters on Capitol Hill.[20]

In key areas of policy, the case for continuity is also persuasive. The initial impulse of the New Dealers was to do what a progressive government had tried to do during World War I — manage the economy during a time of crisis in the interests of all groups.[21] When this effort at a loose corporatist state under the aegis of the National Recovery Administration (NRA) collapsed, the New Deal turned to a sustained attack on big business and finance, utilizing a rhetorical style reminiscent of progressivism at its peak. With legislation such as the Banking Act, Public Utility Holding Company Act, and the Wealth Tax Act (all in 1935), along with an active and vocal antitrust program, the second phase of the New Deal quickened the pulse of many old-line progressives. The New Deal discussion about the federal stance toward big business seems almost a replay of the debate between the New Freedom and the New Nationalism with an outcome not much different from that of the progressive era—a venting of angry big business rhetoric in the grandest antitrust tradition combined with a disinclination to break up any large corporation. As Ellis Hawley has observed, the American people from the beginning of the industrial age have been pulled between a fear of concentrated corporate power and a longing for the benefits of its presumed wealth-generating efficiencies. To this the depression added a sense of the fragility of the economic system; the prospect of dismantling healthy economic units drew little support in such a context. The New Deal confirmed what had been established in the Wilson presidency: antitrustism was to be primarily a regulatory tool against anticompetitive activity, not an ideology of economic fragmentation.[22]

New Deal concern with social welfare likewise had strong roots in the progressive era. The Social Security Act of 1935 was developed by a committee and advisory council with several members who had direct ties to the social work–settlement house wing of progressivism: Perkins, Hopkins, Paul Kellog, Father John Ryan. Its executive director, Edwin Witte, a University of Wisconsin economist, was a member of probably the most socially engaged economics department of the early twentieth century. The act's social welfare provisions gave the federal government an institutional responsibility that had been sought by a generation of earnest middle-class reformers in the late nineteenth and early twentieth centuries.[23]

The triumphant Roosevelt coalition of 1936 was in many respects the ultimate evolution of the Wilson coalition of 1916, a robust adult grown from an anemic infant. Like Wilson, Roosevelt appealed strongly to the independent progressive vote and won over many former Republicans. Like Wilson, he got the support of farmers by providing them with major benefits programs. Like Wilson, he appealed successfully to labor. Like Wilson, he capitalized on traditional reservoirs of Democratic strength in the South and the West, which he enlarged by making the New Deal a major regional development program.[24]

Another New Deal theme—the maturing of the administrative state—also reflects evolutionary continuity. Faith in expertise and bureaucratic management had been a major theme of modernization in the late nineteenth and early twentieth centuries, not limited to progressives but enthusiastically adopted by them in manifold ways that ranged from Tom Johnson's professionalization of municipal services in Cleveland to Robert La Follette Sr.'s array of advisory and regulatory commissions in Wisconsin to federal programs that included conservation, tariff adjustments, transportation regulation, the Federal Trade Commission, and the Federal Reserve System. Political progressivism more often than not had begun as a series of local responses to problems that ranged from corruption to poverty. As the progressive impulse moved up the political ladder in a search for definitive and universally applicable resolutions, progressivism took on a far more national focus than had been the case in 1900. The progressive crusade against politics as usual turned into an offensive against organized party politics; semi-independent agencies became the institutional guarantors of reform.

The New Deal did more of the same in such magnitude that one might argue for a state that was different in kind. Sidney Milkis has persuasively described Franklin Roosevelt's move toward the establishment of an entrenched administrative bureaucracy, buttressed by a supportive unelected judiciary, as the primary implement of liberal government. A byproduct of this trend was a further decline in the importance of political parties and electoral politics—orchestrated by America's greatest master of electoral politics. Moreover, the administrative state inevitably devalued the sentiments of electoral majorities as it went about its tasks of complex regulatory decision-making and the definition of fundamental rights beyond popular restriction. The ironic practical result was a decline in democracy (in the traditional sense of majority rule) or at least a redefinition of it by a movement that constantly asserted its democratic aspirations. One need not endorse Milkis's assertion that this development amounted to a de facto rewriting of the Constitution to recognize the New Deal as a big leap forward in a process that has continued to this day.[25]

The most obvious discontinuity between the 1930s and the early twentieth century—the fact of depression—demonstrates the fundamental evolutionary continuity from progressivism to the New Deal. Progressivism had flowered during an era of prosperity and indeed may have been made possible by the very lack of an economic crisis. The ebbing of class conflict after the turbulent 1890s had made possible a measured debate about the American future, one driven by issues of economic structure, political organization, and social justice—all informed by the moral values and economic interests of a reasonably secure middle class. That discussion had been brought to a halt by World War I and muted by the mass prosperity of the 1920s. The New Dealers tried to take it back to the center of American politics and found the task complicated by the pervasive economic insecurity of the 1930s. Brought to power by a depression and given a mandate to engage in sweeping reforms to combat it, they were very nearly as unsuccessful at the task as Herbert Hoover had been—in large measure because they were children of the progressive era. The experience of progressivism gave them no guidelines, no intellectual capital, for dealing with the business cycle.

The New Deal addressed economic problems with an increasing tendency toward countercyclical federal spending, but it was never clear, even to most of the policymakers, whether this was an economic recovery strategy or simply humanitarian relief (and not so covert vote-buying) on a grand scale. Roosevelt and most of those around him may be forgiven their failure to seize upon the new and strange economic theories of John Maynard Keynes. Moreover, one may question whether Keynes's recommendation of massive spending would have played out so magnificently in the peacetime thirties as in World War II, when a challenge to national survival legitimized the unimaginable. The idea of countercyclical spending (so long as the federal budget was in balance over a period of years) had long been around; the concept, reduced to the idea of pump-priming, was consistent with the progressive heritage. As good progressives, FDR and many of those around him wanted to help the destitute and make work for the unemployed. The policy was both humane and politically shrewd.

Countercyclical spending peaked in 1936 (the first full year of the Works Progress Administration). Apparently bringing recovery into sight, it did much to insure Roosevelt's landslide victory. Yet in 1937, the administration, worried about a rapidly increasing national debt, cut work relief sharply. The result was a sharp recession and a serious political crisis that had to be resolved by a resumption of expenditures. By 1939, to be sure, the Roosevelt administration was more complacent about the prospect of large federal deficits as far into the future as the eye could see. But the Keynesian remedy, which required far greater spending, was too far outside the progressive heritage. The WPA provided work for a fraction of the jobless; here and there it threatened to become a way of life for those on its payroll. The national unemployment rate remained in high double digits and the nation in a state of depression until 1940. Roosevelt's budget deficits were spectacular by previous peacetime standards, but the old heritage of orthodox fiscal management (really neither "progressive" nor "conservative") still controlled policies that rather than beating the depression, simply made it less catastrophic.

If the progressive legacy did not tell the New Dealers how to deal with the business cycle, it did tell them to attack the interests and hope that somehow the depression might thereby be conquered. Roosevelt made some friendly gestures toward business during his first two years in office, and a few programs, notably the Reconstruction Finance Corporation, were of immense help to many corporations. Still, the second most-remembered line of his first inaugural address was his triumphal pronouncement that the money changers had been driven from the temple of government. From the beginning, the New Deal angered the corporate/financial establishment and not infrequently baited it. The attacks would have resonated with progressives of twenty years earlier.

All the same, history never exactly repeats itself. The term "evolutionary continuity" rightly acknowledges some change, most of it in this case related to the shifting character of the progressive/liberal coalition and the politics of pluralism.

The mood and content of the New Deal possessed a more social-democratic tinge than was ever sighted near the mainstream of progressive thought and action. The depression itself discredited capitalism as a system and encouraged ordinary people to examine quasi-socialist welfare-statist alternatives with sympathy. A rising labor movement, even in America, inclined toward narrowing income differentials, punishing wealth, controlling business, and seeking government guarantees of security for the worker. Such tendencies were encouraged by the existence of a strong current of moderate socialism among influential unionists including David Dubinsky, Sidney Hillman, and the young Walter Reuther.[26]

The New Deal appeal to the working class was not based simply on welfarist ideology or interest group mobilization. It also had a frank ethnocultural character from which most progressives would have recoiled. Wilson, only partly motivated by the divisive impact of World War I, denounced "hyphenated Americanism" and clearly was put off by assertions of ethnic identity; Theodore Roosevelt agreed with (as usual) redoubled vehemence. Franklin Roosevelt appealed much more deliberately to ethnic and religious minorities as cultural entities, not just as working-class people. Wilson's relationship with the Democratic machines that organized these constituencies was often distant and uneasy; FDR had little love for the urban bosses, but accepting the big city organizations as facts of life, he dealt with them on a pragmatic basis.[27]

Wilson had appealed with some success to labor unions and their ethnocultural constituencies, but labor was far more important in FDR's coalition. Most progressives had mixed feelings about organized labor. Their biggest priority was the situation of the small entrepreneur, threatened primarily by the trusts but secondarily by irresponsible unions. Despite some rhetorical and programmatic symbolism, the New Deal cared little for small business. By and large, the progressives recoiled from class conflict; the second Roosevelt played the class card with gusto. After an initial hesitation that had its roots in his own progressive past, he aligned himself strongly with a rapidly growing labor movement. The Wagner Act of 1935 provided guarantees for union organization that most progressives surely would have deemed excessive. The agency it created, the National Labor Relations Board (NLRB), operated more as a wing of the union drive than as an impartial arbiter. Labor in turn became Roosevelt's biggest backer, handing him and his party large campaign contributions and providing thousands of highly motivated campaign workers. By FDR's death, the big unions had become the organizational core of the Democratic Party in the northern industrial states. In 1948 Harry Truman would kick off his campaign with a huge union rally in Detroit's Cadillac Square; Adlai Stevenson, John F. Kennedy, Lyndon Johnson, and Hubert Humphrey would follow his example in a symbolic recognition of the party's power center.[28]

If the New Deal lent decisive backing to labor's drive to organize, it went considerably farther with the large, diverse agricultural sector of the economy, which it organized commodity by commodity from Washington. Acreage allotments, federally enforced marketing agreements, the purchase and warehousing of surpluses — all with the objective of establishing a fair price for the products of a farmer's labor — constituted the most extensive federal management of a single economic sector in

American history. The World War I Food Administration had done many of these things, but it was designed as a short-term crisis agency, not a long-term income-support vehicle. Roosevelt may have seen agricultural subsidies as a temporary depression measure, but most program administrators, including Secretary Henry A. Wallace, had other ideas. Moreover, the agricultural program created a large constituency that could not be denied its benefits. In the 1930s approximately 25 percent of the population still lived on farms. And the very fact that farmers tended to vote more independently than labor gave them considerable political leverage. The federal organization of agriculture would endure with adjustments in details for the balance of the century.[29]

A macro view of the political economy that emerged from the New Deal by 1939 yields a picture quite distinct from the past, but not without roots in it. A sector-by-sector look reveals two tiers in each major sector, the top one considerably more assisted (or in the case of business less adversely impacted) by the New Deal than the bottom:

Business

The large corporations constituted the top tier. Harassed a bit by federal regulation and the inconvenience of having to deal with labor unions, they continued to be huge concentrations of economic power. Not as dominant politically as in the 1920s, they still wielded considerable influence. The second tier — ranging from smaller corporations to individual shopkeepers — mostly bitterly resented the New Deal. The regulatory state and the labor unions presented far greater difficulties for them, and only the politically connected few could hope to receive anything in the way of compensatory benefits. The dream of progressivism as a reform program serving (to use Wilson's phrase) "the man on the make" was effectively interred for good.

Labor

At the top was an elite of old-line railway and American Federation of Labor (AFL) craft unions joined by a newly emergent, rapidly growing contingent of industrial unions concentrated in the Congress of Industrial Organizations (CIO). Enjoying a symbiotic relationship with the New Deal, the CIO unions were the most dynamic and politically conscious. The railway unions, politically engaged for decades, already had effectively utilized their strategic position athwart the nation's transportation system to achieve such gains as the Adamson Act (1916) and the Railway Labor Act (1926). By the end of the New Deal, they were among the largest and most powerful American unions. The AFL craft unions, pushed by their members, had abandoned their traditional anti-governmental stance to support Roosevelt and his program. Unionized workers accounted for less than 25 percent of the work force; still, they provided a reservoir of political support for Roosevelt unlike anything seen in America before. The bottom tier, the vast majority, although nonunionized, was probably even more intensely behind him, in part because of what the New Deal accomplished for more fortunate workers, in part because so many of the unorganized received help in the form of public works projects, other forms of relief, and (in a relatively small number of cases) the establishment of a minimum wage.

Agriculture

The top half or so of American agriculture — those farmers with substantial operations who produced for the market — were in many cases literally saved from liquidation by the New Deal. That makes it hard to account for their erratic voting record after 1936, even when one takes a partial price fallback into account. Clearly there was much in the New Deal that conflicted with the entrepreneurial sensibility of the farmer. Culturally there was little attraction to the New Deal's increasing affinity with urban populations and labor unions. Still, "middle-class agriculture" prospered. The bottom half — marginal farmers, tenants, share-croppers — was hardly touched, and when it was, the impact might well be negative. (The agricultural programs, by establishing acreage allotments, allowed many landowners to get rid of a percentage of their sharecroppers; often those that remained never saw a check.) These groups never got beyond a status that might be labeled "relief problem."

Implicit in these outcomes was a belief that it was the responsibility of an enlarged federal establishment to manage the economy in the interest of all groups and especially to use its weight to establish balances of power within the major sectors and between them. From a European point of view, this amounted to a crude form of corporatism, but that concept, with its transatlantic baggage and intimations of fascism, is of questionable utility in understanding American politics. "Organizational society" or "countervailing powers" are more satisfactory descriptive phrases, but even they convey a misleading impression of coherence.

The New Deal system, far from being the implementation of a new and detailed intellectual blueprint, evolved out of the ideas and experience of the Progressive Era, the exigencies of the depression, and changing realities in the sociopolitical environment. At no point, however, did it abandon the progressive idea that a common public interest exists and that the government should pursue it. If it had a "social-democratic tinge," it assuredly did not establish a social democracy, although in later years many of its adherents aspired to that goal. Nor did it foreshadow the synthesis of social democracy and corporatism that exists throughout Western Europe today. It was typically American in its messy liberal democratic pluralism. For most Americans, and most New Dealers, the New Deal was simply Roosevelt, who attracted a following unlike that of any other Western democratic leader in the 1930s.

FDR's appeal was all the more remarkable in light of his economic failure. Battered by the sharp recession of 1937–38, continued mass unemployment, a middle-class backlash against the excesses of organized labor, rejection of the plan to pack the Supreme Court, the misconceived Democratic Party purge of 1938, and the rise of a loose "conservative coalition" in Congress, the New Deal stalled in political gridlock. With unemployment at 18 percent as late as the summer of 1939, Roosevelt appeared destined in the long run to be remembered as one of the more interesting unsuccessful American presidents. Yet seemingly by force of personality he had pulled together a powerful political movement and given it a sense of common purpose.

Beyond the cult of personality there was the coalition. But for what purpose did it exist, once the fight against the depression and the war against totalitarianism had come and gone? Once Roosevelt was no longer there to give it leadership? The Roosevelt coalition would endure for a generation, winning occasional electoral triumphs, making piecemeal gains in the struggle for "liberalism." Increasingly, however, it was less than the sum of its parts, functioning more to achieve benefits for its diverse constituencies than as an agent of reform for the common good.

World War II

In Franklin D. Roosevelt one finds a foreign policy that is a clear synthesis of the styles and ideals of Theodore Roosevelt and Woodrow Wilson — an undergirding of realpolitik, a hefty side-bracing of moralism, and a heavy overlay of quasi-utopian idealism. Understanding the realities of power, Roosevelt did not shrink from the use of force in pursuit of the national interest. Historians have emphasized his political trimming in the face of overwhelming isolationist sentiment during the looming world crisis of the late 1930s: his backing away from sanctions against Italy after the invasion of Ethiopia, his refusal to take sides in the Spanish civil war, his acceptance of the Neutrality Acts, his lack of fol- lowup after the Quarantine speech, his praise for the Munich agree- ments. But these were tactical maneuvers, not indicative of a strategic direction. Sometimes quietly, sometimes ostentatiously, Roosevelt chal- lenged the widespread isolationism that was at least as strong among his liberal supporters as his conservative opponents.

After war broke out in Europe in September 1939, the logic of his policy was unmistakable. Among its most scathing critics were nu- merous old progressives who had opposed war in 1917. It was they, at least as much as Republican right-wingers, with whom Roosevelt had to employ all his considerable guile as he led the nation toward war. Possi- bly he did not actually anticipate full participation in the conflict, but he surely realized that such could be the consequence of one unneutral act of aid after another to Britain — a transfer of naval vessels (disguised as a shrewd bargain called the Destroyers for Bases Deal), extensive credits (misleadingly called Lend-Lease), U.S. naval escorts for British convoys and active participation in the war against German submarines ("Atlan- tic patrols"), a friendly meeting with Prime Minister Winston Churchill and the issuance of a benign "joint declaration of war aims" (the Atlantic Charter), aid to the Soviet Union after it was invaded by Germany, a tightening noose of economic restrictions around the neck of the other Axis belligerent (Japan).

These were the acts of a practitioner of power politics who under- stood the interests of his country. But Roosevelt presented them in terms of the grandest Wilsonian ideals: the Four Freedoms ("everywhere in the world" for "everyone in the world"), the Atlantic Charter (a refor- mulation of Wilson's Fourteen Points), the establishment of a United Nations organization (a recreation of Wilson's League). Such ploys, along with the realization that the Axis powers presented the greatest threat to American democracy in the nation's history, converted the liberals. Pearl Harbor ended the debate. By 1943 the nation was in the midst of a Wilsonian revival. Liberals who persisted in isolationism were relegated one by one to the political dustbin. The World War II Roose-veltian synthesis remains the dominant mode of American thinking about foreign policy.[30]

At home the war was managed along the lines progressives had estab-lished in World War I, but with a heavier hand that reflected the over-whelmingly total character of the conflict. Yet, although enormous war orders produced full employment, the economic control apparatus left few liberals with a sense of great new possibilities. And although public sentiment, unlike that of World War I, was nearly unanimous in its support for the conflict, resentment of the economic controllers was far greater than in the first war. Roosevelt's defeat of Thomas E. Dewey in 1944 was the least substantial of his four presidential election triumphs. The election, conforming to a pattern established in 1938, returned a Congress in which the balance of power tilted toward the center-right, leaving little hope for impressive legislative breakthroughs. Partly in reaction to political adversity, partly as a logical response to the deep American suspicion of the regulatory-organizational creed, American liberalism turned to a consumer-oriented Keynesianism as its primary tool of economic management.[31]

Part of the problem was in the nature of the war itself. Lasting three years and nine months, it was two and a half times the effective length of World War I, and its impact on the civilian population was considerably more pervasive. Much of the World War I managerial effort had been quasi-voluntaristic. Most of it in World War II was mandatory. It in-volved bureaucracy, reams of regulations, enforcement personnel, penal-ties, and, above all, widespread deprivation. Probably necessary but loaded with political peril, a comprehensive system of rationing and price controls affected the lives of virtually all Americans. For the average civilian, government policy meant the management of shortages of every type of consumer good. Never adept at detached comparative perspec-tives, most Americans cared little for their status as the best-fed, best-housed, and safest population among the major belligerents. Rather as consumers, they resented the difficulty of obtaining such comforts of life as gasoline, red meat, coffee, and tires. As farmers or small business people, they hated price controls and all the regulations that went with them, and they reacted with a mixture of anger and despair at being unable to obtain vital equipment.

In the 1930s the New Deal (especially after the demise of the NRA) had meant multiple forms of assistance from a beneficent government. Now it meant the apportionment of discomfort. Running the war with what most people understood to be "New Deal methods" mostly administered by "New Deal administrators," the government held down agricultural prices, put a lid on wages, effectively forbade strikes, severely limited civilian production, and regulated the conduct of business to an extent never before attempted in the United States, all the while presiding over an economy characterized by shortages of consumer goods. There was something in the management of the war to offend almost every interest group, and that management was irretrievably labeled "New Deal."

Here as in other instances, the progressive tradition collided with the fundamental temperament of the classical liberalism from which it had developed. Wartime mobilization enjoyed widespread consent in European nations with traditions that were in varying degrees more corporatist, especially when those nations faced direct military attack. Even Britain — by long tradition the most liberal of the belligerents — in the name of defending the realm, established what amounted to a near-monolithic state that controlled the economy, rationed consumer goods severely, effectively nationalized medical care, resettled bombing victims, and laid the basis for the postwar welfare state. Safe from military attack, possessing almost nothing in the way of a corporatist tradition, the United States was inherently more hostile to the sort of management that total war implies. This hostility easily transferred to the New Deal liberalism identified with that management.

Postwar Years: Fair Deal to Great Society

Harry S. Truman, as fully a child of progressivism as Franklin Roosevelt, carried on the struggle for liberalism after FDR's death. Largely a holding action, his presidency performed a critical role in preserving the Roosevelt coalition and maintaining existing New Deal programs. A liberal movement that had seemed on the verge of defeat and disintegration by the end of 1946 was alive and victorious in 1948, viable and developing an enlarging agenda throughout the 1950s, thanks in large part to Truman's efforts. The culmination would be the Great Society.[32]

Postwar liberalism took on an important issue that had been of marginal interest to early twentieth-century progressives — an increasingly firm and explicit commitment to black civil rights. Here Truman played a role of paramount importance. Beginning his political journey as a rural, upper-South progressive, he had matured into a New Deal urban liberal who accepted blacks as a legitimate political constituency. Propelled by the logic of a belief in equal opportunity that was in many respects derived from his progressive past, he found it natural to oppose blatant racial discrimination. Many liberals who came out of the progressive tradition experienced similar transformations, but more was involved than a series of personal conversions. The liberal political coalition included increasing numbers of voting blacks, driving reform beyond the old progressive agenda while retaining much of progressivism's spirit and ideals.[33]

Truman also continued American foreign policy along the progressive ideological lines in which Roosevelt had directed it. Only the name of the enemy changed. Truman's Cold War rhetoric was Wilsonian, invoking an American mission to achieve self-determination, individual rights, and democracy for almost everyone in the world, based on a vision of liberal capitalism as a political-economic norm. The Marshall Plan and, later, Point Four (aid to the underdeveloped world) captured the imagination of liberals. In the tradition of progressivism they rejected the Popular Front assertion of an underlying unity among all "left-of-center" forces and accepted the struggle against Soviet Communism as the international embodiment of a historic obligation to reshape the world according to progressive values.[34]

Truman's immediate successors as leaders of the Democratic Party—Adlai Stevenson, John F. Kennedy, and Lyndon Johnson—all identified themselves with liberalism, and all accepted the outline of it that Truman had left them: greater development of the social service state and civil rights at home, the Cold War as a drive for liberal values abroad. The culmination was the Great Society and what Allen Matusow has called the unraveling of America.[35]

Taking the reins of the Democratic Party from the twice-defeated Stevenson, Kennedy called for a New Frontier, composed in equal parts of advanced social welfarism, civil rights, economic stimulus, more open trade, and a vigorous, idealistic pursuit of the Cold War. After his assassination, Johnson fulfilled the dream. The results, however, were disheartening. At its moment of greatest achievement, the progressive tradition seemed to self-destruct. In 1964 Johnson received 61 percent of the popular vote. Four years later, his designated heir, Hubert Humphrey, got less than 43 percent. Richard Nixon and George Wallace polled a combined total of nearly 57 percent, signaling a retreat from liberalism that continues after a generation.

What had gone wrong? Three large answers stand out:

1. Liberalism overreached itself, pursuing aims beyond full achievement and reaping the disillusionment that came with failure. Early twentieth-century progressives would have admired aspects of Johnson's Great Society, which was squarely in the progressive tradition of applying pragmatic social science to public policy. Still the overall program was so large and ambitious as to be more a difference in kind than in degree — not simply from progressivism but also from the New Deal. By the 1960s, moreover, most of what remained of the socialist party had established itself on the left wing of the Democratic Party, imparting to liberalism's major political vehicle a stronger social-democratic bias than ever. (The most spectacular example was the way in which the socialist Michael Harrington provided the central rationale and working assumptions of the war on poverty.) Progressives had thought in terms of equal opportunity; Great Society liberals were more likely to think in terms of equal results. Nor did the so-called New Left provide much in the way of intellectual refreshment. Its visions — at times explicitly Marxist, at times simply varieties of confused utopianism — rejected the rational, gradualist pragmatism that had characterized the progressive outlook at its best. Ultimately, whatever the fairest interpretation of a complicated reality, the Great Society's major problem stemmed not from its conceptualization but from its performance. Programs such as medicare or aid to education might appear as triumphs, but the war on poverty was at best a stalemate, and the cities seemed on a downward spiral beyond the remedial ministrations of government. On the surface, the America of 1968 was more ridden with menacing social problems than the America of 1960.

2. From progressivism through the Great Society, American reform had focused primarily on issues of corporate power, social welfare, and income distribution, secondarily on "good government" concerns. While one could always find a few cultural dissenters around the edges, progressivism and New Deal–Fair Deal liberalism had existed comfortably within a consensus of traditional Judeo-Christian morality that provided clear and unmistakable cues for behavior. Monolithically accepted

throughout American culture, the traditional morality was neither a matter of dispute between rich and poor nor a subject of controversy between conservatives and liberals. Conventional religion enjoyed wide acceptance as a rationale for policy formulation. If conservatives might invoke "the Protestant ethic" as a justification for individualistic capitalism, progressives often derived much of their zeal from the social gospel idea of Christian brotherhood. "Onward Christian Soldiers" was the unofficial hymn of the 1912 Progressive Party. Woodrow Wilson's theology was inseparable from his political-diplomatic thinking. Franklin Roosevelt freely invoked God and prayer in his rhetoric. The cultural upheavals of the sixties and seventies shattered this consensus irretrievably, splitting both the liberal political coalition and the elites who led it. By the midseventies, mainstream liberalism disparaged religion and rejected once-unquestioned moral strictures. Cultural politics competed with social welfare politics as a focus of concern, leaving it an open question as to whether liberalism stood primarily for business regulation, social security, and the needs of working people or (to quote Spiro Agnew's notorious formulation) for "acid, amnesty, and abortion."

3. The Vietnam War likewise was a shattering wedge issue, disrupting the always-fragile liberal Cold War consensus. Initially it split the liberals down the middle, but after Lyndon Johnson was succeeded by the hated Richard Nixon, most liberals moved sharply in the direction of neoisolationism and a quasi-pacifist approach to foreign relations. As early as the George McGovern campaign of 1972, they went far beyond simple criticism of an ill-considered military commitment. Fecklessly, liberals tossed the mantle of responsible anti-Sovietism to the Republicans, who seized it, wrapped themselves in it, and used it brilliantly as a primary attraction. It was devastatingly telling that in 1980, a one-time liberal Democrat who had led a struggle against Communist influence in the movie industry won the presidency as a conservative Republican.

The overreaching of social reformism, the rise of the adversary culture, and the abandonment of anticommunism left the liberal-Democratic coalition in shreds. Much of its culturally traditional working-class constituency was demoralized and alienated. Dissenters among its intellectual elite undertook a reevaluation that came to be known as "neoconservatism" and began a move to the Republican Party. By the 1980s the term "liberal" had fallen into such disrepute that politicians of national aspirations ran from it desperately. It seemed reasonable enough to conclude by the time Ronald Reagan buried Walter Mondale — the best and the brightest the liberals had to offer — that liberalism had self-destructed.[36]

What Remains of the Progressive Tradition?

The theme of this essay has been one of evolutionary continuity. Early in this century, a loose political tradition that we may call "progressivism" established itself as a dominant force in American public life. It was an interesting, if not altogether coherent, set of well-articulated ideas about the ends and means of American politics. Behind these ideas were impulses, anxieties, and interests that were more *felt* than articulated — reactions to rapid social-economic change in the form of large-scale corporate capitalism, big finance, the internationalization of commodity markets, labor militance, mass immigration, overwhelming urban problems, and the bureaucratization of American life. Progressivism took shape from the fears of farmers, small entrepreneurs, and a broad swath of the urban middle class. It also emerged from a new sense of professionalism and professional values in endeavors ranging from the Christian ministry and the academy to journalism and public administration. A politics of hope, progressivism drew on both the socialization of traditional Christianity and a faith in the pragmatic social sciences. In the end, however, what gave expression to these forces was the political coalition behind them. As that coalition changed in step with changes in American society, so also did the meaning of "progressivism." The "liberalism" of the late twentieth century may still be a lineal descendant of the "progressivism" of the early twentieth. But we all know that grandparents and grandchildren, however great their fondness for each other, generally have differences of perspective that loom large.

The most significant of these stems from the breakdown of the middle-class, white, Anglo-Saxon, Protestant consensus that animated so much of the progressive movement. Neither religion nor patriotism nor a sense of community can be effectively invoked as a rationale for political reform today. The most common standards are either an abstract sense of justice based on considerations of equity (civil rights and antidiscrimination measures) or simple material betterment at the individual level ("Are you better off now than you were four years ago?"). Standards of morality have shifted so greatly that it is only a bit of a stretch to say that today the moral example of 1900 is thought of as either uninteresting or downright immoral. Conversely, the height of immorality in those days may today be considered moral, or at least a matter of personal choice to be defended without quarter on civil libertarian grounds. Surely neither Theodore Roosevelt nor Woodrow Wilson ever imagined a politics in which "cultural" issues loomed so large. They would have found inconceivable a style of progressivism that defended abortion as a matter of individual choice and envisioned homosexuals as an oppressed minority.

Many progressives actually thought it possible to break up the trusts; most had a strong emotional attraction to the objective. Nearly a century later, antitrust policy is no more than a disciplinary tool that blocks anticompetitive practices and occasionally places some restrictions on corporate mergers. The huge combines that roused progressive fears — those that survive at all — seem for the most part ailing dinosaurs. Microsoft and Bill Gates are often discussed in the same terms as the Standard Oil Trust and John D. Rockefeller; the analogy is at best imperfect. Today's closest counterpart to J. P. Morgan is the chairman of that progressive creation, the Federal Reserve Board. The objects of progressive social welfare aspirations, the working and nonworking poor, are less than half the proportion of the population today than in those days, leaving the middle class as the recipient of most federal largesse. Labor unions are more likely to be composed of public employees than blue collar workers. Farmers, around 50 percent of the population in 1900, are now at 2 percent and no longer up in arms over freight rates and being weaned from government subsidies. The few true family farms are quaint reminders of a simpler past. The world that gave rise to progressivism is gone.

Yet the pace of economic transformation and dislocation at the end of this century is comparable to that at the end of the last. Then as now, the basic institutions and assumptions of the economy were changing rapidly and in the process creating substantial hardship, while corporate chieftains paid themselves princely salaries and engaged in unseemly displays of wealth. Then as now, the gap between rich and poor struck many as unconscionably wide and getting wider, and the establishment wisdom was that such was the price of progress. Consider the urban scene. A huge wave of immigration consisting mostly of non-northern Europeans did not assimilate readily into the dominant culture and seemed a source of multiple social problems. Cities were hard put to provide basic services and maintain order. A large and menacing under-class seemed out of control. Insurgent reformers attacked the political and business establishments as callous or corrupt or both; they urged a transfer of power to either themselves or like-minded defenders of the ordinary person against the forces of exploitation and greed.

Are there counterparts today? Has one described Ralph Nader? Common Cause? Ross Perot? It is intriguing that the term "progressivism" seems to be making its way back into political discourse.[37] Moreover, faith in the power of rational social science continues unabated among today's policy wonks. Proposals for change have little chance of being considered seriously unless supported by "a study" with appropriate statistical tables. Most Americans may write off Nader and Perot as cranks or zealots and yawn at the latest Common Cause press release. Still, TR prematurely dismissed Lincoln Steffens and his friends as unconstructive muckrakers.

Whatever the chances for a rebirth of progressivism, one thing seems clear. Times may change, but ways of thinking die hard. Many of the perspectives of progressivism and much of its language remain with us, shaping our sense of the world around us more than we may realize.

Notes

The author wishes especially to thank Jerome Mileur, Sidney Milkis, Morton Keller, and James Patterson for their extensive and very helpful comments on an earlier draft of this article.

1. For Truman's career, see Alonzo L. Hamby, *Man of the People: A Life of Harry S. Truman* (New York: Oxford University Press, 1995). For specific references, Robert Ferrell, *Dear Bess* (New York: Norton, 1983), 39, 89, 99 (on muckrake magazines and Bryan); Harry S. Truman, "The Military Career of a Missourian" (handwritten World War I memoir), Truman Papers, Senatorial and Vice-Presidential File, Harry S. Truman Library, Independence, Mo.; George B. Tindall, *The Emergence of the New South* (Baton Rouge: Louisiana State University Press, 1967), chap. 7 (on business progressivism).

2. Representative examples of what might be called the primal view of progressivism include the final chapter of John D. Hicks, *The Populist Revolt* (Minneapolis: University of Minnesota Press, 1931); the first two chapters of Theodore Saloutos and John D. Hicks, *Agricultural Discontent in the Middle West, 1900–1939* (Madison: University of Wisconsin Press, 1951); and George Mowry, *Theodore Roosevelt and the Progressive Movement* (Madison: University of Wisconsin Press, 1946).

3. See, e.g., Richard Hofstadter, *The Age of Reform* (New York: Knopf,

1955); John Buenker, *Urban Liberalism and Progressive Reform* (New York: Scribner's, 1973); Nancy Weiss, *Charles Francis Murphy, 1858–1924: Respectability and Responsibility in Tammany Politics* (Northampton, Mass.: Smith College, 1968); Allen F. Davis, *Spearheads for Reform* (New York: Oxford University Press, 1967); Eric F. Goldman, *Rendezvous with Destiny* (New York: Knopf, 1952); Gabriel Kolko, *The Triumph of Conservatism, 1900–1917* (New York: Free Press, 1963); James Weinstein, *The Corporate Ideal in the Liberal State* (Boston: Beacon Press, 1968); Samuel P. Hays, *The Response to Industrialism* (Chicago: University of Chicago Press, 1957); Robert Wiebe, *The Search for Order* (New York: Hill and Wang, 1967); Robyn Muncy, *Creating a Female Dominion in American Reform* (New York: Oxford University Press, 1991).

4. Peter Filene, "An Obituary for the 'Progressive Movement,'" *American Quarterly* 22 (Spring 1970): 20–34; Alan Dawley, *Struggles for Justice* (Cambridge: Harvard University Press, 1991); John Milton Cooper, *Pivotal Decades* (New York: Norton, 1990).

5. See, e.g., Benjamin Rader, "Richard T. Ely: Lay Spokesman for the Social Gospel," *Journal of American History* 53 (June 1966): 61–74, and Harold Wilson, *McClure's and the Muckrakers* (Princeton: Princeton University Press, 1970).

6. Morton Keller, *Regulating a New Economy* (Cambridge: Harvard University Press, 1990), esp. chap. 2; Louis Galambos and Joseph Pratt, *The Rise of the Corporate Commonwealth* (New York: Basic Books, 1988), esp. chap. 3. See also Thomas McCraw's prize-winning *Prophets of Regulation* (Cambridge: Harvard University Press, 1984), especially for its chapters on Louis Brandeis and David Lilienthal.

7. Michael McGerr, *The Decline of Popular Politics* (New York: Oxford University Press, 1986); Samuel P. Hays, "The Politics of Reform in Municipal Government in the Progressive Era," in Samuel P. Hays, *American Political History as Social Analysis* (Knoxville: University of Tennessee Press, 1980), 205–32.

8. David Thelen, *The New Citizenship* (Columbia: University of Missouri Press, 1972).

9. There is no fully satisfactory account of the Democratic Party in the early twentieth century. One can find perhaps the best rendering of the process I have described in Arthur Link's classic works on Woodrow Wilson, especially *Woodrow Wilson and the Progressive Era* (New York: Harper and Brothers, 1954) and *Wilson: Campaigns for Progressivism and Peace* (Princeton: Princeton University Press, 1965). See also David Sarasohn, *Party of Reform* (Jackson: University Press of Mississippi, 1989); Paolo Coletta, *William Jennings Bryan: Political Evangelist* (Lincoln: University of Nebraska Press, 1964) and *William Jennings Bryan: Progressive Politician and Moral Statesman* (Lincoln: University of Nebraska Press, 1969). Many state and local studies track the process at the subnational level.

10. Cooper, *Pivotal Decades,* 250 (photo).

11. John Milton Cooper, *The Warrior and the Priest* (Cambridge: Harvard

University Press, 1983), compares and contrasts Roosevelt and Wilson with far more subtlety than the title indicates. Robert Endicott Osgood, *Ideals and Self-Interest in America's Foreign Relations* (Chicago: University of Chicago Press, 1953), esp. parts 1 and 2, is a still useful classic.

12. A fine recent synthesis that speaks to many of the points raised below is Ronald Schaffer, *America in the Great War* (New York: Oxford University Press, 1991), which should be supplemented with David Kennedy, *Over Here* (New York: Oxford University Press, 1980) and Robert Ferrell, *Woodrow Wilson and World War I* (New York: Harper and Row, 1985).

13. The two standard studies of postwar life and politics are Burl Noggle, *Into the Twenties* (Urbana: University of Illinois Press, 1974) and Wesley Bagby, *The Road to Normalcy* (Baltimore: Johns Hopkins University Press, 1962).

14. Arthur S. Link, *Woodrow Wilson: Revolution, War, and Peace* (Arlington Heights, Ill.: Harlan, Davidson, 1979), chaps. 4 and 5, splendidly summarizes these issues from Wilson's point of view. On Wilson's perspective and his objectives, see also N. Gordon Levin, *Woodrow Wilson and World Politics* (New York: Oxford University Press, 1968), the best "new left" study, and Thomas J. Knock, *To End All Wars* (New York: Oxford University Press, 1992), a strongly argued depiction of Wilson as more an early social democrat than a conventional "liberal capitalist." For the reaction of the progressives, Goldman, *Rendezvous with Destiny*, chap. 12, remains as good a brief account as we have. Astonishingly, the fullest account of the Treaty of Versailles and the League fight is still Thomas Bailey, *Woodrow Wilson and the Lost Peace* (New York: Macmillan, 1944) and *Woodrow Wilson and the Great Betrayal* (New York: Macmillan, 1945).

15. Arthur S. Link, "What Happened to the Progressive Movement in the 1920s?" *American Historical Review* 64 (July 1959): 833–51.

16. Joan Hoff Wilson, *Herbert Hoover: Forgotten Progressive* (Boston: Little, Brown & Co., 1975) is perhaps the definitive statement on Hoover as progressive, but the articles and edited works of Ellis Hawley have been of great importance also. See, esp., Ellis Hawley, ed., *Herbert Hoover as Secretary of Commerce, 1921–1928* (Iowa City: University of Iowa Press, 1981) and Hawley, *The Great War and the Search for a Modern Order*, 2d ed. (New York: St. Martin's Press, 1992), important not only for what it says about Hoover but for its description of an emerging "organizational" political economy, 1917–33.

17. On the thin and divided progressive support for Hoover in 1928, see Hoff Wilson, *Herbert Hoover*, 123–24; Richard Lowitt, *George W. Norris: The Persistence of a Progressive* (Urbana: University of Illinois Press, 1971), esp. 409–14, 549–62; Edward and Frederick Schapsmeier, *Henry A. Wallace of Iowa: The Agrarian Years, 1910–1940* (Ames: Iowa State University Press, 1968), 109–12; Linda Lear, *Harold L. Ickes* (New York: Garland, 1981), 327–28.

18. The standard work on La Guardia is Thomas Kessner, *Fiorello H. La Guardia and the Making of Modern New York* (New York: McGraw-Hill, 1989), but Arthur Mann, *La Guardia: A Fighter Against His Times* (Philadelphia: Lippincott, 1959) remains a classic.

19. Some of the major statements in this argument are Hofstadter, *Age of*

Reform, chap. 7; Carl Degler, *Out of Our Past* (New York: Harper & Row, 1959), chap. 12; William E. Leuchtenburg, *Franklin D. Roosevelt and the New Deal* (New York: Harper & Row, 1963), chap. 14; Richard S. Kirkendall, "The New Deal: Another Watershed in American History," in John Braeman, Robert Bremner, and Everett Walters, eds., *Change and Continuity in Twentieth-Century America* (Columbus: Ohio State University Press, 1964), 145–89; and Otis L. Graham, *An Encore for Reform* (New York: Oxford University Press, 1967). Among important works on the New Deal that address the problem less directly, the first volume of Arthur Schlesinger Jr.'s The Age of Roosevelt series, *The Crisis of the Old Order* (Boston: Houghton Mifflin, 1957) is clearly on the side of continuity. On balance, it seems to me that the same is true of James MacGregor Burns, *Roosevelt: The Lion and the Fox* (New York: Harcourt Brace, 1956) and Frank Freidel, *Franklin D. Roosevelt: A Rendezvous with Destiny* (Boston: Little, Brown, 1990). Alonzo L. Hamby, *Liberalism and Its Challengers: F.D.R. to Bush* (New York: Oxford University Press, 1992) may appear at a surface glance to side with the advocates of discontinuity in a fashion inconsistent with this essay's theme of evolutionary continuity. It does not.

20. Capsule biographies of many New Dealers may be found in Otis L. Graham Jr., and Megan Robinson Wander, eds., *Franklin D. Roosevelt: His Life and Times, an Encyclopedic View* (Boston: G. K. Hall, 1985). Jordan Schwarz, *The New Dealers* (New York: Alfred A. Knopf, 1993) builds its chapters around biographical treatments of individuals and adopts a theme of evolutionary continuity with progressivism. For more extended treatments of the persons listed above, see Jordan Schwarz, *Liberal: Adolf A. Berle and the Vision of an American Era* (New York: Free Press, 1987); Raymond Moley with the assistance of Elliot Rosen, *The First New Deal* (New York: Harcourt Brace and World, 1966); Raymond Moley, *Realities and Illusions,* ed. Frank Freidel (New York: Garland, 1980); Michael V. Namorato, *Rexford G. Tugwell* (New York: Praeger, 1988); Alpheus T. Mason, *Brandeis: A Free Man's Life* (New York: Viking, 1946); Melvin I. Urofsky, *Brandeis and the Progressive Tradition* (Boston: Little, Brown, 1981); Bruce Allen Murphy, *The Brandeis-Frankfurter Connection* (New York: Oxford University Press, 1982); Michael Parrish, *Felix Frankfurter and His Times: The Reform Years* (New York: Free Press, 1982); Steven M. Neuse, *David E. Lilienthal* (Knoxville: University of Tennessee Press, 1996); and, especially for Cohen and Corcoran, Joseph P. Lash, *Dreamers and Dealers* (New York: Doubleday, 1988).

21. William E. Leuchtenburg, "The New Deal and the Analogue of War," originally published in Braeman et al., *Change and Continuity in Twentieth-Century America,* recently updated and reprinted in Leuchtenburg, *The FDR Years: On Roosevelt and His Legacy* (New York: Columbia University Press, 1995), 35–75.

22. Ellis Hawley, *The New Deal and the Problem of Monopoly* (Princeton: Princeton University Press, 1966); Richard Hofstadter, "What Happened to the Antitrust Movement: Notes on the Evolution of an American Creed," in *The Paranoid Style in American Politics and Other Essays* (New York: Alfred A. Knopf,

1965), 188–237; Alan Brinkley, "The Antimonopoly Ideal and the Liberal State: The Case of Thurman Arnold," *Journal of American History* 80 (September 1993): 557–79.

23. Edwin Witte, *The Development of the Social Security Act* (Madison: University of Wisconsin Press, 1962) and J. Douglas Brown, *The Genesis of Social Security in America* (Princeton: Princeton University Industrial Relations Section, 1969) focus on the program's origins. Important broader studies are W. Andrew Achenbaum, *Social Security: Visions and Revisions* (Cambridge: Cambridge University Press, 1986); Edward Berkowitz, *America's Welfare State* (Baltimore: Johns Hopkins University Press, 1991); and Martha Derthick, *Policymaking for Social Security* (Washington: Brookings Institution, 1979).

24. On this point, see esp. Schwarz, *The New Dealers.*

25. Sidney Milkis, *The President and the Parties* (New York: Oxford University Press, 1993), chaps. 1–6.

26. Steve Fraser, *Labor Will Rule: Sidney Hillman and the Rise of American Labor* (New York: Free Press, 1991); Nelson Lichtenstein, *The Most Dangerous Man in Detroit: Walter Reuther and the Fate of American Labor* (New York: Basic Books, 1996). One hopes Robert D. Parmet's projected biography of Dubinsky will some day fill an important gap.

27. See, e.g., George Flynn, *American Catholics and the Roosevelt Presidency* (Lexington: University of Kentucky Press, 1968); David J. O'Brien, *American Catholics and Social Reform: The New Deal Years* (New York: Oxford University Press, 1968); Charles Trout, *Boston, the Great Depression, and the New Deal* (New York: Oxford University Press, 1977); Bruce Stave, *The New Deal and the Last Hurrah: Pittsburgh Machine Politics* (Pittsburgh: University of Pittsburgh Press, 1970), and Lyle W. Dorsett, *Franklin D. Roosevelt and the City Bosses* (Port Washington, N.Y.: Kennikat Press, 1977).

28. On labor in the 1930s, in addition to the books by Fraser and Lichtenstein cited above, see Irving Bernstein, *Turbulent Years* (Boston: Houghton Mifflin, 1970); Robert Zieger, *The CIO, 1935–1955* (Chapel Hill: University of North Carolina Press, 1995) and *John L. Lewis* (Boston: Twayne, 1988), a good short biography; and Melvyn Dubofsky and Warren van Tine, *John L. Lewis* (New York: Quadrangle, 1977), the standard full biography.

29. Theodore Saloutos, *The American Farmer and the New Deal* (Ames: Iowa State University Press, 1982) is the standard survey. Richard S. Kirkendall, *Social Scientists and Farm Politics in the Age of Roosevelt* (Columbia: University of Missouri Press, 1966) is a penetrating look at key policymakers.

30. On Roosevelt as diplomatist, see esp. Robert Dallek, *Franklin D. Roosevelt and American Foreign Policy, 1932–1945,* 2d ed. (New York: Oxford University Press, 1995); Warren Kimball, *The Juggler* (Princeton: Princeton University Press, 1991); and Eric Larabee, *Commander in Chief* (New York: Harper & Row, 1987). On the enduring Wilsonian synthesis, see Tony Smith, *America's Mission* (Princeton: Princeton University Press, 1994).

31. The best comprehensive account of American life and politics in World War II is Richard Polenberg, *War and Society* (Philadelphia: Lippincott, 1972)

closely followed by John Blum, *V Was for Victory* (New York: Harcourt Brace Jovanovich, 1977). Barton J. Bernstein, "America in War and Peace: The Test of Liberalism," in Bernstein, ed., *Towards a New Past* (New York: Pantheon, 1968), 289–321, critiques the liberalism of the 1940s from the left. On labor, see Nelson Lichtenstein, *Labor's War at Home* (New York: Cambridge University Press, 1992) and James Foster, *The Union Politic* (Columbia: University of Missouri Press, 1975). John Jeffries, *Testing the Roosevelt Coalition: Connecticut Society and Politics in the Era of World War II* (Knoxville: University of Tennessee Press, 1979) is a fine case study. The transit of liberalism toward a limited form of consumptionist Keynesianism is trenchantly argued by Alan Brinkley, *The End of Reform* (New York: Knopf, 1995), a very important book despite its overstated title.

32. In addition to the critical Barton Bernstein article cited above, see also Hamby, *Man of the People* and Hamby, *Beyond the New Deal: Harry S. Truman and American Liberalism* (New York: Columbia University Press, 1973). For liberalism beyond the Truman administration, see Steven Gillon, *Politics and Vision: The Americans for Democratic Action* (New York: Oxford University Press, 1987) and Richard Pells, *The Liberal Mind in a Conservative Age* (New York: Harper & Row, 1985).

33. Donald McCoy and Richard Ruetten, *Quest and Response: Minority Rights and the Truman Administration* (Lawrence: University Press of Kansas, 1973) is the standard account of its topic. A still excellent study of liberalism and the civil rights revolution in the 1940s is Richard Dalfiume, *Desegregation of the U.S. Armed Forces* (Columbia: University of Missouri Press, 1969). These works are challenged from the left by William C. Berman, *The Politics of Civil Rights in the Truman Administration* (Columbus: Ohio State University Press, 1970) and Barton J. Bernstein, "The Ambiguous Legacy: The Truman Administration and Civil Rights," in *Politics and Policies of the Truman Administration,* ed. Bernstein (Chicago: Quadrangle Books, 1970). The debate is a fairly typical example of the "mainstream liberal" versus "new left" debate that characterizes much of the scholarship about the Truman presidency.

34. There is a vast literature on the Truman administration, liberalism, the Cold War, and the choices that the liberals had to make. In addition to the works already cited, see Norman Markowitz, *The Rise and Fall of the People's Century: Henry A. Wallace and American Liberalism, 1941–1948* (New York: Free Press, 1973); Athan Theoharis, *Seeds of Repression: Harry S. Truman and the Origins of McCarthyism* (Chicago: Quadrangle Books, 1971); and Michael Paul Rogin, *The Intellectuals and McCarthy: The Radical Specter* (Cambridge: M.I.T. Press, 1967), all written from various points on the left. Richard Fried, *Nightmare in Red* (New York: Oxford University Press, 1990) is written from a more centrist perspective. On the Cold War itself, two major studies with important implications for the problem of liberalism are John L. Gaddis, *Strategies of Containment* (New York: Oxford University Press, 1982) and Melvyn Leffler, *A Preponderance of Power* (Stanford: Stanford University Press, 1992).

35. Allen J. Matusow, *The Unravelling of America* (New York: Harper and

Row, 1984) remains the best single volume on liberalism in the 1960s, but see also Irwin Unger and Debbi Unger, *Turning Point: 1968* (New York: Scribner's, 1988) and John Blum, *Years of Discord* (New York: Norton, 1991).

36. On Mondale and the larger theme of the disintegration of liberalism, see Steven Gillon, *The Democrats' Dilemma: Walter F. Mondale and the Liberal Legacy* (New York: Columbia University Press, 1992). Peter Steinfels, *The Neoconservatives* (New York: Simon & Schuster, 1979) is a useful, if not entirely satisfactory, introduction to its topic. On political coalitions and the disaffection of key Democratic constituencies, see Richard Scammon and Ben Wattenberg, *The Real Majority* (New York: Coward-McCann & McGeoghegan, 1971); Samuel Lubell, *The Hidden Crisis in American Politics* (New York: Norton, 1970); Andrew Greeley, *Building Coalitions* (New York: New Viewpoints, 1974); Everett C. Ladd and Charles Hadley, *Transformations of the American Party System* (New York: Norton, 1975); and Samuel Freedman, *The Inheritance* (New York: Simon & Schuster, 1996).

37. The most recent prominent example is E. J. Dionne, *They Only Look Dead: Why Progressives Will Dominate the New Liberal Era* (New York: Simon & Schuster, 1996).

Progressivism and Federalism

Martha Derthick and John J. Dinan

Progressivism left a greater legacy of political thought about federalism than of deliberate change in the working of the institution. Ironically, perhaps, given the large amount of institutional reform that is associated with the era — expansion of the civil service, strengthening of chief executives, reorganization of municipal governments, numerous measures of direct democracy — there is relatively little in the reform of intergovernmental relations that can be ascribed specifically to it.

Direct election of senators, which replaced election by state legislatures through the seventeenth constitutional amendment in 1913, was of transcendent importance to federalism, marking as it did the abandonment of one of the main constitutional protections of state governments. But this was only superficially a Progressive achievement; it had been many decades in the making.[1] The same may be said of the Sixteenth Amendment, which enabled Congress to impose income taxes, though here the implications for federalism, if no less profound, were less manifest.

Otherwise, unless it would be the development of uniform state laws or, less plausibly, the initiation of governors' conferences, the era produced no milestones in the practice of intergovernmental relations. There was nothing comparable, say, to passage of the Morrill Act of 1862, which overturned an earlier veto by President James Buchanan and established categorical grants-in-aid to the states, or to the rise of

81

federal mandates in the 1960s and 1970s.[2] Several new grant-in-aid programs were enacted, including an important one in 1916 for highway construction, but there was nothing comparable to the Great Society explosion of shared programs. Nevertheless, the period was of utmost importance to the evolution of federalism. Progressive political thought laid an indispensable foundation for the transformations in policy and institutions that were to come later in the twentieth century.

Prior to the Progressive Era, federalism in the United States was conceived of as a constitutional doctrine that prescribed separate sovereignties. The Civil War and the amendments that followed had decisively shifted the terms of nation-state relations to the nation's advantage, but federalism was still understood as a precept of constitutional law, to be interpreted and applied by the Supreme Court. In a celebrated aphorism, the Court rendered the essence of its understanding in *Texas v. White* (1869), saying that the Constitution had created "an indestructible Union, composed of indestructible States."[3] States could not destroy the nation by seceding, but neither could the nation abolish states. When the Civil War presented an opportunity to abolish some, the opportunity was not used. Nonetheless, the relation between the two levels of government was still understood to be largely conflictual. The task of the Court was to define and enforce the boundaries between nation and states.

The Progressive Era advanced a new way of thinking about federalism, grounded less in constitutional law than in conceptions of community and political ideology. It taught that Americans were one people who would improve themselves individually and socially by cooperating in pursuit of shared social ideals. Cooperation among governments in the federal system was one of many forms of cooperation advocated. This shift, with its emphasis on construction of a national community, could easily have denied the importance of federalism altogether, but we will argue that this was not the case. The Progressive attack was qualified.[4] We will first take up the attack, then proceed to the qualifications.

The Attack

Progressive Era political thought assaulted the conventional conception of federalism in three main ways. First, it both challenged the Constitution as a governing instrument and propounded radically new ways of interpreting it that would have virtually abolished any limitation on the powers of the federal government. Second, by propounding an explanation of the causes of centralization that blamed the victim — the states — it justified and facilitated further centralization. Third, it began constructing a social and philosophical conception of federalism as a substitute for the legalistic one that had dominated American political thought.

Constitutional Doctrine

The principal barrier to the expansion of federal power was the Constitution, or, more precisely, the prevailing Supreme Court interpretation of the Constitution. Particularly troubling to the Progressives were a series of Court decisions that were handed down in the final decade of the nineteenth century and that overturned a number of important federal economic regulations. The Progressives tried to overcome these decisions in a variety of ways.[5]

Their first strategy was to devalue both the federal judiciary as an institution and judicial review as an instrument of government. J. Allen Smith, among others, contended that judicial review was illegitimate because it was neither specified in the Constitution nor intended by its drafters.[6] Others followed Charles Beard in concluding that the delegates to the constitutional convention did expect that courts would exercise judicial review, but that they had done so for illegitimate reasons, to better secure property.[7]

Several institutional reforms were proposed to restrain the federal courts, although none was ultimately enacted. Bills backed by Progressives were introduced in Congress to curtail the courts' jurisdiction and to require a supermajority or a unanimous vote before the Supreme Court could invalidate legislation.[8] Some Progressives were also attracted to Theodore Roosevelt's proposed recall of judicial decisions or Robert LaFollette's motion to permit Congress to reenact statutes that the Court declared unconstitutional.[9]

Amendment was another avenue through which Progressives sought to overcome the prevailing constitutional interpretation. But as Judge Charles Amidon argued in 1906, "the vast enlargement of our country has made the method of amendment provided by the fathers far more difficult than they contemplated at the time, [and in fact,] there is a very general understanding that formal amendment is impossible." Although Amidon's estimate of the difficulty of amendment proved to be overstated in that four amendments were adopted between 1913 and 1920, proposed amendments to permit federal regulation of child labor, minimum wages, and a number of other areas were all defeated. In any event, constitutional amendment was viewed as "not suitable to bring about those slight but steady modifications of fundamental law which adapt it to the progressive law of the nation. It is far too violent a remedy for that purpose. The Constitution has been and ought to be accommodated to the ever-changing conditions of society by a process as gradual as the changes themselves."[10]

Accordingly, the most prominent Progressive strategy was to challenge the existing understanding of constitutionalism and to put forth a new interpretation of the constitutional balance of powers between the state and federal governments. Until the late nineteenth century, political scientists, historians, and statesmen had been prone to venerate the Constitution. It was viewed as the product of a unique set of circumstances and the embodiment of enduring institutions and principles. This understanding was challenged on several fronts in the Progressive Era. Political scientists began to suggest that the Constitution was no longer an accurate guide to understanding the operation of American governing institutions. In 1885 Woodrow Wilson, in his book *Congressional Government,* criticized those who engaged in "an undiscriminating and almost blind worship of [the Constitution's] principles, and of that delicate dual system of sovereignty, and that complicated scheme of dual administration that it established." In 1906 Albert Bushnell Hart opened his American government textbook by proclaiming the necessity of studying "the actual workings of government: the text of constitutions and of statutes is only the enveloping husk; the real kernel is that personal interest which vitalizes governments."[11]

These initial doubts soon turned into a full-blown critique of constitutionalism itself. J. Allen Smith offered the clearest statement of this view when he argued that a democratic age required a new understanding of the purpose of a constitution. "A constitution can not be regarded as a check upon the people themselves," he argued. It is properly viewed as "the means of securing the supremacy of public opinion and not an instrument for thwarting it, [and therefore] must yield readily to changes in public opinion."[12]

Judge Amidon held to a more moderate view of constitutionalism, but one that differed from the conventional understanding nonetheless. He believed that "the constitution performs its chief service when it holds the nation back from hasty and passionate action, and compels it to investigate, consider and weigh until it is made sure that the proposed action does not embody the passion of the hour, but the settled purpose of the years." But, "a changeless constitution becomes the protector not only of vested rights but of vested wrongs."[13]

The Progressives were particularly troubled by what Frank Goodnow described as the tendency "to emphasize the rights of the states rather than the powers of the federal government [and to adopt] an extremely individualistic conception of the powers of government [that has] resulted in a constitutional tradition which is apt not to accord to the federal government powers it unquestionably ought to have the constitutional right to exercise." In light of the economic changes that had taken place since the Founding as well as the experience of other countries that had drafted constitutions in the course of the nineteenth century, Goodnow concluded: "We are justified, therefore, in assuming that, if the American people were called upon at the present time, to frame a scheme of federal government, they would adopt one which departed in a number of respects from the one under which we now live, and which would resemble that of Germany or Canada in that it would make provision for greater ease of constitutional amendment and for securing to the national government greater powers than are believed by many to be accorded to the government of the United States under the present constitution."[14]

The Progressives challenged the well-established convention that the federal government was one of enumerated powers. A series of Supreme Court decisions had relied upon this doctrine to permit federal regulation of interstate commerce in prostitution, lottery tickets, and adulterated food and drugs, but to limit the ability of the federal government to regulate monopolies and prohibit child labor. A central aim of the Progressive movement, which was expressed most clearly by President Theodore Roosevelt in a speech in 1906, was to introduce a more expansive understanding of national power, particularly with respect to the regulation of interstate commerce. Condemning the Supreme Court's construction of the powers of the national government as too narrow, he called for a return to James Wilson's view. Roosevelt attributed to Wilson the doctrine "that an inherent power rested in the nation, outside of the enumerated powers conferred upon it by the Constitution, in all cases where the object involved was beyond the power of the several states and was a power ordinarily exercised by sovereign nations." He was drawn in particular to Wilson's belief that "whenever the states cannot act, because the need to be met is not one of merely a single locality, then the national government, representing all the people, should have complete power to act. [Under a] wise and farseeing interpretation of the interstate commerce clause," Roosevelt concluded, "the national government should have complete power to deal with all of this wealth which in any way goes into the commerce between the States."[15] The chief concern, as Roosevelt made clear in an address to the Colorado legislature in 1910, was that "the courts, instead of leading in the recognition of the new conditions, have lagged behind; and . . . have tended by a series of negative decisions to create a sphere in which neither nation nor state has effective control; and where the great business interests that can call to their aid the ability of the greatest corporation lawyers escape all control whatsoever."[16]

The Progressives also challenged limitations on federal power that were grounded in conventional understandings of dual sovereignty and the due process clause. The prevailing judicial conception was that federal power was limited not only by the specific enumeration of powers in Article 1 of the Constitution but also by the reservation of certain powers to the states in the Tenth Amendment and limitations on federal power in the Fifth Amendment. The Progressives argued that the concept of dual sovereignty was outdated. Goodnow complained that it "laid emphasis on preserving for all time the same degree of state sovereignty and independence as was recognized to exist in the latter part of the eighteenth century."[17] But it was evident, as constitutional scholar John Jameson argued, that in the aftermath of the Civil War and in view of the increasing scope of political problems, "no theory of sovereignty but that of the people as a whole is in harmony with the facts of American political life."[18]

Additionally, the Progressives sought to bring a halt to expansive interpretations of the due process clause of the Fifth Amendment that served to limit federal power. In light of the fact that many of the most important questions of government were no longer political in nature, they agreed with Walter Weyl that the conception of individual rights had to be "extended and given a social interpretation" so that it might cease to serve as a barrier to national regulation of the conditions under which men, women, and children labored.[19]

Political Theory

The Progressive Era was a period of centralization in measures of public policy. These might have been understood as constitutional usurpations, or as the partisan acts of congressional majorities. Critics of centralization, defenders of the established way of thinking, did so conceive of them.[20] Progressive thinkers, however, justified them as necessary responses to the default and incapacity of state governments.

The classic statement of this view, widely noticed at the time and cited since, came in a speech late in 1906 by Elihu Root, Theodore Roosevelt's secretary of state. Delivered in New York to a dinner of the Pennsylvania Society, this speech argued that state lines were being obliterated by three forces: an increase in national sentiment, domestic free trade, and technological changes in transportation and communication. Under the new conditions of economic and social interdependence on a national scale, the states were no longer capable of performing such functions as the regulation of railroad rates, the inspection of meat, and the guaranteeing of the safety of foods and drugs.

The states could only be preserved, Root continued, if they awakened to "their own duties to the country at large." To survive, states must act in the national interest, submerging particular agendas to the greater good, which was of course defined by the agenda of Progressivism:

> If any state maintains laws which promote and foster the enormous over-capitalization of corporations condemned by the people of the country generally; if any state maintains laws designed to make easy the formation of trusts and the creation of monopolies; if any state maintains laws which permit conditions of child labor revolting to the sense of mankind; if any state maintains laws of marriage and divorce so far inconsistent with the general standard of the nation as violently to derange the domestic relations, which the majority of the states desire to preserve, that state is promoting the tendency of the people of the country to seek relief through the national government and to press forward the movement for national control and the extinction of local control. The intervention of the national government in many of the matters which it has recently undertaken would have been wholly unnecessary if the states themselves had been alive to their duty toward the general body of the country.[21]

Root's explanation for centralization was that of a statesman — an eminent lawyer, party leader, and public servant. More penetrating theories, cast in terms arguably more devastating to state governments, came from academic sources.

The political scientist Henry Jones Ford of Princeton University argued that quite apart from the inadequate scope of their individual jurisdictions, states as governments were flawed structurally. They were premodern democracies in decay, the symptoms of which were "the historic perversions of democracy—namely, oligarchy and ochlocracy. . . . " Formed in the eighteenth century when it was believed that government power should be diffused, they lacked "appropriate organs of authority." Power, therefore, flowed to that government which *did* have an appropriate authority, namely, the federal government, "the sole, competent organ of sovereignty in this country," at the pinnacle of which was a powerful, responsible unitary executive. Ford simultaneously condemned the state governments and celebrated the emergence of the active presidency, and his condemnation of the states was savage: "Our state politics exhibit the characteristic phenomena which occur with monotonous regularity in all ages, as republican forms of polity degenerate. They are all there—the growth of plutocratic privilege, the violence of demagogues, the infirmity of legislation, the decay of justice, the substitution of private vengeance for judicial process, the increase of crime and disorder, and the growth of associations formed for self-help in the redress of grievances, and resorting to night-riding, torture and assassination in furtherance of their purpose."[22]

Still, a different academic theory was advanced by the economist Simon N. Patten, who located the cause of the decay of state and local governments in processes of development. Patten noted with dismay that state and local offices had "lost their former independent position" and had come to be valued "largely for the places they furnish for partisans of national politics." State and local officials—even the least of them, such as constables—were chosen not because they advanced individual policies, or exhibited any special fitness for office, but because they had served a national party. State and local governments had been reduced to a "mere nominal existence."

This decay had occurred, Patten argued, because as population spread across the continent and new state and local governments were formed, they had ceased to have the character of communities defined by shared interests. The original colonies along the Atlantic seaboard and their towns had arisen "naturally" and were held together by common bonds of religion or national origin of the settlers. "Each town in this region became a centre of a group of families having common aims and interests which bound them together in a real unit." As development proceeded west of the Alleghenies, however, units of local government were formed arbitrarily, suiting the convenience of surveyors. States similarly were formed without regard to commonality of interest or the logic of geography and climate. Patten cited north-south divisions in Ohio, Indiana, and Illinois, marked by differing climates, crops, and currents of migration. Political communities so haphazardly and illogically constituted were certain to lack vitality, he argued, and farther west, this problem was compounded by the extreme size of the states and corresponding thinness of population.[23]

The view that defects of the states were the cause of centralization took hold widely, as is suggested by its appearance in 1925 in a Memorial Day speech by President Calvin Coolidge at Arlington National Cemetery. Unlike Root, Coolidge spoke as an ardent defender of individualism and local self-government, which he judged to be crucial to both the preservation of American liberty and Western civilization. He deplored the tendency toward centralization in the federal system, but also found the source of it in the default of the states: "Without doubt, the reason for increasing demands on the Federal government is that the states have not discharged their full duties."[24]

Progressive Era defenders of state sovereignty did their best to meet this challenge by fashioning uniform state laws, an effort that originated in the late nineteenth century in the New York state legislature and the American Bar Association (ABA) and was supported financially by some of the states and state bar associations as well as the ABA. This was the constitutional conservatives' strategy of constructive response to the demands of the time.[25]

The Great Community

The formation of American nationhood and nationality had been under way for a long time before the Progressives arrived on the scene. They did not invent national consciousness, but they sought to alter its content. They spoke of a national "community," having in mind that the nation should have purposes both moral and public that all of its members shared. This conception — indeed, this political ideology — had implications for government that of course went well beyond the institutions of federalism. To illustrate what it meant specifically for federalism, we draw on the work of Mary Parker Follett, who was one of the few

Progressive authors to employ the term in a self-conscious way. Follett's work, *The New State,* contains a revealing chapter on "Political Pluralism and the True Federal State," though it needs to be read in conjunction with a chapter entitled "From Contract to Community," which draws on Roscoe Pound to develop a concept of law as the product and instrument of community life.

Follett rejects individualism, contract theory, divided sovereignty, and divided powers or interests. She objects to the concept of balanced powers because to be balanced powers must first be divided, and "there are no absolute divisions in a true federal union." She argues for a state that is unifying, inclusive, dynamic, and internally cooperative. It embraces all groups — and it is only through group life that individual fulfillment and democracy are realized. It embraces new groups as they emerge. Thus, the true federal state is "the unifying state." "Only in the unifying state do we get the full advantage of diversity where it is gathered up into significance and pointed action. . . . [A]ny whole is always the element of a larger whole. . . . Democracy depends on the blending, not the balancing, of interests and thoughts and wills."

As this language suggests, the work is more than a little mystical and does not often address directly the subject of relations between levels of government in a federal system however federalism is defined. Where it does, it endorses the growing practice of federal grants-in-aid as an instance of "true federal," i.e., cooperative, action. Using the example of grants for vocational education, Follett says that the federal government does not impose something from without; states must take responsibility and determine how their own needs can best be satisfied. "The experience of one state joins with the experience of other states to form a collective experience."[26] Attitudes toward grants-in-aid differentiated Progressives, who favored them, from defenders of the old order of dual sovereignty, who did not.

The Reprieve

This attack on federalism was indubitably powerful. It underpinned or complemented the centralizing changes in public policy of the Progressive Era as well as its far-reaching successors in the New Deal and Great Society. At the same time, it is important to note the several ways in which the attack was qualified. Though powerful, it was not total. The

Progressives did not mount a frontal attack on the constitutional principle. To attack federalism fundamentally would have required an assault on the form of the Senate, which was the principal federal feature remaining in the Constitution after the framing convention of 1787.

The logical next step for Progressivism following adoption of the Seventeenth Amendment in 1913 would have been to attack equal representation of the states in the Senate. While the literature of the period occasionally advances this proposal, as for example J. Allen Smith's *The Spirit of American Government,* it did not become a Progressive cause.[27] Woodrow Wilson, who may or may not be regarded as an authentic voice of Progressivism, celebrated the Senate as the embodiment of regional representation, which he argued was necessary "in a country physically as various as ours and therefore certain to exhibit a very great variety of social and economic and even political conditions."[28]

More appealing to Progressives was a proposal to make constitutional amendment easier by substituting popular ratification of amendments for ratification by three-fourths of the state legislatures. Herbert Croly took up this cause in his second book, *Progressive Democracy,* and Wisconsin's great Progressive leader, Robert M. LaFollette, sponsored it in the Senate. But this was less an attack on federalism than on judicial supremacy. By making the Constitution easier to amend, Progressives hoped to reduce the need and the scope for judicial discretion. "The guardianship of the robe," Croly explained, "was based in practice upon the extreme difficulty of amending the Constitution."[29] Ending that guardianship was a Progressive priority of utmost importance.

If Progressives had attached greater importance to constitutional forms, they might have devoted more effort to changing them. What mattered for the arch-nationalist Croly, and for Progressives generally, was not the specific allocation of power among governments, but the fidelity of all governments to the common purpose. Croly distinguished between centralization, for which he claimed no presumption, and nationalization, which he declared to be "an essentially formative and enlightening transformation [in which the] political, economic and social organization or policy [of a people was coordinated with] their actual needs and their moral and political ideals."[30] Follett would have eschewed the term "nationalization" in favor of "true federalism," but they were alike in stressing the overriding importance of shared social ideals.

Particularly in framing an agenda of institutional reform, Progressive

Era political thought treated all levels of government as important and distinct. To people bent on political change, the states had an exceptional attractiveness because of the flexibility of their constitutions. This was true whether the change was sought in policy or institutions. Benjamin DeWitt, who was both a chronicler and a voice of the Progressive movement, wrote of the states that "because they are not so strictly limited by their constitutions, because they can more easily amend their constitutions when they are limited, because of the liberal interpretation of the so-called police power, states are able to grapple with modern social and economic problems much more effectively than the federal government can."[31]

In *The Promise of American Life,* Croly dismissed most constitutional reform at the federal level as a waste of time but then wrote a lengthy chapter on reform of the state governments, arguing for greater concentration of power and responsibility. He had very benign, positive expectations of the role that state governments so reformed might play. He saw them — and could be cited more convincingly than Brandeis on this point — as places of experiment. As such, they would be far superior to the federal government: "Obviously a state government is a much better political agency for the making of . . . experiments than is a government whose errors would affect the population of the whole country. No better machinery for the accomplishment of a progressive programme of social reform could be advised [*sic*] than a collection of governments endowed with the powers of an American state. . . . Such a system would be flexible; it would provoke emulation; it would encourage initiative; and it would take advantage of local ebullitions of courage and insight and any peculiarly happy local collection of circumstances." He went on to suggest that governors, endowed with greater powers so that they would be the real political leaders of their states, should meet periodically "for the purpose of comparing notes obtained under widely different conditions and as the result of different legislative experiments."[32] Late in 1907 President Roosevelt invited all the governors to convene at the White House in 1908 to discuss conservation; this meeting laid the foundation for subsequent governors' conferences.[33]

In regard to municipal governments, Progressives likewise expressed disappointment with experience of the past but held out high hopes for the future. Much of the energy of Progressivism went into the reform of municipal governments. Croly wrote of this movement in 1909 with great optimism: "In all probability, the American city will become in the near future the most fruitful field for economically and socially constructive experimentation." Like Progressives generally, he endorsed home rule. In respect to that which was exclusively local, cities should be able to govern themselves without interference from the states.[34]

Most important, perhaps, Progressives exhibited no profound or consistent bias against small-scale polities per se. Simon Patten's plan for reversing the decay of state and local governments was to have smaller units of greater homogeneity. As a group, Progressives made no important contribution to that strand of American political thought running from James Madison in *Federalist 10* to Grant McConnell in *Private Power and American Democracy,* which has held that small-scale democracy is inherently defective — more prone to tyranny than the large scale and less able to protect diffuse, intangible, "public" interests.[35] On the contrary, the communitarians among them, such as Follett, John Dewey, and Josiah Royce, rested their theories explicitly on respect for small-scale societies, leaving an important legacy in defense of the local.[36]

Follett constructed her ideal democracy on the foundations of neighborhood association. So did Dewey, who declared that "Democracy must begin at home, and its home is the neighborly community. . . . Unless local communal life can be restored, the public cannot adequately resolve its most urgent problem: to find and identify itself."[37] But it was Royce who advanced the most compelling and elaborate case for what he chose to call "provincialism." He defined a province as any part of a national domain that had a consciousness of its own unity, was proud of its own ideals and customs, and possessed a sense of its distinction. Provincial*ism* was the tendency of a province to possess its own customs and ideals; the totality of the customs and ideals themselves; and the love and pride that led the inhabitants of a province to cherish these traditions, beliefs, and aspirations.

He then argued that a "wholesome provincialism" is "the absolute necessity for our welfare" because it is a bulwark safeguarding individuality against mob spirit and the homogenizing, leveling tendencies of modern life that breed mediocrity. "Keep the province awake," he counseled, "that the nation may be saved from the disastrous hypnotic slumber so characteristic of excited masses of mankind." Individuals and provinces should both learn freely from abroad, but then insist on their interpretation of the common good.[38] Royce spoke as did Tocqueville, but in a native tongue — that of a Californian who became a professor of philosophy at Harvard and who all but apologized to his listeners and readers for having left his province. His continuing fidelity to it is manifest in his history of California, written after the move to Cambridge — a "labor of love" in which he undertook to comprehend "the process whereby a new and great community first came to a true consciousness of itself."[39] While Progressives wanted to construct a great national community, it was not part of their project to deny claims of community, or yet of greatness, elsewhere.

Conclusion

Progressive Era thought on the subject of federalism is of enduring interest both for the effects that it had and for those that it did not seek. It marks a critical stage in the transition from compact-based, conflictual federalism to what Samuel Beer has called "national federalism," rooted in a conception of popular sovereignty and presuming cooperation rather than conflict in intergovernmental relations. The passing of "dual federalism," which Edward S. Corwin announced in a classic article in 1950 and seemed to locate in the New Deal, is more properly traceable to intellectual developments of the Progressive Era.[40] It also helped lay the basis for a more elastic, forgiving constitutional law and for putting to rest the doctrine that the federal government was a government of limited powers.

Nevertheless, it did not root federalism out of the constitutional framework, or even try very hard to do so. By accepting a federal system of distinct and constitutionally protected governments and by failing to conceive of egalitarian measures of public policy, at least implicitly (though in some cases explicitly), it accepted spatially defined political societies within the larger society that differed from one another. The attack on federalism, though powerful, was arguably half-hearted. Why? As a constitutional principle, federalism may have been too deeply embedded to attack. Yet Progressives did not shrink from proposing constitutional amendments, nor from making the Constitution easier to amend.

Unlike modern liberals, who disdain federalism because they associate it with racism, Progressives were insensitive to issues of race or were pessimistic about the ability of the national government to deal with those issues. Some of them appear to have believed in the superiority of the Anglo-Saxon race, as they would have called it. Others may have harbored the illusion that the Civil War had disposed of racial questions. Thus, James A. Garfield could say in 1869, in a speech that foreshadowed Progressivism, "Now that the great question of slavery is removed from the arena of American politics, the next great question to be confronted will be that of the corporations and their relation to the interests of the people."[41] Later, having witnessed the end of Reconstruction, others tended to dismiss the federal government as ineffectual in respect to civil rights for Negroes. Henry Jones Ford wrote that "Federal authority showed itself signally incompetent in dealing with the race problem."[42]

Progressives may also have been insufficiently radical to attack the income inequalities that modern liberals decry and more loosely associate with federalism. Croly inveighs against inequalities in wealth only to recommend a graduated inheritance tax—doubtless anticlimactic to a modern liberal reader. Our view is that modern liberals can take the positions they do, including recommendations for interlocal and interstate redistribution of wealth, because the Progressives laid foundations for them. Progressives took the first giant steps toward destroying laissez-faire and constructing the welfare state. For their modern heirs to object that they failed to take steps even more gigantic ignores the way democracy works, which is for the most part gradually, by discussion, except in times of crisis.

We believe that the Progressives were half-hearted because they were reluctant to mount a full-scale attack on localism and regionalism in American public life. Many of them valued what would be destroyed in such an attack. Even in their most radical measure of constitutional change—the proposal for a popular vote on constitutional amendments—they preserved an element of regionalism. They did not call for a national referendum on amendments, but referenda within the states, with a requirement that protected regional interests by making approval depend on a majority of the people in a majority of the states. In the tension between nation and locality, they sought, for the most part, a middle way, be it balance or blend. Whether it should be a balance, which presumed a large measure of autonomy for all communities, or a blend, which threatened to submerge if not extinguish the local, they never agreed. There was no single Progressive Era prescription for community or federalism; one is hard put to reconcile the views of Patten and Follett.

Their legacy to us is an engagement with the dilemma of scale in a democracy, a dilemma that contemporary political science has failed to treat with the seriousness it deserves. To a student of federalism and of American political institutions generally, the Progressive Era is of interest because its political thinkers grappled with the central question of the American political experiment: whether it is possible to realize self-government on a grand scale. This was the question that had pitted federalists against antifederalists at the framing. One could argue that early experience vindicated the antifederalist claims. They had said that the heterogeneity of the large nation would cause instability. Instability is a mild term for the cataclysm of the Civil War, but the Civil War, ending in Union victory, only imparted new drama to the experiment, which then entered a different phase. So decentralized was the pre–Civil War United States that it had not seriously tested the antifederalist claim that democracies must be small. This was a nation of isolated, self-governing hamlets — the little rural republics immortalized by Tocqueville. Not until the nation developed more fully would it become necessary to confront the question of whether development was compatible with democracy.

That task awaited the Progressives soon after the turn of the century, in a nation now populous, continental, industrializing, urbanizing, increasingly interdependent, stratified, and strained by industrial conflict — in short, "modern." What they said about federalism constituted one important component of their response. United in a desire to strengthen the national character of American democracy, they were also concerned, though in different ways and to varying degrees, with preserving the virtues of decentralization and provincialism. Their work may or may not seem satisfying at the end of the twentieth century, but its impact is such that it requires the attention of anyone who wishes to understand the evolution of America's federal institutions. Moreover, its intellectual ambition, depth, and seriousness were such that it deserves to be studied, along with contemporaneous rejoinders, by anyone who would prescribe a direction for federalism today.

We began by suggesting that what Progressives said about federalism was of greater long-run significance than any deliberate reform of the institution that they undertook. However, one ought not to overlook the consequences for federalism of the institutional changes that they fashioned with other ends primarily in view. As institutional reformers, they sought above all to perfect democracy by eliciting the purest possible expression of the public will. This had consequences for federalism whether intended or not.

Most political scientists today would probably agree that the Progressive assault on organized political parties weakened a critical underpinning of the decentralized constitutional form.[43] They would also probably agree that the development of the rhetorical and plebiscitary presidency, speaking directly to and for the people, as fashioned by Theodore Roosevelt and Woodrow Wilson, was a critical step toward a perceived union of democracy and nationality, the particular project of Roosevelt and Croly, whose work remains for many students the quintessence of Progressive Era political thought.[44] Scholars would probably concur that the Progressives' expansion of the civil service at the federal and municipal levels and their promotion generally of professional expertise in government became a force for centralization as professional leaders found positions in large-scale governments.[45]

Perhaps more intriguing and debatable in its implications for federalism was the promotion of direct democracy at the state level. If some Progressives sought to fashion a union of democracy and nationality, some also elected to make use of the smaller-scale polities to institutionalize popular sovereignty, bypassing representative institutions altogether. Roosevelt stood with accustomed vigor for both causes. Arguably, in their political practices as distinct from their elaborated thoughts, Progressives collectively managed to deny that there was any dilemma of scale. Democracy could be realized, and realized in something that aspired to pure form, on any scale.

The ever trenchant Henry Jones Ford argued that the movement for direct democracy arose in response to the corruption of state legislatures. "The American people despise legislatures, not because they are averse to representative government, but because legislatures are in fact despicable." The initiative and referendum were ways of bypassing them and rendering them irrelevant. By providing an alternative and at least superficially superior method of obtaining the popular will, measures of direct democracy served to discredit state legislatures further and to diminish them by comparison to Congress, although the Oregon-based sponsors of this movement, according to Ford, thought of their measures as temporary, to be abandoned except for emergency use once the probity of legislatures was secured through reform.[46]

Yet the changes endured and even flourished in some places, and the existence of direct democracy in the state governments, but not in the federal government, was to mean that public opinion would be expressed most directly and explicitly at the subnational level, thereby increasing the capacity of the states to be in the vanguard of policy development and to serve as laboratories of policy experimentation. To be sure, the states were already serving as policy initiators even prior to the Progressive Era, by virtue of their numbers, their diversity, and a historically privileged constitutional position. The measures of direct democracy that were enacted in the first two decades of the twentieth century had the effect of increasing their ability to do so.

Thus, in the last quarter of the twentieth century, a number of significant political movements have originated in initiative and referendum campaigns at the state level. The tax-limitation movement of the late 1970s and 1980s, which won its first major victory with the passage of Proposition 13 in California in 1978, is the leading example, but one could also point to the contemporary movement for limiting legislative terms, which enjoyed its initial success through the initiative process in Oklahoma in 1990, as well as the movement to require color-blind procedures in college admissions and government contracting, which gained significant momentum after a successful initiative campaign in California in 1996. Direct democratic institutions have also served as the vehicles through which states have experimented with revised public policies in the areas of bilingual education, immigration, and assisted suicide. In this regard, it is noteworthy that California, which has done more than any other state (and possibly more even than any other political actor) to set the national agenda in recent years, is also the most vigorous in its use of direct democracy.

Whether viewed as political thought or as institutional change, Progressivism's legacy remains nationalizing in its central tendency, yet ambiguous in its implications for federalism. One might add "appropriately so," given the essential ambiguity of the federal form itself.

Notes

Miss Derthick thanks the White Burkett Miller Center of the University of Virginia for financial support.

1. William H. Riker, "The Senate and American Federalism," *American Political Science Review* 49 (June 1955): 452–69.

2. On uniform state laws as a Progressive reform, see William Graebner, "Federalism in the Progressive Era: A Structural Interpretation of Reform," *Journal of American History* 64 (September 1977): 331–57. On the governors' conference, see Glenn E. Brooks, *When Governors Convene* (Baltimore: Johns Hopkins University Press, 1961).

3. *Texas v White*, 47 US 700 (1869).

4. For a contrary interpretation, arguing the wholehearted commitment of Progressives to "the national idea," see Michael S. Joyce and William A. Schambra, "A New Civic Life," in *To Empower People: From State to Civil Society*, ed. Peter L. Berger and Richard John Neuhaus (Washington: American Enterprise Press, 1996), 11–29.

5. The decisions that generated the most hostile reactions were *United States v E. C. Knight Co*, 156 US 1 (1895), which limited Congress's ability to restrain monopolistic trade practices; the *First Employers' Liability Cases*, 207 US 463 (1908), which overturned a federal statute that required railroads to assume liability for workplace injuries; *Adair v United States*, 208 US 161 (1908), which overturned a statute that sought to prohibit companies that were engaged in interstate commerce from making use of yellow-dog contracts, which required workers to give up their rights to join labor unions; and *Hammer v Dagenhart*, 247 US 251 (1918), and *Bailey v Drexel Furniture Co*, 259 US 20 (1920), which prevented Congress from regulating child labor, either by prohibiting interstate commerce in goods that were made by children or by imposing a tax on such products. For an overview of the various Progressive responses to these decisions, see William G. Ross, *A Muted Fury: Populists, Progressives, and Labor Unions Confront the Courts, 1890–1937* (Princeton: Princeton University Press, 1994), 20.

6. J. Allen Smith, *The Spirit of American Government* (New York: Macmillan, 1907), 90. See also Louis Boudin, "Government by Judiciary," *Political Science Quarterly* 26 (1911): 238.

7. Charles A. Beard, *An Economic Interpretation of the Constitution of the United States* (New York: Macmillan, 1913), 163.

8. Ross, *Muted Fury*, 57–59.

9. Ibid., 145, 194.

10. Charles Amidon, "The Nation and the Constitution," address delivered before the American Bar Association in 1907, reprinted in *Selected Articles on States Rights*, ed. Lamar T. Beman (New York: H. W. Wilson, 1926), 129–30. Beman's compilation of Progressive Era sources on federalism has been invalu-

able to us, as subsequent citations will show. Amidon was a federal judge in North Dakota.

11. Woodrow Wilson, *Congressional Government* (1885; reprint, New York: Meridian Books, 1956), 27, and Albert B. Hart, *Actual Government as Applied under American Conditions* (New York: Longmans, Green and Co., 1906), vii. We are indebted for these references to Herman Belz, "The Constitution in the Gilded Age: The Beginnings of Constitutional Realism in American Scholarship," *American Journal of Legal History* 13 (1969): 110, quotations: 118, 123.

12. Smith, *Spirit of American Government,* 40 (quotations rearranged).

13. Amidon, "The Nation and the Constitution," 128.

14. Frank Goodnow, *Social Reform and the Constitution* (New York: Macmillan, 1911), 16, 13. A professor at Columbia University, Goodnow was the first president of the American Political Science Association and arguably the most eminent political scientist of his day. This book grew out of lectures sponsored by the Charity Organization Society of the City of New York and was delivered before the New York School of Philanthropy. While Goodnow professed in the preface to take no position on measures of social reform, the book was a comprehensive brief for the constitutionality of uniform commercial regulation, the power of Congress to charter interstate corporations, the power of Congress over private law, and the constitutionality of political reform, government regulation, and grants-in-aid.

15. Theodore Roosevelt, "State and Federal Powers," Address delivered at Harrisburg, Pennsylvania, 4 October 1906, reprinted in Beman, *States Rights,* 148–58.

16. "The Nation and the States," speech before the Colorado Legislature, 29 August 1910, in Theodore Roosevelt, *The New Nationalism* (New York: Outlook, 1910), 34–48; quotation at 38–39.

17. Goodnow, *Social Reform and the Constitution,* 9.

18. John A. Jameson, "National Sovereignty," *Political Science Quarterly* 5 (1890): 213.

19. Walter Weyl, *The New Democracy* (New York: Macmillan, 1912), 161.

20. A powerful rebuttal came from Henry Wade Rogers, dean of the Yale Law School, in the *North American Review* 108 (1908): 321–25. See, too, John Sharp Williams, "Federal Usurpations," *Annals of the American Academy of Political and Social Science* 32 (1908): 185–211. Williams was a member of Congress from Mississippi.

21. Reprinted in Beman, *States Rights,* 61–68 and in Paul S. Reinsch, *Readings on American Federal Government* (Boston: Ginn and Company, 1909), 731–36. For a discussion of its historical importance, see W. Brooke Graves, *American Intergovernmental Relations: Their Origins, Historical Development, and Current Status* (New York: Scribners, 1964), 797.

22. Henry Jones Ford, "The Influence of State Politics in Expanding Federal Power," *Proceedings of the American Political Science Association* (Fifth annual meeting, Washington, D.C., and Richmond, Va., 28–31 December 1908 (Baltimore: Waverly Press, 1909), 53–63; quotation at 62.

23. Simon N. Patten, "The Decay of State and Local Governments," *Annals of the American Academy of Political and Social Science* 1 (1890): 26.

24. Calvin Coolidge, "Responsibilities of the States," in Beman, *States Rights,* 68–78.

25. "The Effort to Secure Uniform State Laws," excerpted from the report of the forty-seventh annual meeting of the American Bar Association, 1924, reprinted in Beman, *States Rights,* 81–87. See, too, Graebner, "Federalism in the Progressive Era."

26. Mary Parker Follett, *The New State: Group Organization the Solution of Popular Government* (New York: Longmans, Green and Co., 1918), chap. 31. Quotations appear at pages 296, 300, 301, 306, 307, and 309, but have been rearranged.

27. Smith mentions the possibility in one brief paragraph: *The Spirit of American Government,* 339. Progressives may have been discouraged from making any such proposal by the Constitution itself, Article 5 of which stipulates that no state shall be deprived of equal suffrage in the Senate without its consent.

28. Woodrow Wilson, *Constitutional Government in the United States* (New York: Columbia University Press, 1908), 116.

29. Herbert Croly, *Progressive Democracy* (New York: Macmillan, 1915), 244.

30. Herbert Croly, *The Promise of American Life* (Indianapolis: Bobbs-Merrill, 1965), 273. See also *Progressive Democracy,* 241–43, in which the same argument appears.

31. Benjamin Parke DeWitt, *The Progressive Movement* (New York: Macmillan, 1915), 244.

32. Croly, *Promise of American Life,* 347.

33. Proceedings of a Conference of Governors in the White House, Washington, D.C., 13–15 May 1908 (Washington: Government Printing Office, 1909). For an illuminating account of the significance of this conference, which puts it in the context of Progressive policies toward conservation and development, see Michael J. Lacey, "Federalism and National Planning: The Nineteenth-Century Legacy," in *The American Planning Tradition: Culture and Policy,* ed. Robert Fishman (forthcoming, Woodrow Wilson Center Press).

34. Croly, *Promise of American Life,* 349.

35. *The Federalist Papers* (New York: New American Library, 1961), 77–84; Grant McConnell, *Private Power and American Democracy* (New York: Alfred A. Knopf, 1966), esp. chap. 4.

36. For illuminating secondary analyses, see Jean B. Quandt, *From the Small Town to the Great Community: The Social Thought of Progressive Intellectuals* (New Brunswick: Rutgers University Press, 1970) and David E. Price, "Community and Control: Critical Democratic Theory in the Progressive Period," *American Political Science Review* 68 (December 1974): 1663–78.

37. John Dewey, *The Public and Its Problems* (Denver: Alan Swallow; copyright 1927 by Mrs. John Dewey), 213, 216.

38. John J. McDermott, ed., *The Basic Writings of Josiah Royce,* vol. 2 (Chicago: University of Chicago Press, 1969), 1067–88.

39. Josiah Royce, *California* (Boston: Houghton Mifflin and Co., 1886), vii–xii.

40. Edward S. Corwin, "The Passing of Dual Federalism," *Virginia Law Review* 36 (1950), reprinted in Alpheus T. Mason and Gerald Garvey, eds., *American Constitutional History: Essays by Edward S. Corwin* (New York: Harper & Row, 1964), 145–64.

41. "Ninth Census: Speech of the Honorable James A. Garfield of Ohio, Delivered in the House of Representatives December 16, 1869," cited in Michael J. Lacey, "The World of the Bureaus: Government and the Positivist Project in the Late Nineteenth Century," in *The State and Social Investigation in Britain and the United States,* eds., Michael J. Lacey and Mary O. Furner (Cambridge and New York: Woodrow Wilson Center Press and Cambridge University Press, 1993), 141.

42. Ford, "The Influence of State Politics," 62.

43. For a powerful statement, see Sidney M. Milkis, "Localism, Political Parties, and Civic Virtue," in *Dilemmas of Scale in America's Federal Democracy,* ed. Martha Derthick (forthcoming, Cambridge University Press).

44. On the rhetorical presidency, see Jeffrey K. Tulis, *The Rhetorical Presidency* (Princeton: Princeton University Press, 1987), and Richard J. Ellis, ed., *Speaking to the People: Presidential Rhetoric and Popular Leadership in Historical Perspective* (Amherst: University of Massachusetts Press, 1998).

45. For a case study that illustrates the point, see Martha Derthick, *The Influence of Federal Grants: Public Assistance in Massachusetts* (Cambridge: Harvard University Press, 1970), chap. 7.

46. Henry Jones Ford, "Direct Legislation and the Recall," *Annals of the American Academy of Political and Social Science* 43 (1912): 65–77, quotation at 72.

Standing at Armageddon

Morality and Religion in Progressive Thought

Wilson Carey McWilliams

Progressivism was more disposition than doctrine, its ideas developed by thinkers who were almost relentlessly idiosyncratic and at least suspicious of the forms, in logic if not in society.[1] Necessarily, the movement was somewhat amorphous, and almost every generalization about it calls to mind an obvious exception, e.g., Progressives, pretty much across the board, were critics of local party organizations and especially of "boss rule," yet no one wrote more appreciatively about ward politics than the remarkable Mary K. Simkhovitch.[2] And Brand Whitlock — successful both as a novelist and as a reform mayor of To-ledo — came to suspect that the old ward bosses, in their flawed and florid humanity, were "more nearly right after all than the cold and formal and precise gentlemen who denounced their records."[3] It is not surprising, then, that contemporary historians call attention to the Heinz-like varieties of Progressivism, or even deny that the movement had any real coherence.[4]

Still, Progressives saw and spoke of *themselves* as part of an identifiable movement or tendency, and while I will pay some homage to their diversity later on, I want to begin by focusing on some of their com-monalities in life and thought.

In the first place, they were almost all born in the twenty-year period from just before the Civil War (like Ida Tarbell and Woodrow Wilson) to just before the end of Reconstruction (like Charles Merriam, born in

1874). Unlike their parents, they took the war and its aftermath largely for granted. They were the first generation shaped by the problems of late-century America and ready to give them more or less undivided attention.

Second, with few exceptions they were Protestants raised in mainline denominations who had attended similarly denominational colleges (e.g., Oberlin, Amherst, Grinnell) or public universities (Dewey attended the University of Vermont; Charles Herbert Cooley was a graduate of Michigan). With only slightly less frequency, they had at best a strained relation to churches and organized religion; even the Social Gospel clergy found that relationship heavy going. Nevertheless, they brought to the "search for order"—for Robert Wiebe is right, it was that—a distinctly Protestant and often evangelical tone.[5]

Yet while Progressives drew on that heritage, they were both more troubled and more confident than their teachers. As I will be arguing, they felt caught up in something close to a secular Armageddon, just as Theodore Roosevelt said in 1912, a political battle with supremely high stakes.[6] Beyond mere order, Progressives were engaged in a quest for democracy on the grand scale, informed by the belief that the human spirit or conscience, guided by social science, could eventually create a vast and brotherly republic of public-spirited citizens. That high ambition moved Progressives to humanize American life in any number of ways, but it also led them to endanger the foundations of their own virtues; their legacy deserves to be appreciated, but it is also an occasion for regret.

Progressives, with few exceptions, were trained in a grand moral school, one that sought to address an enduring problem in American culture. Tocqueville had observed that their laws and social condition pushed Americans toward the pursuit of "worldly welfare," distracting them from, and discouraging attention to, the nurturance of the soul. But the wants of the soul—"the taste for the infinite and the love of what is immortal"—inhere in human nature and will make themselves felt, Tocqueville argued, and when they do, the untrained and unformed soul is likely to express itself in a "fanatical and almost wild spiritualism" devoid of "common sense."[7]

Midcentury America, especially in the Protestant mainstream, recognized the danger of materialism and religious excess, and it set out to supplement the laws, producing what D. H. Meyer calls an "instructed conscience" on the basis of a pervasive and remarkably coherent attempt at synthesizing religion and science.[8] Everywhere, this persuasion was broadly pragmatic, more concerned with moral order than philosophic rigor, but it reached a reasonably high intellectual level in the senior-year course in Moral Science (or some similar title) which was a feature of American higher education down to the end of the nineteenth century.[9]

The curriculum of Moral Science tended to draw on Thomas Reid's "common sense" philosophy, but invariably it presumed the moral sovereignty of *conscience,* a term at least ambiguously acceptable to both liberalism and Protestantism, as in Reid's claim that conscience reveals to the individual both the "intention of nature" and the "law of God written in his heart."[10] Note that Reid's nature has intention as well as order: his teaching was attractive, in part, because it provided a stronger natural basis for obligation than its chief rival, utilitarianism. As Meyer indicates, the great teachers of Moral Science were social conservatives who aimed to overcome the anarchical potential of the doctrine of conscience, hoping, through reason, to link *conscience* to *form* — to the Bible, to laws, and to institutions generally.[11] And they hoped to improve and elevate human moral faculties by the discipline and practice of the logic of morals, aiming to instill in their students that inner constraint that Mark Hopkins called the "Law of Limitation."[12]

They saw nature as a moral government, divinely ordained, in which the moral law is roughly equivalent to a "Law of Nature" imposed on moral agents by their "nature or constitution."[13] It is a small step from this to a moralized laissez-faire in which interests — if not naturally harmonic — are believed to work toward good ends, so that self-interest, pursued in a free market, will be at least *socially* redemptive. Thus, James McCosh could argue that "[o]ne who pursues an honest and industrious course of life will commonly be successful, by the arrangement of Him who hath appointed all things." Yet McCosh was too honest not to include the fatal word "commonly," acknowledging the exceptions. These were crucial, since Moral Science also characteristically held that government is natural, divinely appointed and intended to promote virtue.[14] Following an old Puritan line of argument, Joseph Haven held that while human beings are free to vary the form of government according to circumstance, they are naturally constrained to *be* political. In the same way, he insisted that no contract or consent is valid unless it conforms to the moral law, so that one has a duty to struggle against any government or law that endangers either liberty or virtue (Haven was almost certainly thinking of slavery though not slavery alone).[15] Many, of course, were more moderate: in the years before the Civil War, Francis Wayland argued that the "wickedness" of slavery did not justify abolitionist zealotry.[16] Nevertheless, it is impossible to understand the Progressive impulse without recognizing its foundation in the enduring conviction that government has a moral and magisterial mission.

In Moral Science and for Progressives, the inclination toward the Moral State was reinforced by the familiar argument that advances in human ability — in wealth, skill, or power — are accompanied by a parallel increase in human responsibility. Consequently, both for individuals and political communities, material or scientific improvements create greater duties.[17] Certainly, most teachers of Moral Science argued that scientific and technological power went hand in hand with moral progress, an unfolding of the spirit that, in practice, virtually identified secular progress with moral law.[18] (The slavery crisis encouraged this view, a point to which I will return later.)[19]

Still, "progress," in this theorizing, was measured in terms of the increasing approximation of standards of right and of excellence that were thought to be rooted in nature, and hence tolerably known. The exponents of Moral Science, well aware of human frailty, were less confident that material progress brings moral achievement than they were that it imposes moral *obligation*. They knew that power in human hands is perennially dangerous, and they regarded moral progress less as a process than as an imperative, as in Lowell's call to battle in the unending struggle between truth and falsehood:

> New occasions teach new duties,
> Time makes ancient good uncouth.
> They must upward still and onward,
> Who would keep abreast of truth.[20]

From their predecessors and teachers, Progressives learned and retained (1) a *pragmatic* temper, concerned with action and synthesis more than philosophic systems, (2) a reliance on *conscience* or *spirit* as the ruling tribunal of morals, (3) the conviction that material progress imposes an accompanying *duty* to promote *moral progress,* and (4) the belief that *government* has a broad responsibility for uplifting society.[21]

What they did *not* retain, however, was the core of Moral Science, the confidence in the compatibility of science and faith, and the assurance that it is possible to derive morals from nature.

Even in the victorious North, post–Civil War America found itself amid an increasingly perceptible crisis of culture. It may belong to Americans, Alexander Hamilton had written, "to decide by their conduct and example . . . whether societies of men are really capable or not of establishing good government from reflection and choice, or whether they are forever destined to depend, for their political constitutions, on accident and force."[22] The Civil War answered, "On force," a teaching thundered worldwide by politics at midcentury.

Reason, experience seemed to indicate, persuades too few, too slowly — or not at all — and cannot *rule* events. It was in response to that perception, after all, that socialism made its decisive turn from an ideal rooted in the Enlightenment to a doctrine of "class struggle," with force and dictatorship harnessed to historical inevitabilities.[23] But the great voice of the zeitgeist was Bismarck's: "The great questions of the time will not be decided by speeches and majority votes — that was the error of 1848 and 1849 — but by blood and iron."[24]

So they were, and it underlined the point that the Second Reich was the political success story of the late nineteenth century. A striking number of Progressive intellectuals studied in Germany, and even those who did not were typically influenced by German politics — especially by the example of the State as an agent of economic and social planning and reconstruction — and by German social science, with its appeal to the diversities of history and culture.[25]

In general, in the politics that succeeded the Civil War, more and more Americans came to share at least a part of Henry Adams's dark conviction that the hopes of the eighteenth century had gone a-glimmering and "the system of 1789 had broken down, and with it the eighteenth-century fabric of a priori or moral principles. Society hesitated, wavered, oscillated between harshness and laxity, pitilessly sacrificing the weak, and deferentially following the strong. . . . The moral law had expired — like the Constitution."[26]

Nature, in fact, was coming to seem at best indifferent to morality and perhaps to seem its implacable antagonist. In the physical sciences, Darwin and Lyall, increasingly influential among younger Americans, described a nature that is violent, cataclysmic, and wasteful. It is also, as Henry Adams reminded American teachers of history, part of a universe that is slowly dying, according to the laws of thermodynamics.[27] In the new understanding, nature offered no fixed species or qualities, and the status of humanity itself was contingent, so that toward the end of the Progressive Era, J. Howard Moore wrote confidently that "the earth and its contents were not made for man. . . . Man is not the end; he is but an incident."[28] In the spring of 1864, speaking to the Sanitary Fair in Baltimore, Lincoln had denounced what he described as the wolf's definition of liberty.[29] Now, however, it seemed that human beings were like wolves. At the very least, Darwinism implied, as John Bascom wrote, that the rules and forms of moral conduct necessarily change or vary with the progress of civilization.[30]

Progressives celebrated the moral possibility inherent in the growth of human power over nature, that by transcending old limits, human beings might more closely approach the ideal. History, Richard Ely urged, had been virtually transformed; the expansion of knowledge had taken humanity beyond the limits of purely biological evolution. Society, not the individual, was now the primary unit in the process, one capable of improving on and overcoming the competition for survival of nature's own flawed design.[31]

But at the same time, Progressives were haunted by old doubts about the ability of human beings to master and direct the new energies, especially because the escalating possibilities for destruction and evil made mistakes more or less intolerable. Human beings might be improving over time, but civilization was still only a *second* nature, a veneer of habit built on "natural moral motives" — primarily sympathy and the desire for approbation — but resting on fundamental self-interest and the will to power. Human nature, Howard Moore wrote, is a "product of the jungle, [and human beings are], in some respects, the lowest in the animal kingdom." He hoped that such "vestigial instincts" would waste away — like the appendix and the human tail — until they were next to nothing, but they were still with us, and even Moore's overheated imagination did not envision them disappearing altogether.[32]

Progressives quarreled with William Graham Sumner, but they recognized the force of his case. Civilization, and democratic civilization especially, depends on an abundance that allows for a relaxation of the struggle for survival, but with a closed frontier and an increasing population, maintaining a favorable "Man/Land Ratio" requires increasing capital, a kind of artificial "land."[33] Progressives shared this sense that civilization is a defense against nature, as well as Sumner's belief that civilized life faces an ongoing imperative to grow or perish. What they rejected was Sumner's willingness, in general, to leave the protection of civilization to private initiatives and to the market.

The case was more compelling, in Progressive thinking, than even grim Sumner had allowed. "Common sense," William James noted, had become incapable of keeping pace with force.[34] Hence, the familiar Progressive pursuit of social sciences endowed with technical mastery, capable of predicting and harnessing nature and force in the interest of civilized life. The governing of the outer world seemed a more urgent priority than the preoccupation of Moral Science with the government of the self.

That new ranking, however, is an indication of the fact that Progressivism was a search for a new intellectual and moral order as much as for social reconstruction.[35] Henry Adams's wistful yearning for the Virgin was the inner voice of the movement. More or less desperately, Progressives were seeking some way of *comprehending,* as well as *controlling,* the energies in the "power house" of industrial civilization.[36] It is a mark of urgency and the radicalism of the Progressive impulse that Progressive theorists adopted the most transforming elements of the existing alternatives, a liberal *theology* and *philosophy* associated, up to the Progressive Era, with advocates of laissez-faire like Sumner or Henry Ward Beecher, and a *political reformism* hitherto linked to theological conservatives like Joseph Cook, Jesse Henry Jones or — most famously — William Jennings Bryan.[37]

Relativism, especially of a historical sort, occupied a critical but essentially negative place in Progressive argument. "Reform Darwinism," as Eric Goldman observed, provided a critique that denied existing beliefs and institutions any claim to permanence.[38] It allowed Progressives to treat established authority as only obsolescence in process, a decomposing old waiting to give birth to the new. Even more important, relativism lent itself to the denial that there are fixed or natural *limits* to human aspiration. Human nature, Progressives were fond of arguing, is far more plastic than had been believed, offering in evidence any number of moral gentlings, like the success in curbing dueling, once regarded as a necessary outlet for human violence. Progressives, in other words, were inclined to reject or downplay original sin in favor of the kind of sins that are mitigable or eradicable through education and law.[39] Modern social life, Dewey and Tufts declared, includes "not only what has become institutionalized and more or less fossilized, but also what is still growing (forming and reforming), [so that] not order, but orderly progress represents the social ideal."[40]

The *positive* foundation for the Progressive belief in history, however, was the belief that the spirit—or in a slightly more secular form, the conscience—guides and sets moral direction amid change, acting as the voice of telos in the soul.[41] In Emersonian philosophy, in Moral Science, or in evangelical religion, Progressives had been trained in a locution that played down forms, sacraments, and laws in favor of being "right in the soul."[42] "Why," Emerson had asked, "should we be such hard pedants and magnify a few forms? . . . Why should we make account of time, or of magnitude or of form? The soul knows them not. . . . "[43] And a variety of the same teaching informs Samuel Longfellow's great hymn:

> Holy Spirit, Right Divine,
> Make my conscience wholly thine.
> Be my law, and I shall be
> Firmly bound, forever free.[44]

In this tradition, even—and especially—the Bible was to be read and interpreted under the guidance of the Spirit.[45] Other implications aside, that doctrine had been crucial to the antislavery movement that, for so many Progressives, typified moral heroism. The letter of the Scripture regards slavery as undesirable, perhaps even unnatural in a high sense, but it *accepts* it as a legitimate secular institution. Trying for the best construction, Francis Wayland had to concede that the Bible teaches the "duty of slaves," while denying that it recognizes the "right of masters."[46]

In order to argue that slavery was *wicked*—and even Wayland, not inclined to justify abolitionism, went that far—it was necessary to go beyond the text to the testimony of the Spirit, which discerns the meaning and validity of all laws.[47] Hence, in his 1865 amendment to *Moral Science*, Wayland subjected the Bible to a *historical* reading, rejecting the idea that "whatever God allows at one time, he allows for all time." Moses, Wayland contended, made some concessions to the "cherished practices" of a "rude, ignorant and sensual people," but in a way that would "tend ultimately to abolish them."[48]

But that, of course, referred to the Hebrew Scriptures, which Christians had long regarded as a "preparatory dispensation." It is more striking that Wayland subjected the Christian Testament to the same reading, discerning the "subversive" intention or spirit underlying Jesus' concession to the times.[49] Southern critics, outraged, pointed out that, in addition to disregarding the text, Wayland was claiming that Jesus and the apostles were bowing to expediency.[50] Our more enlightened times, Wayland concluded, call for abolition "without delay," and though he still denied that religion authorized the use of force, his argument left lawful, secular government more room for maneuver.[51]

This appeal from the letter to the spirit, so fundamental to Lincoln's great, resounding cadence at Gettysburg, was even more necessary when Progressives and other reformers turned to the rights of *women* against the patriarchal and Pauline texts.[52] In the end, it became an unchallenged principle of exegesis: by 1894, for example, G. Stanley Hall — confident in the authority of science — could proclaim a transition from the idea that morality is a *code* revealed by God in Scripture to the assurance that it is a *disposition* founded on "innate intuitions and sentiments."[53] Similarly, Dewey and Tufts traced the evolution of ethics "from custom to conscience," a historical process culminating in the development of the scientific method, so indispensable, especially in the social sciences, for bringing a moral society into being. *Conscientiousness,* Dewey and Tufts argued, differs from the older idea of wisdom as an attainment, something possessed by an elite; the modern principle "rests in the active desire and effort, in pursuit rather than possession." In these terms, the good human being

> measures his acts by a standard, but he is concerned to revise his standard. His sense of the ideal, of the undefinable because ever-expanding value of special deeds, forbids his resting satisfied with any formulated standard; for the very formulation gives the standard a technical quality, while the good can be maintained only in enlarging excellence. The highest form of conscientiousness is interest in constant progress.

So understood, Dewey and Tufts trusted, "genuine conscientiousness" is the "guarantee of all virtue."[54]

Of course, Progressives were not discarding the moral law: they relied almost "instinctively," as Mark Noll observes, on biblical morality and expected conscience to sustain and enhance it.[55] They did, however, run the risk of taking a complex moral heritage too much for granted, including such far from evident propositions as the duty to sacrifice and the contempt for merely material success.[56]

Progressives certainly followed tradition, however, in believing that the spirit strains toward the universal and the vision of human fraternity. But historic faith had held — as in Mark Hopkins's "law of limitation" — that the Old Adam, life in the flesh, both demands the support of immediate, particular persons and communities *and* indicates that any human devotion to the universal, short of Grace, will be imperfect.[57] Progressives, by contrast, were more apt to credit Emerson's famous vision, "one day all men will be lovers, and every calamity will be dissolved in the universal sunshine."[58] Some Progressives remained more or less orthodox; some listened to new doctrines, like the Comtean "religion of humanity" that influenced Croly: Washington Gladden's hymn, with its appeal to "the future's broadening way," was a song for all choirs.[59] While, of course, there were racist and nationalistic notes in the Progressive anthem, the movement's dominant teaching made the "Great Community" the end in secular history.[60] Dewey and Tufts were emphatic: "the divine kingdom is to come, the divine will to be done *on earth* as it is in heaven."[61]

Progressives saw science, commerce, and education enlarging and extending human sympathy and altruism in a gradual march toward a kind of "species being."[62] Love, Richard Ely argued, has been the unifying principle of earlier, narrow human communities but individualism had shattered old bonds and old boundaries. Strengthening distrust, it had also opened the door to civilization, making it possible to build the material basis for a new, universal solidarity.[63] As yet, Ely contended, modernity had not advanced beyond the externals: European socialism was bound to fail because its doctrine was materialistic, not a new synthesis or a transformation, but the mirror image of the theory of economic man — individualism constrained into an outward equality. The true socialist goal — and the end of history — was a kind of inwardness, an equality of spirit.[64]

Similarly, looking beyond individualism, Charles Herbert Cooley — like Dewey — saw a continuing need for primary groups preserving and nurturing the "instinctive solidarity" of early society in a limited, subordinate sphere. But Cooley's argument included a severe critique of secondary groups — interest groups, but also parties and representative institutions — that pretend to more than their real, instrumental status: Cooley envisioned the sovereignty of what Dewey called a "fraternally associated public," a national citizenry with the qualities of a primary group, as a way station on the road to the universal.[65] Human beings, Cooley declared, are rightly guided by the spirit of "onwardness," which leads them beyond parochialities toward the realization of the principle that "men live for one another."[66]

Progressives, in other words, inclined toward the view that when technology or trade overcomes material limits, the spirit can extend itself almost indefinitely with little or no effective loss of force. Moral progress, Dewey and Tufts taught, combines an extension in the size and scope of the social group with an intensification of the individual's social interest.[67]

That attitude implies a decisively pre-Freudian slighting of the continuing claims of the body and the erotic. (J. Howard Moore, an extreme case to be sure, suggested that progress pointed in the direction of "sloughing off . . . this inherited animality.")[68] Worse, it can easily slide into a dangerous neglect of the human need for particular attachments and very personal bonds and obligations.[69] And despite the trumpeting about science, at critical points the Progressive faith proves to have been more than a little mystical.[70]

Edward Bellamy's universalism, for example, left him convinced that, in the great administrative collectivity he saw in the future, the feeling of brotherhood en masse would be as "real and vital" as in the family and small communities. That fact, his Dr. Leete tells the time-traveler, Julian West, is "a key to the mysteries of our civilization."[71] But it is a mystery that Bellamy never explained. The skeptical may note that despite teaching a "merger with nature," Bellamy was at pains to deny that this implied a "commingling" of the races.[72]

Dewey wrestled with the problem. He affirmed the permanence of the human need for the local — "as near to an absolute as exists" — and he sometimes indicated that broader, more national allegiances would necessarily be more diffuse: it will be sufficient, he wrote, if "interaction and interdependence" give us "enough similarity of ideas and sentiments to keep the thing going."[73] But keeping the thing going, in Dewey's terms, presumed the sovereignty of public claims akin to the general will.[74] Consequently, Dewey fell back on the hope that locality can be wedded to larger loyalties—and that opinion can be empowered to rule over expert government—by a radically improved "art of communication," hoped for but not described, yet able, as Howard Moore wrote, "to make real and vivid . . . phenomena that are more distant in time and space."[75] It ought to be clear, however, that despite their power, the contemporary mass media—so episodic and so tied to superficial and essentially private sensibilities—are not what Dewey had in mind.

In any case, Progressives had no doubt that history was moving humanity into larger and more complicated social units, and that evolution—pace Darwinian individualism—rewarded the capacity for cooperative action. Bees, so selfless and hardworking, had always had a special charm for Protestant moralists: "Drones," Oberlin College had warned prospective students, "are not welcome in this hive of industry." In the late nineteenth century, however, bees—more attractive than militaristic ants or pestiferous termites—came to be praised for their power. "These," Kipling had Kaa teach Mowgli, "are the real masters of the jungle."[76] And Moore only amplified the argument in claiming that bees manifest "the ideal relations of living beings to each other."[77]

Most Progressives, of course, stopped short of such proto-totalitarian claims, but they were apt to grow lyrical about patriotism or to cross the line into nationalism or imperialism; and racism had its advocates, although most Progressives were guilty chiefly of indifference.[78] Even Walter Rauschenbusch, who detested war, spoke of the prophets as part of a "national" and "patriotic" movement, and Shailer Mathews, during World War I, proclaimed patriotism "the religion of tomorrow."[79]

Before 1914, the nation-state seemed only a step in humankind's march toward the universal—"Nothing could be more absurd from the historic point of view," Dewey and Tufts contended, "than to regard the conception of an international state of federated humanity as a mere dream"—and Wilson's rhetoric, for a time, fused the state and the dream into a single cause.[80]

It was really only in the aftermath of World War I that Progressives, in general, began to think seriously about the two-sided quality of patriotism, altruistic within the country, but, as Niebuhr was to write, largely "collective egotism" without.[81] And while the critique of nationalism is easily compatible with Progressive universalism, it is also true that the moral problem of patriotism points to a problem for Progressive teaching: The solidarity of large groups — and nations especially — rivals or overrides the claims of erotic and primary groups chiefly in war, and it is not so easy to find the "moral equivalent" of that aspect of war in peaceful civic life, as more than one movement is discovering in contemporary America.[82] Certainly, it is unmistakable that, after World War I, Progressivism lost much of its moral confidence. If older Progressives kept the flame — and many fell away — the younger generations lacked the old trust in the positive, ruling qualities of the spirit, confining themselves more and more to relativism's narrower negations.

Progressivism helped direct American moral impulses into political and social life, and it deserves much of the credit for building a government even remotely adequate to the problems of the twentieth century. As moral theory and in moral education, however, it gets lower marks; as Eisenach argues, crucial aspects of Progressive doctrine disintegrated or self-destructed.[83]

Progressives were moralists with bells on and altogether happy to make judgments — for Dewey, Morton White writes, "a judgement that something is desirable is just as scientific as a judgement that something is desired."[84] But their very confidence that conscience or spirit leads toward the goal encouraged them to substitute training in scientific method for moral education, virtually identifying technique with the end.[85] The "interest in technique," Dewey declared, "is precisely the thing which is most promising in our civilization, the thing which in the end will break down devotion to external standardization and the mass-quantity ideal."[86]

Similarly, Progressives appeared not to notice that their relativism and pragmatism worked in the direction of drift, supporting a tendency to accept prevailing terms and understandings, not simply as constraints on action — as surely they are — but as proper limits on thought. In that too-familiar persuasion, "adjustment" came to be treated as equivalent to well-being in the soul.[87] It only reinforced this logic that so many Progressives, if not as disdainful of "soul stuff" as Arthur Bentley, were inclined to let appearances and behaviors define reality.[88] The long-term danger of Progressivism, especially if one remembers Progressive enthusiasm for mass communications, points in the direction of the "tyranny of the majority" and the sort of happy nihilism that is apt to be celebrated in our time.

Progressives like Dewey saw the need human beings have for groups smaller than the state as nurturers and protectors against the mass. But they tiptoed around the fact that beyond the mere existence of local or functional groups, the development of citizens — people who extend themselves into public life — presumes relatively *stable* institutions and forms, the bases of civic trust. Progressives seemed surprisingly blind to the tension between democracy and rapid change, and only half aware that their embrace of progress itself threatened their higher, republican hopes.[89]

While Progressives did recognize the need to nurture and develop the emotions and moral faculties in a local sphere, they ignored or slighted the implication: we all begin in a world of particulars, from which the human spirit ascends, on any account, only slowly and with difficulty. The highest, most universal ranges of the spirit, consequently, are not achieved universally at any given time, and very likely, are something most of us can hope to see only in the mirror of the few. Humanity and equality, in that sense, are most broadly discerned in speech and in theory; in political practice, by contrast, the dominating categories are likely to be identity and difference.[90] Still, while the Progressives may have overestimated the reach of the spirit, unlike so many of our contemporaries, they never forgot that its yearning perennially strains against the possibilities.

To this point, I have been emphasizing — and criticizing — general themes and patterns in Progressive thought, and I want to conclude on a different note by giving some attention to two thinkers — Walter Rauschenbusch and W.E.B. Du Bois — who (among many) were exceptions, in important respects, to the Progressive rule.

Rauschenbusch was the great theorist of the Social Gospel, and that status carries its own ambivalence. The exponents of the Social Gospel were sometimes mawkishly sentimental and, more often, were tempted to tailor religious teaching to the measure of social utility. But at its best, it offered (and offers) an invaluable witness, and Rauschenbusch is not a bad exemplar.

He does strike many notes that jar our sensibilities: He took virtually no notice of race, for example, and worried that the church might become "feminized."[91] Similarly, he was apt, especially in perorations, to soar into a startlingly Progressive idiom, speaking of human "elasticity and capacity for change," appealing to history and social science and asserting that "the largest and hardest part of Christianizing the social order has been done."[92]

But there was also a strongly orthodox dimension to Rauschenbusch's thought: he believed, for example, in a fixed human nature, with sin included — "[h]istory is never antiquated because humanity is always fundamentally the same." Against religious conservatives, in fact, Rauschenbusch argued that it is precisely the ubiquity of sin that demands criticism of the world.[93]

Jesus, Rauschenbusch pointed out, was no modern social reformer, since he worked from the soul outward, beginning with the "sin of the heart" and the soul's need for meaning, aiming at the "inauguration of a new humanity" as the foundation for an attack on the sins of society, themselves rooted in the lust for dominion and for "easy and unearned gain."[94]

While Rauschenbusch hoped for moral improvement, his view of history presumed a permanent dialectic between priest and prophet, ceremonial form and righteous life. Consequently, when Rauschenbusch insisted that we understand Jesus in relation to "his times," he meant that Jesus must be freed from later, Hellenizing mysticism, understood as he understood himself, in a tradition that is Hebrew and public.[95]

Even one of his more startling assertions — that ethical conduct, *in principle,* is the "supreme and sufficient religious act" — had Scriptural and even Pauline referents.[96] Rauschenbusch did, however, reject what he took to be Paul's expectation of a spiritually transformed cosmos: human beings, Rauschenbusch maintained, cannot expect to be freed apocalyptically from the limits of sin and bodiliness; the spirit will have to work within the limits of the world. In that sense, Rauschenbusch is less "postmillennial" (a description more easily applied to John Locke) than he is *anti*-pre-millennial.[97]

True to the prophetic tradition, he was at least immediately pessimistic. Progress, he thought, was anything but guaranteed, especially since the new, potentially destructive energies at human command seemed to call for a new humanity as well as new forms of organization. He ruled out the hope for political transformation: revolutions are showy, but superficial; humanly produced change must follow the "law of organic development." But Rauschenbusch allowed himself to hope that it was a crucial moment, a time "at the turning of the ways," when Christianity, by applying moral force to the material world, might hope to turn human beings toward first things. Following the early Christians, he thought in terms of a small beginning and a "Brotherhood of the King-dom"—a few people, principally young, scattered throughout society and capable, by the "contagion" of speech and example, of creating a new moral discourse, a "new life" set to growing amid the old.[98]

With the ordinary fate of prophets, Rauschenbusch fell well short of achieving his vision, and along with its virtues, his theorizing has short-comings to spare. But warts and all, Rauschenbusch's teaching reminds reformers that the proper aim and starting point of change is the educa-tion of the soul.

On that point, however, W.E.B. Du Bois is an even better instructor. Race still muddles us enough that we are apt to forget how thoroughly Du Bois fits the Progressive paradigm—raised in Protestant, New En-gland culture; educated at Fisk in the Moral Science of James McCosh, trained at Harvard and Berlin in the most advanced social science; and the champion of an educated elite; Du Bois was even gulled, for a consid-erable period, by Woodrow Wilson and the imagined social promise of World War I.[99]

But *The Souls of Black Folk* does not speak of, or even suggest, evolu-tion or historical progress. Quite the contrary, Du Bois's chapter, "On the Meaning of Progress," describes the decline and the tragedies of the community in rural Tennessee where he once taught school. There, change had meant defeat and disappointment and death: "How shall man measure Progress there where the dark-faced Josie lies?" Even the replacement of the old log schoolhouse appeared as loss. "In its place stood Progress, and Progress, I understand, is necessarily ugly."[100] He had come there, walking and lighthearted, in the old time; he left, ten years later, riding the train in the Jim Crow car.

Race pointed Du Bois to the failure of any social science that could not pierce appearances. He spoke (and to our time?) of the inadequacy of sociologists who "gleefully count . . . bastards and . . . prostitutes," and his great affirmation—that "the problem of the twentieth century is the problem of the color-line"—indicated that the then-coming century would be measured by its ability to reach beyond the visible to a knowledge of the soul. The "tragedy of the age," Du Bois wrote, is "not that men are poor, . . . not that men are wicked, . . . not that men are ignorant, . . . [but] that men know so little of men."[101]

The Souls of Black Folk reaches broadly. It includes some social science and some very personal loss, some stories and some poetry and a grand discussion of the music of the "sorrow songs," and Du Bois invoked, too, the centrality of the church and its vision in African American life: "Some day the Awakening will come when the pent up vigor of ten million souls shall sweep irresistibly toward the Goal, out of the Valley of the Shadow of Death. . . . "[102]

But beyond evoking the experience and culture of black folk, Du Bois called for the education of an elite, one not defined in terms of the mastery of technical skills. Du Bois was always an "elitist," even at his most radically democratic (and certainly in his latter-day Marxist-Leninism) because he was convinced of the need for exceptional individuals, the "higher individualism" of those who see beyond the practical and the possible, exerting the *pull* of high culture and theory that Du Bois saw — in *The Souls of Black Folk,* at any rate — as the dynamic and meaning of progress.[103]

Liberation, so conceived, requires access to the Great Conversation and its discipline, the "chance to soar in the dim blue air above the smoke" where it is possible to discern the human truth.

> I sit with Shakespeare and he winces not. Across the color line I move arm in arm with Balzac and Dumas, where smiling men and welcoming women glide in gilded halls. From out of the caves of evening that swing between the strong-limbed earth and the tracery of the stars, I summon Aristotle and Aurelius and what soul I will, and they come all graciously, with no scorn nor condescension. So, wed with Truth, I dwell above the veil.[104]

If Progressivism has any claim to include that passage in its legacy, and I think it does, then it has left us an inheritance rich enough to excuse many faults.

Notes

1. Morton White, *Social Thought in America: The Revolt Against Formalism* (Boston: Beacon, 1957).

2. Mary K. Simkhovitch, "Friendship and Politics," *Political Science Quarterly* 17 (1902): 189–205.

3. Brand Whitlock, *Forty Years of It* (New York: Appleton, 1925), 204; Whitlock's sympathy for traditional politicos is also evident in his political novel, *Big Matt* (New York: Appleton, 1928).

4. James Kloppenberg, *Uncertain Victory: Social Democracy and Progressivism in European and American Thought, 1870–1920* (New York: Oxford University Press, 1986) presents the major variations on the Progressive theme. For the argument that there was no coherent movement, see Peter G. Filene, "An Obituary for the Progressive Movement," *American Quarterly* 20 (1970): 20–34.

5. Robert Wiebe, *The Search for Order, 1877–1920* (New York: Hill and Wang, 1967); John Buenker, *Urban Liberalism and Progressive Reform* (New York: Scribner, 1973) points to urban and ethnic dimensions of Progressivism, but I am persuaded that Robert Crunden is right in treating leaders like Al Smith or Msgr. John Ryan more as precursors of the New Deal. *Ministers of Reform: The Progressives' Achievement in American Civilization, 1889–1920* (New York: Basic Books, 1982).

6. Roosevelt twice used the trope "We stand at Armageddon and we battle for the Lord," first in a speech given at the time of the Republican convention (17 June 1912), and then in "Confession of Faith," which he gave at the end of the Progressive convention, 6 August 1912. *The Works of Theodore Roosevelt,* National edition (New York: Charles Scribner's Sons, 1926), 17:231, 239.

7. Alexis de Tocqueville, *Democracy in America* (New York: Knopf, 1980), 2:134–35.

8. D. H. Meyer, *The Instructed Conscience: The Shaping of the American National Ethic* (Philadelphia: University of Pennsylvania Press, 1972). See, too, Mark A. Noll, *The Scandal of the Evangelical Mind* (Grand Rapids: Eerdmans, 1994); John G. West Jr., *The Politics of Revelation and Reason: Religion and Civic Life in the New Nation* (Lawrence: University Press of Kansas, 1996), 121–22.

9. One of a handful of similar courses in contemporary American colleges is Hadley Arkes's class in Political Obligations at Amherst College, built around the argument in Arkes's *First Things: An Inquiry into the First Principles of Morals and Justice* (Princeton: Princeton University Press, 1986).

10. *Works of Thomas Reid,* Sir William Hamilton, ed. (Edinburgh: Maclaclan Stewart, 1863), 2:594–99, 638. See, too, Mark Hopkins, *Lectures on Moral Science* (Boston: Gould and Lincoln, 1862), 205–27; Archibald Alexander, *Outlines of Moral Science* (New York: Scribner, 1852), 86.

11. Meyer, *Instructed Conscience,* 6–9, 16–17, 28–30, 71; for one example, see Francis Wayland, *The Elements of Moral Science* (1835), Joseph Blau, ed. (Cambridge: Harvard University Press, 1963), 100–106.

12. Mark Hopkins, *The Law of Love and Love as Law* (New York: Scribner, 1869), 129–31; Hopkins, *Lectures on Moral Science,* 59–78.

13. Charles G. Finney, *Lectures on Systematic Theology* (Oberlin: J. M. Fitch, 1846), 1:6; Nathaniel William Taylor, *Lectures on the Moral Government of God* (New York: Clark, Austin and Smith, 1859), 1:7–17, 63–68.

14. James McCosh, *Our Moral Nature, Being a Brief System of Ethics* (New York: Scribners, 1892), 19, 47. See, too, Hopkins, *The Law of Love,* 268–70;

Wayland, *Moral Science,* 311–16, argued along these lines, although he also adhered to a broadly Jeffersonian version of social contract theory. On the general point, see Sydney Ahlstrom, *A Religious History of the American People* (New Haven: Yale University Press, 1972), 787.

15. Joseph Haven, *Moral Philosophy* (New York: Sheldon, 1880), 228–29, 276–77.

16. Edward Madden, "Francis Wayland and the Limits of Moral Responsibility," *Proceedings of the American Philosophical Society* 106 (1962):352–58; James Murray, *Francis Wayland* (Boston: Houghton Mifflin, 1891), 204–11. Wayland, however, did justify resistance to the Fugitive Slave Law. Idem, 274.

17. Meyer, *Instructed Conscience,* 82–85; Asa Mahan, *The Scripture Doctrine of Christian Perfection* (Boston: D. S. King, 1839), 9.

18. Emerson Davis, *The Half-Century* (Boston: Tappan and Whittemore, 1851), 222; Francis Wayland, *Occasional Discourses* (Boston: James Loring, 1833), 321–23, 341–43.

19. By 1865 Wayland had strengthened the antislavery argument in his widely used text by reference to the "progressive development" of the moral law from the "rude and ignorant" early Hebrews to the teaching of Jesus. *Moral Science,* 377–78.

20. "Once to Every Man and Nation," *Hymnal for Youth* (Chicago: Pilgrim, 1941), 221.

21. Eldon Eisenach, *The Lost Promise of Progressivism* (Lawrence: University Press of Kansas), 3.

22. *The Federalist* #1.

23. Stephen Eric Bronner, *Socialism Unbound* (New York: Routledge, 1990).

24. Speech to the Prussian Diet, 30 September 1862. "Nicht durch Reden und Majoritätsbeschlüsse werden die grossen Fragen der Zeit entschieden — das ist die grosse Fehler von 1848 und 1849 gewesen — sondern durch Blut und Eisen," *Die politischen Reden des Fürsten Bismarck,* Horst Kohl, ed. (Stuttgart: Cotta, 1892–1905), 2:29–30.

25. Eisenach, *Lost Promise,* 92–102; David Noble, *The Paradox of Progressive Thought* (Minneapolis: University of Minnesota Press, 1958), 160–61, 166.

26. Henry Adams, *The Education of Henry Adams,* ed. Ernest Samuels (Boston: Houghton Mifflin, 1974), 280–81.

27. Henry Adams, *A Letter to American Teachers of History* (Baltimore: J. H. Furst, 1910).

28. J. Howard Moore, *The Universal Kinship* (Chicago: Kerr, 1916), 317, 319.

29. Abraham Lincoln, *The Complete Works of Abraham Lincoln,* ed. Roy Basler (New Brunswick: Rutgers University Press, 1953), 7:302.

30. John Bascom, *Ethics, or The Science of Duty* (New York: Putnam, 1879), 354–78; Garry Wills, *Under God: Religion and American Politics* (New York: Simon and Schuster, 1990), 97–106.

31. Richard Ely, *Studies in the Evolution of Industrial Society* (New York: Macmillan, 1913).

32. E. A. Ross, *Social Control* (New York: Macmillan, 1914), 49–50, 59–60, 411–12; Moore, *Universal Kinship,* 245, 239, 132. On the other hand, as part of her feminist utopia, where it was social policy to "breed out" the "lowest types," Charlotte Perkins Gilman did imagine cats bred to kill rodents, but leave birds unharmed. Ross, *Herland* (New York: Pantheon, 1979), 82, 49.

33. William Graham Sumner, *What Social Classes Owe to Each Other* (1883) (Caldwell, Idaho: Caxton, 1978), especially 63–70; Sumner, *Earth Hunger and Other Essays* (New Haven: Yale University Press, 1913).

34. William James, *Pragmatism* (Cleveland and New York: World, 1968), 123.

35. Wiebe, *The Search for Order;* Grant A. Wacker, "The Holy Spirit and the Spirit of the Age in American Protestantism, 1880–1910," *Journal of American History* 72 (1985):45–62.

36. Adams, *The Education of Henry Adams,* 379–90, 421–22.

37. Ahlstrom, *Religious History,* 787–88; Charles H. Hopkins, *The Rise of the Social Gospel in American Protestantism* (New Haven: Yale University Press, 1940), 39; Henry F. May, *The Protestant Churches and Industrial America* (New York: Harper, 1949), 79.

38. Eric Goldman, *Rendezvous with Destiny* (New York: Knopf, 1953).

39. Ahlstrom, *Religious History,* 779; Charles H. Cooley, *Social Process* (New York: Scribners, 1920), 103, 418. On dueling, see West, *Revolution and Reason,* 88–97.

40. John Dewey and James H. Tufts, *Ethics* (New York: Henry Holt, 1908), 434, 485.

41. Richard Ely, *Social Aspects of Christianity* (New York: Crowell, 1889).

42. Nathan O. Hatch, *The Democratization of American Christianity* (New Haven: Yale University Press, 1989), 5–9, 17–46, 182.

43. Ralph Waldo Emerson, "History," in *Emerson's Essays,* ed. Sherman Paul (New York: Dutton, 1976), 13.

44. "Holy Spirit, Truth Divine" (1864), *Presbyterian Hymnal* (Louisville: Westminster/John Knox Press, 1990), #321.

45. Horace Bushnell, *Building Eras in Religion* (New York: Scribners, 1881), 269–80.

46. Wayland, *Moral Science,* 394.

47. Ibid., 380–81; Finney, *Lectures on Systematic Theology,* 1:20–24.

48. Wayland, *Moral Science,* 388–90.

49. Ibid., 389, 391–93.

50. Joseph Blau, Introduction to Wayland, *Moral Science,* xliv–xlvi.

51. Wayland, *Moral Science,* 394–96 and *Occasional Discourses,* 80–97.

52. Garry Wills, *Lincoln at Gettysburg: The Words that Remade America* (New York: Simon and Schuster, 1992), 37–38.

53. G. Stanley Hall, "On the History of American College Textbooks and Teaching in Logic, Ethics, Psychology and Allied Subjects," *Proceedings of the American Antiquarian Society* 9, 2 (1894):152.

54. Dewey and Tufts, *Ethics,* 167–68, 419–20, 422, 419.

55. Noll, *Scandal,* 162.

56. Sigmund Freud, *Civilization and Its Discontents,* in *Complete Psychological Works of Sigmund Freud,* ed. James Strachey (London: Hogarth, 1966), 21:112.

57. Hopkins, *Moral Science,* 59–78; Hopkins, *Law of Love,* 129–31.

58. Ralph Waldo Emerson, "Man the Reformer," in *Selected Essays of Ralph Waldo Emerson,* ed. Larzer Ziff (Harmondsworth: Penguin, 1982), 146.

59. Gladden's hymn, "O Master, Let Me Walk With Thee," may be found in the *Presbyterian Hymnal,* #357. On Comte's influence, see Edward Stettner, *Shaping Modern Liberalism: Herbert Croly and Progressive Thought* (Lawrence: University Press of Kansas, 1993) and Gillis J. Harp, *Positivist Republic: Auguste Comte and the Reconstruction of American Liberalism, 1865–1920* (University Park: Penn State University Press, 1995).

60. John Dewey, *The Public and Its Problems* (New York: Holt, 1927), 142, 148. Progressive distaste for ethnic communities — like the anti-Semitic and anti-immigrant asides in Gilman's writing — often rested on the belief that such groups were "tribal" or otherwise backward, resisting history's march toward the universal. See Ann J. Lane's introduction to Ross, *Herland,* xvii–xviii.

61. Dewey and Tufts, *Ethics,* 109.

62. John Dewey, *Democracy and Education* (New York: Macmillan, 1916), 73–74; Richard Ely, *Social Aspects of Christianity.*

63. Richard Ely, *The Social Law of Service* (New York: Methodist Book Concern), 1896.

64. Richard Ely, *Socialism and Social Reform* (New York: Crowell, 1894), 50–55.

65. Charles H. Cooley, *Social Process,* 42, 103, 109, 395, 400–401, 418; Cooley, *Social Organization: A Study of the Larger Mind* (New York: Scribners, 1909), 90, 118; Dewey, *The Public and Its Problems,* 109, 127, 131–34.

66. Charles H. Cooley, *Human Nature and the Social Order* (1902) (New York: Scribners, 1922), 118–19; Cooley, *Social Process,* 105; see also Cooley, "The Process of Social Change," *Political Science Quarterly* 12 (1897): 63–87.

67. Dewey and Tufts, *Ethics,* 428–30, 435.

68. Moore, *Universal Kinship,* 246. In Gilman's utopia, women reproduce by parthenogenesis, but are attracted by the possibility of "bisexual" reproduction. However, sexual feeling has disappeared, from disuse, and the heroines are shocked when Gilman's male characters suggest sex without a procreative aim. Even Ellador, who can see something beautiful in the idea of sexual intimacy, associates sexual passion with men; sexual desire in women, she says, "seems . . . against nature." Ross, *Herland,* 92, 126–29, 138.

69. Wills, *Under God,* 97–106; Christopher Lasch, *The True and Only Heaven: Progress and Its Critics* (New York: Norton, 1991).

70. There are many interesting parallels and connections between Progressivism and the late-century vogue of spiritualism. See Kenneth R. Andrews, *Nook Farm: Mark Twain's Hartford Circle* (Cambridge: Harvard University Press, 1950), 53–66.

71. Edward Bellamy, *Looking Backward* (1887) (New York: New American Library, 1960), 99.

72. On the union with nature and similar concepts, see Bellamy, *Looking Backward*, 49, 77, 194 and Bellamy, *Equality* (1897) (New York: Appleton-Century, 1937), 267–69, 341; on the races, see Bellamy, *Equality*, 37, 365.

73. Dewey, *The Public and Its Problems*, 113–14.

74. Ibid., 206–10; Dewey and Tufts, *Ethics*, 435.

75. Dewey, *The Public and Its Problems*, 114, 152–53, 183–84, 206–10; Moore, *Universal Kinship*, 268–69.

76. Rudyard Kipling, *The Jungle Books*, (New York: New American Library, 1961), 288.

77. Moore, *Universal Kinship*, 235. Praising *Herland*, Gilman's character, Jeff, likens that utopian community to bees, who "manage to cooperate and to love." Jeff even has admiring words to say about anthills. Ross, *Herland*, 67. It is useful to compare Hobbes's comments in *Leviathan*, chap. 17.

78. See Dorothea Muller, "The Social Philosophy of Josiah Strong: Social Christianity and American Progressivism," *Church History* 28 (1959):183–201.

79. Walter Rauschenbusch, *Christianity and the Social Crisis* (New York: Macmillan, 1913), 337, 350; Shailer Mathews, *Patriotism and Religion* (New York: Macmillan, 1918).

80. Dewey and Tufts, *Ethics*, 481–82.

81. Reinhold Niebuhr, *Moral Man and Immoral Society* (New York: Scribners, 1932).

82. William James, *Memories and Studies* (New York: Longmans Green, 1911), 267–96; present-day conservatives, particularly, feel the loss of the unifying force of the Cold War. E. J. Dionne, Jr., *Why Americans Hate Politics* (New York: Simon and Schuster, 1991).

83. Eisenach, *Lost Promise*, 3.

84. White, *Social Thought*, 242–43.

85. Meyer, *Instructed Conscience*, 137.

86. John Dewey, *Individualism Old and New* (New York: Minton Balch, 1930), 30.

87. Ibid., 67–69, 124–27, 130, 143, 148; Dewey, *The Public and Its Problems*, 31–32; Dewey, *Reconstruction in Philosophy* (New York: New American Library, 1950), 62, 65, 102, 141, 147. For a striking example, see Muzafer Sherif, *The Psychology of Social Norms* (New York: Harper, 1936), 15.

88. Arthur F. Bentley, *The Process of Government* (Bloomington: Principia, 1949); for a particularly fine critical response, see Lewis Lipsitz, "If, as Verba says, the state functions as a religion, what are we to do then to save our souls?" *American Political Science Review* 62 (1968):527–35.

89. Jacques Ellul, *The Technological Society* (New York: Vintage, 1964), 208–18.

90. William Connolly, *Identity/Difference: Democratic Negations of Political Paradox* (Ithaca, N.Y.: Cornell University Press, 1991).

91. Rauschenbusch, *Christianity and the Social Crisis*, 367.

92. Rauschenbusch, *Christianizing the Social Order* (New York: Macmillan, 1912), 124; see also 3, 6, 114, 119, 136ff, 209; Rauschenbusch, *Christianity and the Social Crisis,* 209; see also 100–105, 420–22.

93. Rauschenbusch, *Christianity and the Social Crisis,* 1, 17, 349, 39, 213.

94. Ibid., 47, 71; Rauschenbusch, *A Theology for the Social Gospel* (New York: Macmillan, 1917), 4.

95. Rauschenbusch, *Christianity and the Social Crisis,* 5, 8, 55.

96. Ibid., 7.

97. Ibid., 45ff, 104–5; "premillennial" teachings hold that, until the Second Coming, the world is sufficiently lost in sin that secular action offers only pretensions and low possibilities, emphasizing instead a soul that waits expectantly for Christ's return. "Postmillennial" doctrine, by contrast, sees the Kingdom of God as coming into being in and through history. Ahlstrom, *Religious History,* 808–12.

98. Rauschenbusch, *Christianity and the Social Crisis,* 59, 64, 210, 213, 279, 330–31, 353, 356, 363, 400.

99. David Levering Lewis, *W.E.B. Du Bois: Biography of a Race,* vol. 1, 1868–1919 (New York: Holt, 1994).

100. W.E.B. Du Bois, *The Souls of Black Folk* (1901) (New York: Everyman's/Knopf, 1993), 62, 60.

101. Ibid., 13, 16, 178–79.

102. Ibid., 163; the church, Du Bois observed, "antedates the Negro home." (156) On Du Bois's style, see Arnold Rampersad, *The Art and Imagination of W. E. B. Du Bois* (New York: Schocken, 1990).

103. Du Bois, *The Souls of Black Folk,* 70–71, 78.

104. Ibid., 88–89.

Social and Economic Regulation in the Progressive Era

Morton Keller

Our government is the most successful contrivance the world has ever known for preventing things from being done.

—Charles Evans Hughes

Continuity with the past is only a necessity, and not a duty.

—Oliver Wendell Holmes

Once upon a time, American historical writing was past politics; political science (not yet so named) was political history brought up to date. Woodrow Wilson could be—and indeed was—president of both the American Historical and the American Political Science Associations.

After that, political science and political history followed divergent paths. Political science evolved from the *staatspolitik* of Wilson, Westel W. Willoughby, and the rest of the out-of-Germany-by-Johns-Hopkins generation, to the interest-group tradition that began with Arthur F. Bentley and proceeded through Charles Merriam and E. E. Schattschneider to its apotheosis in Robert Dahl, V. O. Key, Nelson Polsby, and Aaron Wildavsky.

More recently, the study of American politics appears to consist of two

wings. One may be called the Great Tradition approach, blending traditional institutional and interest-group analysis with the more normative
concerns of political theory. Its practitioners include Theodore Lowi,
James Q. Wilson, state-formationists Stephen Skowronek and Theda
Skocpol, and public philosophers Michael Walzer, Michael Sandel, and
Robert Putnam (some of whom appear to be trying to craft, out of the
ruins of Socialism, a new social democracy with a communitarian face).

The other wing—currently, perhaps, the more influential in the
field—consists of those political scientists more or less indiscriminately
lumped together as practitioners of the rational-choice approach: essentially an application of the theoretical and analytical practices of Economics, the reigning Queen of the social sciences.

While all this was going on, political history as practiced by historians
went into a Rip Van Winkle–like slumber, stirred only by a rumble of
thunder named Richard Hofstadter—a slumber from which it has been
roused only in recent decades. It awoke to a world changed in two major
respects. A new social history had come into place, in which the concerns
of class, race, and gender took primacy over the pluralist constructs of
past political history and much political science. And rational choice and
other thoroughly modern methodologies gave political science a language and a set of concerns that, so far, have been difficult for political
historians to assimilate or even to address.

One revealing measure of this misfit is the degree to which the quantitative analysis of past electoral behavior, a branch of political history
that flourished from the 1950s to the 1970s in the work of Lee Benson,
Paul Kleppner, and Richard Jensen, has gone out of favor (and to a
considerable degree out of practice) in recent decades: precisely the time
when rational choice has come into its own among political scientists.

But now—and the conference out of which this and the other papers
in this volume emerged is a sign of the times—there is a fair prospect for
convergence between political science and political history, and in a most
unexpected venue.

For some time now, early twentieth-century American public life has
had a growing attraction for political scientists and political historians of
every persuasion. The structure of the American state and the funda-
ments of modern public policy are major themes of modern political
science, and the Progressive period is a mother lode for inquiry and
insight into these concerns. Polsby, Joseph Cooper, David Brady, Morris

Fiorina, and Eileen McDonagh are among those who have found fruitful source material in the turn-of-the-century Congress for the study of that complex branch of government. State formationists Skowronek and Skocpol, and social capitalist Robert Putnam, find in the public life of that period institutional and public policy developments highly relevant to our own time and to the contemporary concerns of their discipline.[1]

Recent political history has been more entangled than its political science counterpart in the race-class-culture Tong wars and the strictures of Marxist and post-Marxist analysis. But an approach that sets American politics and government in a broader social and cultural context is slowly gaining favor and is bringing to political history something of the insight and (relative) objectivity that has been perhaps more evident in its sister discipline in recent decades.[2]

This is a roundabout way of getting to the theme of the present essay: the polity's response to major economic and social issues in the early twentieth century. On its face this is a story of change: of the rise of a new set of political and governmental responses to a new set of economic and social realities. But while change is the chosen theme of most twentieth-century political history, this essay proposes a somewhat different perspective: one that keeps firmly in mind the massive, inertial persistence of existing institutions, interests, and ideas, and that looks upon political change as the product of special conditions rather than as the normal state of being of our political system.

It is well at the outset to keep in mind the degree to which the twentieth-century framework of American politics and government was inherited from nineteenth-century America and would persist with relatively little constitutional change. Amendments to the Constitution in the twentieth century have been most notable for the degree to which they have dealt with particularities, and not with the basic structure, of politics and government. Aside from Prohibition—soon negated by repeal—the only constitutional change that would have a significant effect on government policy was the Sixteenth (income tax) Amendment. Otherwise, constitutional change in this century has focused on who votes (women, eighteen-year-olds, residents of the District of Columbia); on for whom and how votes are cast (directly for senators, without a poll tax); and on adjustments to the machinery of government (when a new Congress and president take office, presidential term limits, the presidential succession). If anything, substantive change in the charter of American government has become more difficult during the course of the twentieth century, as demonstrated by the failed child labor, ERA, and balanced budget amendment campaigns.

No less striking is the persistence of the major political parties. True, the makeup and loyalty of party constituencies, the culture and structure of party organization, and the extent to which party affiliation determines public policy have undergone vast sea changes over the course of this century. And the parties themselves are in deep dis-esteem today — as, on a more limited scale, they were in the Progressive Era. But no recent challenge to two-party hegemony has matched the one mounted by the Progressives in 1912. From the Populists of the 1890s and the Progressives of 1912 and 1924 to George Wallace in 1968 and Ross Perot in 1992, the ground rules of the Constitution, and the utility of large, diverse parties, have prevented the rise of a major or permanent new political organization in the United States.

But what of government and public policy? Surely here the winds of change have blown long and hard and to great effect. In its fiscal scale, in its impact on people's lives, American government today is a presence unimaginable at the turn of the century.

Political scientists appear to be drawn increasingly to the view that the origins of the modern American state lie not in the New Deal or post-1960 America (as historian Arthur Schlesinger Jr. and political scientist Theodore Lowi have suggested), but in the Progressive Era. It is here that Stephen Skowronek finds the American administrative state taking form, that Theda Skocpol locates the origin of the modern welfare state, that Robert Putnam finds a rich store of social capital upon which the Progressive polity was able to draw.[3]

Is this right? Or wrong?

Perhaps.

While this answer would be perfectly satisfactory to historians, political scientists want — and are entitled to — something more in the way of explication. That requires a closer look at early twentieth-century public policy and some inquiry into what it tells us about the character of the developing twentieth-century American state.

The most notable features of public policy-making in the Progressive Era were a sudden and broad-scaled increase in the number, character, and salience of public issues, and a marked decline in the degree to which they were defined by the parties. The absence of constitutional amendments from 1870 to 1913 is an eloquent silence: mute testimony to the primacy of party government. Then four amendments were enacted between 1913 and 1920: testimony to the rise of a different sort of policy-making.

A comparison of the most salient concerns of the late nineteenth and early twentieth centuries also makes the point. The pre-1900 polity was concerned above all with the tariff and the currency, and (less so) with issues involving labor, mores, religion, public health, and the railroads. The parties substantially controlled the policy agenda, which is why third parties — farmer, labor, prohibitionist — cropped up so frequently, touting themes that the major parties sought to avoid. Government itself had a thin, insubstantial regulatory framework, resting almost entirely on the courts and the states.

After 1900 both the agenda and the structure of public life exploded. Dramatic increases occurred in federal and state lawmaking and in new modes of administrative regulation. Public opinion, mobilized by a newly party-free newspaper and magazine press and by a flood of extra-party pressure groups, took up a greatly expanded range of political and governmental, economic, and social/cultural issues. Presidents, congressional leaders, governors, and local officials were far more independent and policy-minded than their predecessors. It is noteworthy that none of the Progressive amendments to the Constitution — neither the income tax, direct election of senators, Prohibition, nor woman's suffrage — was the product of partisan politics. Put another way, they were responses to political pressures that transcended party lines.

These were the lineaments of the new world of Progressive policy-making, a world that seems familiar, or at least recognizable, today. But the question remains: was it an epiphenomenon, a unique response to unique early twentieth-century conditions? Or did it mark a basic change in the character of American governance, comparable to those of the Founding or of Jacksonian democracy?

One answer, currently the received one, is that here indeed are the beginnings of the modern American state. Certainly the most prominent issues of the Progressive Era — corruption and efficiency in government, corporate consolidation and maldistribution of wealth in the economy, race and gender relations, and the place of immigration and cultural pluralism in American life — are with us today. So too are the techniques by which policy was formulated, public support secured, and legislation passed: in particular, the ability of the mass media to mobilize public opinion (there is a direct line of descent from muckraking to today's investigative journalism) and the proliferation of special-interest groups pushing their political agendas outside the party system. Much of what we perceive as modern American society — rapid urbanization, quality-of-life-altering technological change, the rise of big business, professionals, white-collar workers, and consumers as significant factors in American life — came with a rush around the turn of the century. It would have been surprising indeed if these changes had not left their imprint on the polity.

But while the conditions of American life were in violent flux, no less real was the persistence of established values and institutions. This is where the historian has something to offer to the theme of twentieth-century American state-building that is the special province of the political scientist. Just as the Bismarckian/Wilhelmine welfare/warfare state, or early twentieth-century British Liberalism's social welfare policies, are comprehensible only in terms of the inherited social and governmental structures of those countries, so too is the encounter of American politics and government with the conditions of modern society, which began at the turn of the century and continues today, comprehensible only in terms of the peculiar history of this country's culture, politics, and law.

The interplay between continuity and change may be seen in the realms of social and economic policy. These became major new arenas in the early twentieth century: "major" in that they raised issues of very broad public concern, and "new" in that they reflected the cultural and technological changes that lie at the heart of what we mean by modernity.

The most notable new economic developments of the time were the sudden appearance on a large scale of big business, public utilities, and motor transportation. There were two fairly distinct policy reactions to the rise of big business. In the case of what were seen as purely private corporations, the response was the Sherman Antitrust Act of 1890. This gave the federal government — or more precisely, the federal courts — the authority to enforce ancient common law prohibitions of conspiracies in restraint of trade.[4]

Administrative oversight of antitrust policy — the Bureau of Corporations in 1902, the Federal Trade Commission in 1914, the Tariff Commission in 1916 — came laggardly, and was notable more for its regulatory weakness and susceptibility to corporate capture than for its bureaucratic vigor. More important, antitrust was subsumed within a process of judicial decision-making that quickly became the primary regulatory reality.

It is true that presidential administrations varied in their readiness to instruct the Justice Department to bring antitrust suits. But the basic guidelines — and much of the fine-tuning — of antitrust policy stayed in the hands of the courts. The uniqueness of this situation from an international perspective is evident when it is compared to the much more bureaucratic regulation of big business in early twentieth-century Britain, Germany, and France.

The court-driven character of corporate regulation in the United States had a solid grounding in nineteenth-century experience. For all their size and power, the "trusts" — a generic term for large extractive, manufacturing, or transportation companies — fit readily enough into the prevailing legal tradition that private corporations were chartered creations of the states. When the time for regulation came, it was logical to subject them to a form of oversight in which the federal courts, taking a common-law-like approach to the interpretation of a statute barring "conspiracies in restraint of trade," applied the law as readily to the trusts as they did to individual entrepreneurs. Thus an essentially nineteenth-century view of how and what to regulate was applied to the quite modern phenomenon of big business.

The second Progressive response to big business — drawing a sharp distinction between private trusts and public enterprises — was also very much in an established regulatory tradition. Businesses defined as having a public purpose — railroads first, and then more inclusively "public utilities" (water, streetcar and subway, gas and electric and telephone companies) — called for a substantially different regulatory response. The goal here was not so much to break them up — their quasi-monopolistic character made that infeasible — but to oversee pricing and the provision of service.

The private-public distinction is troublesome to many contemporary political and legal theorists. But what was private and what was public, and the separation of the one from the other, had an important place in the minds of the Founders. This, in part, was what the Revolution was about. Nineteenth-century American political thought deepened the public-private distinction, not least in that most powerful instrument of governance, the law. Indeed, contemporary Neoconservative, Libertarian, and New Democrat political approaches suggest that the distinction continues to have an important place in American political culture. It is not surprising that Progressive economic policy reflected it as well.

The Interstate Commerce Commission of 1887, the first federal regulatory agency, came directly out of the small cache of nineteenth-century American regulatory experience. In part, the ICC was a national version of existing state railroad commissions. And in part it was what Thomas M. Cooley, one of the first commissioners, called "a new court," designed "to lay the foundations of a new body of American law" — a common law of railroad regulation.[5]

But the newer public utilities raised special regulatory problems of their own. True, in their corporate form they differed little from firms that made steel, mined coal, extracted oil, or turned out consumer products. But their output was not so easily taken or left by customers. What they provided were "public services," as distinguished from the satisfaction of private wants.

Nor did their business consist of the one-off, essentially contractual, transactions that characterized the dealings of steel, coal, and oil firms, or even railroads, with their customers. What they provided was a steady, continuous *flow* of services: water, gas, electricity, telephone calls, commuter transportation. By their very nature these posed problems for the contractual model, which implied that an injured party had due and sufficient recourse in the courts.

One possible policy response to this distinction was public ownership and operation, an option widely adopted in Europe. But aside from municipal waterworks, publicly owned utilities were rare birds in turn-of-the-century America. Along with the political clout of the existing private companies, public ownership was stunted by a widespread inclination, fed by a century of experience, to identify government not with disinterested public service but with the self-serving wiles of politicians and parties.

How to deal with enterprises not quite private, yet not wholly public? The answer was the public utilities commission (PUC). An adaptation (sometimes merely an extension) of the state railroad commissions of the late nineteenth century, PUCs were peculiarly American creations, particularly in the assumption that they would be objective, removed regulatory bodies, like the courts from which they so clearly derived. Their British counterparts — the Railway Rates Tribunal, metropolitan transport committees, the Central Electricity Board — were, on the contrary, explicitly corporative, composed of interest groups (management, labor, the public) under the oversight of the relevant ministries of the central government.

In one sense this was regulatory innovation. The very terms "public utility" and "public service company" were new ones, born around the turn of the century, and they had no place in European law or practice. But this was innovation steeped in tradition. In defining the public responsibility of utilities, the courts resurrected the venerable common law of public callings. Roscoe Pound wryly observed in 1921, "It is significant that progress in our law of public service companies has taken the form of abandonment of nineteenth century views for doctrines which may be found in the [medieval and early modern] Year Books."[6]

Nor did public utilities regulation constitute a great leap forward in the formation of the American administrative state. State public utilities commissions assiduously held hearings and ground out rate and operations orders (142,704 of them in twenty-one states between 1921 and 1928). But two factors kept the PUCs from becoming effective instruments of bureaucratic control. One was the prevalence of commission capture by the utilities: a list in 1930 of state PUC members who had gone to work for the companies they regulated stretched over four pages. The other was the oversight role of the courts — important both for what they actually did and said, and for the implicit threat of judicial review.

Regulatory bodies were shaky in their autonomy, beset by the pressure of industry capture and court review, trammeled by a polity dominated by party politicos and a public suspicious of active government. This matched nobody's idea of a well-tempered administrative state. Just how ineffectual this system of regulation could be appeared in two feckless quests for the Holy Grail of effective PUC rate-setting.

One was the ICC's response to a 1913 Congressional mandate that it come up with a valuation of the material assets of the railroads. On that basis, it was fondly hoped, "rational" rate-setting might go forward. Endless hearings and a flood of data attempted to quantify unquantifiables such as "reproduction cost," "cost value," "present value," "fair value," and "value of the service." After more than a decade, $100 million had been spent on examining and valuing 260,000 miles of track, countless rails and ties, bridges and terminals; on judging the age and condition of masonry; and on preparing elaborate depreciation tables. But the ICC never did determine how to weigh the difference between "historical" (original) cost and reproduction cost as bases for rate-setting.

State public utilities commission rate-determination got hung up on a similarly unresolvable conflict between returns based on "fair value," as defined by each of the numerous interests involved, and "social welfare in rate-making." The idea here was to use utility rates for purposes such as relieving congestion, promoting community and industrial development, fostering education, or raising the standard of living by reducing utility rates.

This hopeless enterprise produced the same endless round of commission hearings and court reviews that attended railroad rate-setting. The early twentieth-century administrative state in action is fairly seen in PUC hearings during the 1920s on the New York Telephone Company. After 625 witnesses and 37,000 pages of testimony, the Commission had to pick its way through estimates of the company's fair value that ranged from $367 million to $615 million. One judge observed with understandable cynicism that any two estimates within 10 percent of each other suggested collusion.[7]

Surely the motor vehicle did as much as any technological innovation in early twentieth-century American life to alter the social and cultural (and indeed the built) landscape of the country. Yet the response of the state to this new technology has gotten short shrift in the literature on economic regulation. This is so primarily because the regulatory response was so muted, so localized, and above all so noninnovative, in the sense that old forms and principles were applied to this most powerful of new technologies.

The earliest regulation of commercial motor vehicle activity was intensely local. Municipal ordinances licensed and regulated taxis; their numbers and routes were subject to the familiar constraints of counterinterests (street railways especially) and industry capture (with existing licensees seeking to limit entry). But the mobility that was at the core of this new technology, and the explosive growth of trucks and buses, soon demanded a larger framework: statewide, then interstate. State motor vehicle regulation acts came with a rush in the 1920s, subjecting commercial vehicles to oversight by existing railroad or public utilities commissions. The courts approved this as a valid exercise of the police power.

So rapid and easy was entry into the taxi, bus, or truck business that the regulation (or elimination) of competition was more important than rate-setting. The larger bus operators, and railroads smarting from bus competition, were great proponents of regulation. The more numerous and independent truckers, and shippers who welcomed the rate-reducing effects of competition, were less favorably inclined. In this sense the politics of motor-vehicle regulation closely resembled that of railroad regulation.

Perhaps the most striking thing about this early regulatory record was how rarely a public-interest perspective emerged. As in the case of the railroads almost a century earlier, most of the public was content (or expected) to allow, and benefit from, headlong expansion and wide-open competition. Indeed the Supreme Court, in the mid-1920s, decided that private motor carriers were not public utilities at all, and it invalidated state licensing of motor transport in interstate commerce. Brandeis argued that licensing was "not regulation with a view to safety or to conservation of the highways, but the prohibition of competition."[8]

In a sequence very similar to the evolution of nineteenth-century railroad regulation, the immediate consequence of this Liberty Hall approach was "consternation and confusion" among carriers and regulators. The former quickly sought to take advantage of the regulatory void: bus companies in the New York–New Jersey–Philadelphia corridor often built terminals straddling state lines, thus avoiding any state regulation. And then there was a public reaction. In 1932 the Supreme Court in effect reversed itself, saying that the state could indeed certify motor carriers in the interest of highway maintenance and safety. And Congress passed the Motor Carrier Act of 1935, which empowered the ICC to license and regulate interstate trucks and buses.

Because of the pressure to restrict entry, and the sheer number, variety, and elusiveness of trucks, buses, and taxis, licensing became the major instrument of commercial vehicle regulation. A new legal device, the certificate of public convenience and necessity, was devised for the purpose. These were permits to operate that, unlike railroad charters or streetcar franchises, were granted for relatively short periods of time and conferred no property rights. Besides protecting established carriers from new entrants, they obligated bus companies to serve less as well as more profitable routes and had more flexible regulatory potential than street railway franchises.

But again, this was innovation steeped in the past. Licensing — a form of regulation that had fallen into disfavor during the nineteenth century because it smacked of privilege and monopoly — now reemerged, as did the law of public callings for utilities: venerable devices resurrected to deal with unsettling new technologies.

The most life-altering of the new technologies of the twentieth century was the family automobile. Governments everywhere had to register cars and drivers, define and regulate dangerous driving, and develop rules of liability and compensation for the harms that emerged from this potent new machine. The net effect was that the state became involved in its citizens' everyday lives on a scale not known before.

The regulatory response was shaped by extraordinarily rapid growth in the number of cars and drivers, and by oversight by state and local rather than federal government. This was an inevitable development, given the place that the police power of the states had come to assume in the American constitutional order. During the first quarter of the twentieth century, a mass of local and state ordinances, licensing and registration provisions, speed and other safety and policing rules came into being. Calls for federal supervision were weak and infrequent. By the end of the 1920s the modern structure of automobile registration — state and local in origin, but increasingly responsive to the need for interstate comity and based on more or less uniform ground rules throughout the nation — was in place.

As striking as the persistence of state and local regulation of this intrinsically national technology was the story — or, better, the non-story — of the impact of the automobile on the courts. For all the scale of auto-induced litigation — car accident liability and injury cases were by far the dominant source of civil litigation by the early 1920s — the courts almost effortlessly absorbed automobile liability law within the traditional torts framework. One of the most conspicuous of the nonbarking dogs of twentieth-century American law is the lack of major doctrinal change (save for allowing intrafamily suits for insurance purposes) traceable to the coming of the automobile.

Looked at in the large, the record of the Progressive polity's response to economic change in the early twentieth century strongly supports Charles Evans Hughes's observation that American government "is the most successful contrivance the world has ever known for preventing things from being done." "Things" — in the sense of close and active state regulation — were just not done in response to the turn-of-the-century economic and technological transformation. Big business, public utilities, motor vehicles grew like Topsy; the response of the state was minimal, traditional. And those regulatory devices that did get put in place revealed how great was the tendency — perhaps the necessity — of American government to respond to dramatic new conditions in time-honored ways.

When we turn to what were, arguably, the most substantial social policies of the early twentieth century, a very different picture emerges: one that lends support to Oliver Wendell Holmes's aphorism that "continuity with the past is only a necessity, and not a duty." In this case a politically engendered "duty" to innovate recurrently overcame the "necessity" of continuity with the past. To put it another way: if Progressive economic regulation illustrates the force of persistence in American government, then the Progressive social policy experience reveals the preconditions for substantial policy change.

The three major social policy achievements of the Progressive period were Prohibition, woman's suffrage, and immigration restriction. Admittedly, much has been made in recent years of the early twentieth century as the seedbed of social welfare policy. But in terms of their impact on large numbers of people, and in what they tell us of the cultural content of early twentieth-century social policy, these three enactments are in a class by themselves.[9]

Prohibition is traditionally identified with rural and small-town religious fundamentalism; woman's suffrage with the organized suffrage movement; immigration restriction with racist-minded xenophobes. These were indeed the leading edge — the vanguard — groups. But federal legislation and, in the cases of Prohibition and woman's suffrage, constitutional amendments were feasible only with the backing of broad coalitions cutting across party, class, and sectional lines. These social policies most certainly had such support. They also had the benefit of a traumatic national event — the First World War — which created as receptive a political context for them as the Great Depression would do, a generation later, for the economic legislation of the New Deal.

The success of Prohibition lay not so much in its small-town/evangelical core, exemplified by the Prohibition Party and the WCTU in the late nineteenth century, as in its expansion around the turn of the century into an issue that appealed to a much wider variety of groups. When liquor regulation came to be seen, in *echt*-Progressive terms, as "part of the question of public sanitation and social control," then social conservatives fearful of the effects of drink on the behavior of the lower classes, and social reformers decrying its effect on poverty, crime, race relations, and family life found common cause.[10]

Under these conditions sea changes in opinion occurred. Southern Democratic congressmen were traditionally reluctant to support national prohibition because of its threat to states' rights and to their tenuous alliance with their urban, often Catholic, northern Democratic compatriots. But they found in the linkage of drink with growing tension in race relations sufficient reason to change their minds. The rise of the Anti-Saloon League as the most potent prohibitionist pressure group involved not only innovative political mobilization, but a freshened alliance between fundamentalism and social reform. Saloon League director Wayne Wheeler championed a national child labor amendment, while the Women's Christian Temperance Union supported an eighthour law, peace through arbitration, juvenile courts, and industrial education.

Woman's suffrage underwent a strikingly similar development. It, too, was started with a late nineteenth-century activist core, and like Prohibition languished as a national cause around the turn of the century. No state adopted woman's suffrage between 1896 and 1910. Powerful cultural predispositions stood in the way of votes for women. A considerable literature dwelt on the threat that it posed to the family, to the tender character of the sex, to apolitical, woman-led charity and poverty work. Nor were women themselves readily mobilized. In 1913 the *New York Evening Sun* polled female schoolteachers, factory workers, stenographers, bookkeepers, and saleswomen in 132 locations on the issue. Of the 2,000 who responded, 571 favored, 651 opposed, and 778 were indifferent to the cause.[11]

But like Prohibition, woman's suffrage became more and more an issue to which large and varied groups could respond. It, too, benefited from the ability of the new mass media and nationally organized pressure groups to foster public support beyond the constraints of a party-defined policy agenda. Suffrage "came to be attractive to the 'clean government' school of thought, the Americanizers of immigrants, the declared enemies of corrupt boss-ridden city politics." Conservatives saw it as a way of increasing the native-born middle-class electorate.

Politicians more and more sensitive to social concerns began to vie with one another to be on the right side of an issue with such manifest electoral implications. Colorado governor Alva Adams assured the timorous that female voting in his state had not altered the character of the sex: "I have known personally at least 10,000 women voters of Colorado, and I have never known one to be less a woman, or less a mother, or less a housekeeper, or less a heart keeper, from the fact that she voted — not one."[12]

Still, the going was slow. By the end of 1914, after sixty years of effort, only three million women in ten states and Alaska could vote. But as the new context and the new policy-formation instrumentalities of the Progressive Era took hold, the pace quickened. The role that women played in America's participation in the First World War, and the ideology of democracy that attached to it, gave woman's suffrage a powerful boost (as it did Prohibition). A New York suffrage-referendum victory in November 1917 led to a favorable vote in the national House of Representatives in January 1918. The Senate endorsed the suffrage amendment in June 1919; state ratification followed by August 1920.

The triumph of immigration restriction is a tale very similar to those of Prohibition and woman's suffrage. Besides its common source in the anxieties bred by rapid social change, restriction resembled the others in the diversity of its supporters, and in the way in which it battened on the distinctive features of the Progressive polity: a media-fostered national public opinion, an increase in reliance on massive fact-gathering, belief in government's social-regulatory role.

Immigration restriction became the cause of a broad popular alliance by the early twentieth century, very similar in its variety, in its blend of old and new social anxieties, to those of Prohibition and woman's suffrage. Its supporters included social elites exercised over the unwashed foreign masses, backwoods xenophobes, academics and intellectuals enamored of new racial and eugenics theories, organized labor, and Progressive reformers who saw in reduced immigration a way of lessening poverty, crime, and social disorder. "The plan for a proper restriction of immigration rests upon an even higher plane than the [Pure] Food Law; it is to benefit not alone our bodies but to insure the welfare of our homes, our States and our nation," said one Progressive restrictionist.

"The problem of immigration is but a part of the greater conservation movement. It has to do with the conservation of the American people, all that it stands for," said another. The forward-looking Boston department-store owner Edward A. Filene contended that it was "important to business that we produce more consumers rather than produce more commodities," and held that a half century of restriction would create a better educated, more efficient, more prosperous, and hence more highly consuming population.[13]

As in the cases of Prohibition and woman's suffrage, the First World War created a situation in which broad restrictionist sentiment led to significant legislation. When Wilson in January 1917, on the eve of American entry into the war, vetoed a literacy test act (the third chief executive to do so), Congress overrode him. After the war ended, Congress, in its Immigration Act of 1921, established a quota system and set an annual maximum intake, reversing a receptivity to immigrants as old as the Republic. The new policy was extended, and tightened, in 1924, with the Progressive-minded *New Republic* accepting restriction "as a political and social necessity in the present condition of the United States."[14]

Prohibition moved to its ultimate triumph because the growing number of reasons to support it turned it into a national cause. Opposition became the province of special interests: brewers, particular immigrant groups, libertarian-minded intellectuals. But the final passage of national legislation was spurred by a galvanizing event: American entry into the First World War. The identification of the war with reform, which lay at the heart of Wilson's rhetoric, helped to create the political environment that made possible the Eighteenth Amendment and the Volstead Act.

The same thing happened with woman's suffrage. By 1917 the movement had broad national support. Once the United States entered the war, the argument for suffrage as a proper recognition of the role of women in the war effort became as irresistible as the argument that Prohibition would make the nation morally fit for returning veterans.

And exactly the same thing happened with immigration restriction. Fervid wartime patriotism, and then a postwar xenophobic, antiradical backlash, provided the seedbed for the restrictions of the 1920s.

It is perhaps inherent in the historian's trade to dwell on continuity and persistence. As (in Mr. Dooley's words) a lawyer is a man who can turn a stone wall into a triumphal arch, so a historian may be counted on to seek the opposite: to turn the triumphal arch of change into the stone wall of resistance to change. But while there is much in the record of Progressive economic and social policy that fits Charles Evans Hughes's skepticism as to the potential of the American state, much of it echoes Holmes's subtle challenge to historical stasis.

The differences that separate Progressive economic from social policy—the past-laden, incremental and particularistic, generally ineffective character of the former; the bold, sweeping, assertive character of the latter—tell us much about the shape and limits of twentieth-century public policy-making. The response to economic change as large-scale as the rise of big business and the coming of motor vehicles was, in many respects, as lame and halting as Hughes's dictum suggests. Why? Because of the political power of the interests affected? Surely so—in part. But surely, too, because of the strong tradition of government subsidization but not close supervision of economic activity, and the equally strong suspicion of regulatory power wielded by a boss-and-party-ridden polity. Perhaps it is the case that the (sometimes creative) destructive forces of market capitalism and technology do not readily lend themselves to tighter and more purposeful governmental constraints. Nor, it may be added, does the diversity of American life. On the record, it appears that little short of a widely shared economic catastrophe such as the Great Depression of the 1930s is likely to make for significant change in economic policy.

The regulatory history of this century is clear: unless the multitudinous interests of a diverse people are welded by experience or attitude into a large-scale political coalition, or some major development, on the scale of war or depression, concentrates the American mind, the likelihood of large-scale regulation is not high. Both of these conditions were at work in the realm of social policy during the early decades of this century, and the consequence was the most notable legislative achievements of the time. It should be said that the results hardly merit our unalloyed enthusiasm. Who would hail prohibition and immigration restriction as triumphs of American politics and government? But the system does allow for the repair of policy mistakes, though it took thirteen years in the case of prohibition and forty-four years in the case of quota-based immigration restriction.

The social policies of the Progressive Era were hardly this century's last instance of large-scale legislative enactment. The same thing happened with the New Deal legislation of the 1930s, when the Great Depression focused the national mind on economic problems. And surely the Great Society's racial and poverty laws of the 1960s, and the environmental legislation of the 1970s, were the products of a widespread public sense of crisis — racial, ecological — and the mobilization of national coalitions that created the conditions for substantial policy change.

Recent failures — Clinton's health care proposal, the more ambitious goals of the Republicans' Contract with America — make the same point in a negative way. In each case there was no broad popular coalition; there was no perceived national crisis; and there was no legislative triumph.

The conclusion of this essay is: that is the way things were; and, pretty much, that is the way things are and will be. The conditions that make for American legislative breakthroughs appear to be at least as harsh and demanding today as they ever were. It might be thought that the greatly expanded mass media, the enlarged body of public policy expertise, and the more nationalized society that have come into being in this century would expedite policy formation and the recruitment of public support. Instead, it appears that these conditions have made for a public and a polity ever more complexly aware of its own interests, ever more difficult to weld into coalitions sufficiently large to surmount the enormous obstacles to policy implementation in the American system.

Notes

1. Nelson W. Polsby, "The Institutionalization of the House of Representatives," *American Political Science Review* 62 (1968): 144–68; Joseph Cooper and David W. Brady, "Institutional Context and Leadership Style: The House from Cannon to Rayburn," *American Political Science Review* 75 (1981): 411–25; David Brady, *Congressional Voting in a Partisan Era: A Study of the McKinley House and a Comparison to the Modern House of Representatives* (Lawrence: University Press of Kansas, 1971); Eileen McDonagh, "The 'Welfare Rights State' and 'Civil Rights State': Policy Paradox and State Building in the Progressive Era," *Studies in American Political Development* 7 (Fall 1993): 225–74; Stephen Skowronek, *Building a New American State: The Expansion of National Administrative Capacities, 1877–1920* (Cambridge: Cambridge University Press, 1982); Theda Skocpol, *Protecting Soldiers and Mothers: The Political Origins of Social Policy in the United States* (Cambridge: Harvard University Press, 1992).

2. Morton Keller, *Affairs of State: Public Life in Late Nineteenth-Century America* (Cambridge: Harvard University Press, 1977); Lizabeth Cohen, *Making a*

New Deal: Industrial Workers in Chicago, 1919–1939 (Cambridge: Cambridge University Press, 1990).

3. Skowronek, *Building;* and Skocpol, *Protecting;* Robert D. Putnam, untitled work in progress on social capital and American public policy.

4. This discussion draws substantially from Morton Keller, *Regulating a New Economy: Public Policy and Economic Change in America, 1900–1933* (Cambridge: Harvard University Press, 1990), chap. 2 (antitrust), chap. 3 (public utilities), and pages 66–74 (motor vehicles).

5. Allan Jones, "Thomas M. Cooley and the ICC: Continuity and Change in the Doctrine of Equal Rights," *Political Science Quarterly* 81 (1966):613.

6. Roscoe Pound, *The Spirit of the Common Law* (Boston: Marshall Jones, 1921), 289.

7. Cited in Keller, *Regulating a New Economy,* 63.

8. Brandeis in *Buck v Kuykendall,* 267 US 307, 315 (1925).

9. The following discussion draws heavily on Morton Keller, *Regulating a New Society: Public Policy and Social Change in America, 1900–1933* (Cambridge: Harvard University Press, 1994), 125–48 (Prohibition), 293–307 (woman's suffrage), and 219–35 (immigration restriction).

10. Samuel J. Barrows, "The Temperance Tidal Wave," *Outlook* 89 (1908): 515.

11. *Outlook* 104 (1913):268–69.

12. Quoted in David Morgan, "Woman Suffrage in Britain and America in the Early Twentieth Century," in *Contrast and Connection: Bicentennial Essays in Anglo-American History,* ed. H. C. Allen and Roger Thompson (Athens: Ohio University Press, 1976), 274; 'Ignota,' "How the Vote Has Affected Womanhood in Colorado," *Westminster Review* 163 (1905):268.

13. Francis E. Hamilton, "Restriction of Immigration," *Forum* 42 (1909): 558; Henry P. Fairchild, "The Restriction of Immigration," *American Economic Review (Supplement)* 2 (1912): 60; Edward A. Filene, "Immigration, Progress and Prosperity," *Saturday Evening Post* 196 (28 June 1923):8, 70–71.

14. "The Immigration Question," *New Republic* 38 (1924):6–7.

Race, Class, and Gender in the Progressive Era

Restructuring State and Society

Eileen L. McDonagh

Scholars engaged in cross-national comparisons of democratic processes and attitudes find many diverse meanings of democracy. Robert Putnam, for example, in his study of Britain and Italy, while cautioning against simplifying too much, nevertheless argues that "government by the people . . . [is] the root meaning of 'democracy'." Although he found that both the British and the Italians contributed to this definition of democracy, there nevertheless were cross-national differences. Italians were more likely to define government by the people very literally to mean "direct popular participation," while in Britain, the term meant such things as "responsible government or public attention to political affairs." Putnam found that some in Britain even went "out of their way to *reject* direct popular participation as a defining characteristic of democracy." Instead, the British were more likely than the Italians, when defining democracy, to mention "specific political institutions such as elections and parliamentary government." While both the Italians and the British frequently mentioned "[p]olitical liberties, such as free speech and freedom of association," those in Britain more often than in Italy mentioned "limitations on government power and discretion," such as "the rule of law, dispersed governmental powers, laissez-faire social and economic policy," as the defining characteristic of democracy.[1]

We can think of democracy, therefore, in terms of two axes: institutional and participatory.[2] The *institutional axis* is defined by rules of law, the structural arrangement of governance and governmental institutions, and the scope and centralization of state power. All of these attributes of a democratic political system refer to institutional arrangements defining the scope and centralization of the power of the state to act. Following Jürgen Habermas, we might think of the institutional axis as the "liberal model" of democracy, one that defines government "as an apparatus of public administration, and society as a market-structured network of interactions among private persons," in which government translates the diverse interests of a heterogeneous polity into cohesive policies.[3]

The second axis of democratic governance is the *participatory axis,* defined by who has access to political power in the exercise of governance. With Jürgen Habermas we can think of the participatory axis as the "republican model" of democracy, defined as "constitutive for the processes of society as a whole." According to this model, politics is the "medium by which the members of . . . solitary communities become aware of their dependence on one another and, acting with full deliberation as citizens, further shape and develop existing relations of reciprocal recognition into an association of free and equal consociates under law."[4] Analysis of the participatory axis, therefore, focuses on how expansive or restrictive the policies are that define membership in the political community (such as immigration laws); on the degree to which the franchise is expanded or contracted to include marginal groups; and on the status of basic civil liberties affecting the everyday lives of members of the polity.[5]

Sidney Milkis and others portray the Progressive Era as a second founding of the American state, by which they mean, in part, that it was a time during which the social contract defining the scope and structure of state power, and the participatory components of the electorate, were renegotiated.[6] The Progressive Era thus invites investigation along not just one, but both axes of democratic governance of the newly configured polity. As a key stage in the development of the modern American state,[7] it is important to ask what the developmental relationship was between the institutional axis and the participatory axis, i.e., whether expansion on the institutional axis of democratic governance in the Progressive Era, which successfully increases the capacity of the state to meet the reform agendas of the time, goes hand in hand with an increase in the participatory axis giving marginal groups greater access to political power.

This essay focuses on the place of race, class, and gender in the politics of the Progressive Era, specifically on how these categories connect to patterns of political development and the legacy of that development for subsequent periods of reform, particularly the civil rights revolution of the sixties and seventies. By doing so, we may assess, for example, whether the New Freedom of Woodrow Wilson and Louis Brandeis advanced "democratic participation over statism" in the Progressive Era,[8] as well as gain insights about the relationship of the Progressive Era to the dynamics of political change at the end of the twentieth century.

The Institutional Axis

The Active Use of Government

The American liberal and democratic heritage, as exemplified in the Declaration of Independence, includes a commitment to principles of equality and liberty. Progressivism is a reform orientation that seeks to implement the power of state authority and government institutions — in contradistinction to dependence upon private, philanthropic institutions — to solve social and economic inequalities viewed as the source of societal ills. The Progressive Era at the onset of the twentieth century as a period of such change is often compared to contemporary reform initiatives. Hugh Heclo observes, for example, that there is something familiar to us in the Progressives' deep worry that, "despite living in an era of relative peace and prosperity, something had gone seriously wrong in the internal life of the nation."[9]

The commonality of progressive reformers in such pivotal periods as the Progressive Era, the New Deal, and the Great Society lies in their attempt to use government as a tool for reducing social and economic inequalities. As E. J. Dionne states, the "progressive tradition" devised in the early twentieth century made "*active use of government* to temper markets and enhance individual opportunities."[10] So, too, at the end of the twentieth century, many advocates of reform turn to government. In the words of Robert Putnam, "political leaders Jack Kemp and Jesse Jackson both survey the inner city and emerge talking about the importance of 'empowerment' and *the government's role in the process*. . . . There is, in short, a growing sense that the solutions to our problems and the courage to implement them will emerge again. Central to that courage, however, will be a change in *how we see government.* "[11] Similarly, historian Morton Keller identifies a conspicuous feature of the Progressive Era to be the use of government and law "to control the behavior of institutions, individuals, and groups."[12]

The Regulatory State

One of the more innovative accomplishments of the Progressive Era on the institutional axis of democracy was expanding the legitimate use of public power by establishing the regulatory state to promote people's welfare.[13] As Morton Keller has shown, it is in the Progressive Era that reformers established regulatory policies encompassing the wide range of "factors of production: labor, land, trade, capital, and taxation."[14] Furthermore, the establishment of new regulatory policies was accomplished not as a reactive response to crises generated by war or economic collapse, but rather in a proactive mode that initiated reforms during a time of peace and general prosperity.

The assumption that social and economic problems were beyond the individual's control had been an obvious rationale for state intervention in the aftermath of such serious disruptions as war. Consequently, pensions for veterans of the Civil War were the first economic assistance provided by the federal government to individuals for income security. Extending this principle of causation to processes of laissez-faire capitalism itself, however, represented a profound departure from earlier, long dominant premises in American liberal culture that had stressed just the opposite.[15] It is the magnitude of this departure that leads John Buenker to mark this period as "launching" the American welfare state.[16]

It is in the Progressive Era, therefore, that those disadvantaged by the market system came more and more to be seen as the victims of forces beyond their control, and the use of governmental power to intervene on their behalf became more legitimate.[17] As James Weinstein puts it, one of the major changes that took place in the liberal state at this time is the "replacement of the ideological concept of laissez-faire" with an "ideal of a responsible social order in which all classes could look forward to some form of recognition and sharing in the benefits of an ever-expanding economy."[18] As a result, millions of middle-class citizens as well as policy elites came to believe that the adverse effects of industrial capitalism could be humanized through regulatory legislation that limited business and purified politics. As Richard Hofstadter has said, the "pioneers of the welfare state" were those in the Progressive Era who were the "first to assert with any real practical success that government should be a positive agent responsible for the welfare of its citizens, and for the poor and powerless citizens."[19]

A key characteristic of economic and welfare policies in the Progressive Era, therefore, was their legitimation of state regulation as a principle setting limits to the damaging effects of uncontrolled industrial capitalism.[20] With rare exceptions, legislation stopped short of monetary provision or social insurance.[21] Yet, not only were the regulatory policies that were passed innovative in content, but they also reformulated the scope and authority of the American state to include intervention in what hitherto had been the sacrosanct laissez-faire relationships between employers and laborers, and between consumers and business. This development alone would designate the early twentieth century as a preeminent institution-building reform era.[22]

Notable policy inventions of the Progressive Era, however, also include establishing new instruments of democratic governance, such as the referendum, initiative, recall, direct election of senators, direct primary, and electoral regulation and civil service legislation. In addition, it is in the Progressive Era that the innovative use of government is legislatively reconfigured to empower government to intervene in the realm of market relationships. While inroads begin in the late 1890s, it is in the Progressive Era decades of 1900–20 that state legislatures successfully pass more and more reforms regulating conditions of employment, protecting consumers, and even authorizing social welfare provisions for mothers and children.[23] In many instances, these state-level policies, when spread across all regions of the country, become the foundation for their centralization by congressional passage of similar legislation.

Heading the Progressive Era agenda, therefore, we find such policies as antitrust legislation; social justice measures, such as workmen's compensation, minimum wage and hours, vocational educational legislation; urban housing codes; and child welfare legislation, such as child-labor laws, educational programs, mothers' pensions, and maternal health

Table 1. Passage of Hours Laws

Time Period	Region			
	Northeast	Central	South	West
pre-1900	+Connecticut (1855) +Maine (1848) +New Hampshire (1847) +New York (1867) +Pennsylvania (1848) +Rhode Island (1853) *Massachusetts (1890) *New York (1853, 1899) *Pennsylvania (1847)	+Illinois (1867) +Indiana (1889) +Michigan (1885) +Minnesota (1878) +Missouri (1867) +Nebraska (1887) +Ohio (1852) *Indiana (1889) *Kansas (1891) *Nebraska (1891) *Ohio *Minnesota	+Florida (1874) *Louisiana (1868) *Maryland (1892) *Texas (1879) *W. Virginia (1899)	+California (1853, 1899) +Montana (1895) *Colorado (1893) *Idaho (1891) *Utah (1894) *Washington (1899) *Wyoming (1889)
1900				
1901				
1902				
1903	*Delaware	*Kansas		*Nevada
1904				
1905				*Montana
1906				
1907				*Oregon
1908			*Oklahoma	
1909		*Wisconsin	*Oklahoma	
1910			*Kentucky	
1911	*New Jersey			New Mexico
1912				Arizona
1913		*Missouri		
1914–31		Illinois (1931)		

*Applies to public works
+General legal day's work

Table 2. Passage of Men's Work Hour Laws, for Railroad and Street Railroads

Time Period	Region			
	Northeast	Central	South	West
Pre-1900	Massachusetts (1884) New Jersey (1887) New York (1887) Pennsylvania (1887)	Michigan (1893) Minnesota (1893) Nebraska (1899) Ohio (1890, 1892)	Florida (1893) Georgia (1891) Louisiana (1886) Maryland (1898) S. Carolina (1897)	California 1887 Washington (1895)
1900				
1901				
1902	Rhode Island			
1903		Indiana	Arkansas Texas	Arizona
1905		Kansas		
1906			Maryland	
1907	Connecticut	Iowa N. Dakota S. Dakota Wisconsin	N. Carolina W. Virginia	Montana Nevada Oregon Washington

Note: In 1907 Congress passed a railroad regulation law with scope that virtually put a stop to further state legislative action. In 1914 the Court ruled that congressional action in this field precluded additional state laws, even where state legislation attempted to set higher standards. (Lescohier and Brandeis, *History of Labor in the United States, 1896–1932,* 1935, 3: 549) services.[24] By 1913, for example, as shown in table 1, forty-six states had passed laws regulating hours of work. By 1907, as table 2 documents, thirty-three states had passed laws regulating men's work hours for railroad and street railroad workers. Further legislation of this type was made unnecessary at the state level by congressional legislation in 1907 that required train men to have ten hours of rest after sixteen consecutive hours of work and that train dispatchers must have a nine-hour working day. This law applied to the territories, the District of Columbia, and to

Table 3. Passage of Workingmen's Compensation Laws

Time Period	Region			
	Northeast	Central	South	West
1910	New York			
1911	Massachusetts New Hampshire New Jersey	Illinois Kansas Ohio Wisconsin		California Nevada Washington
1912	Rhode Island New York	Michigan	Maryland	Arizona
1913	Connecticut	Iowa Minnesota Nebraska Kansas Illinois	Texas W. Virginia	Oregon
1914		Ohio	Louisiana Maryland	
1915	Maine Pennsylvania Vermont New York	Indiana Michigan Wisconsin	Oklahoma	Colorado Montana Wyoming Nevada Washington
1916			Kentucky	
1917	Delaware New Jersey	S. Dakota Nebraska Illinois		Idaho New Mexico Utah California Nevada
1918			Virginia	
1919		Missouri N. Dakota	Alabama Tennessee	
1920s		Missouri (1922)	Georgia (1920)	Arizona (1925)

Table 4. Passage of Minimum Wage Laws

Time Period	Region			
	Northeast	Central	South	West
1912	Massachusetts			
1913		Minnesota		California
		Nebraska		Colorado
		Wisconsin		Oregon
				Utah
				Washington
1914				
1915			Arkansas	
1916				
1917				Arizona
1918				
1919		N. Dakota	Texas	
1920–31		S. Dakota (1923)		

virtually all employees engaged in the movement of trains. The scope of this coverage virtually put a stop to further state legislation, and indeed, in 1914 the Supreme Court ruled in *Erie R. Co. v. N.Y.* that congressional action in this field precluded additional state laws, even where state legislation attempted to set higher standards.[25]

Workmen's compensation legislation also exemplifies the success of social welfare policies in the Progressive Era. By 1920, as table 3 shows, all but five states had enacted workmen's compensation legislation[26] and major bills had been passed at the national level in 1909 and 1916, thus covering "about one-fourth of the civilian employees of the United States."[27] At the state level, fourteen states enacted the more controversial minimum wage legislation between 1912 and 1923, as documented in table 4. States also actively passed women's hours laws and mothers' pensions, as tables 5 and 6 document.[28]

At the national level, the Progressive Era is notable for major pieces of legislation redefining the role of government in the relationship between employer and employee. The Fifty-ninth Congress passed the Pure Food and Drug Act in 1906, which successfully nationalized a myriad of state-level regulations, as well as the Hepburn Act that increased the power of the Interstate Commerce Commission (ICC). The Fifty-ninth Congress passed the Federal Employee's Compensation Act

Table 5. Passage of Women's Hours Laws

Time Period	Region			
	Northeast	Central	South	West
1900	Massachusetts			
1901	Massachusetts			Washington
1902	Rhode Island Pennsylvania			
1903			N. Carolina+	Colorado
1904				
1905	Pennsylvania			
1906				
1907	Connecticut Massachusetts* New Hampshire	Michigan	Tennessee S. Carolina+	
1908	Massachusetts		Louisiana	
1909	Maine	Illinois Michigan Minnesota Missouri		
1910				
1911	Massachusetts	Illinois Ohio Wisconsin++	Georgia N. Carolina S. Carolina**	
1912	New Jersey Vermont New York		Kentucky Maryland**	
1913	Connecticut Massachusetts++ New Hampshire** New York** Rhode Island Pennsylvania Delaware**	S. Dakota Nebraska Michigan++ Ohio++ Minnesota	Texas Virginia Tennessee Louisiana	California Idaho California++ Oregon Washington
1914			Mississippi	Arizona
1915	Maine	Kansas***	Oklahoma Tennessee Arkansas	Colorado++ Nevada Oregon**
1916	Delaware			Utah++
1917	New Hampshire++ New York**			
1918				
1919	Massachusetts	N. Dakota++		Nevada Washington++
1920				Oregon++

*Prohibited night work of women
+Women's hours restriction covered by general hours law
++Effective administrative unit established to implement women's hours legislation
**Prohibited night work and restricted women's hours of work
***Kansas law effective 1917

Table 6. Passage of Mothers' Pension Laws

Time Period	Region			
	Northeast	Central	South	West
1911–13	Massachusetts	Illinois		California
	New Hampshire	Iowa		Colorado
	New Jersey	Michigan		Idaho
	Pennsylvania	Minnesota		Nevada
		Missouri*		Oregon
		Nebraska		Utah
		Ohio		Washington
		S. Dakota		
		Wisconsin		
1914–19	Connecticut	Indiana	Arkansas	Alaska
	Maine	Kansas	Delaware	Arizona
	New York	N. Dakota	Florida	Hawaii
	Vermont		Maryland	Montana
			Oklahoma	Wyoming
			Tennessee	
			Texas	
			Virginia	
			W. Virginia	
1920–31	Rhode Island		Alabama	New Mexico
			District of Columbia	
			Kentucky	
			Louisiana	
			Mississippi	
			N. Carolina	

Source: Mark Leff, "Consensus for Reform: The Mothers' Pension Movement in the Progressive Era," *Social Service Review* 47 (1973): 401.
*Law not made statewide until 1917.

in 1908, which was the first workmen's compensation law established at the national level. The Sixty-first Congress passed the Railroad Brotherhoods Act in 1910, which established a ten-hour workday. The Sixty-second Congress passed a Child Labor Act in 1912. President Wilson's first Congress, the Sixty-third, passed the Federal Reserve Act, additional child-labor legislation, the La Follette-Peters Eight-Hour Act, the Federal Trade Commission Act, the Clayton Anti-Trust Act, and the Seaman's Act (which freed sailors from bondage to their contracts). In 1916 the Sixty-fourth Congress passed the Smith-Hughes Act, which established federal aid to state vocational education, the Adamson Eight Hour Day, the Keating-Owen Child Labor Act, the Rural Credits Act, and a new Federal Workmen's Compensation Act.

The Participatory Axis

When we turn to the participatory axis defining democratic develop-ment in the Progressive Era, however, we do not see an increase in the political participation of marginalized groups that matches the innova-tive expansion of policies characterizing the institutional axis. Instead, we see legislatures and courts pursuing policies that not only fail to enlarge the rights of groups excluded on the basis of their race, class, and gender status, but that in some instances actually intensify restrictions and obstacles preventing the full exercise of their civil rights and civil liberties. Accompanying legislative policies that returned power to the people by means of new, direct democracy mechanisms of government, for example, we also find legislation constricting political participation by means of voting qualifications and new electoral procedures that had the ad hoc effect of disqualifying large groups of immigrants in the North, blacks in the South, and Asians in the West. In addition, while legislators at the state and national levels devised new, innovative legisla-tion protecting the needs of workers vulnerable to a market system unre-sponsive to their interests, Progressive Era legislation also is notable for policies — such as eugenics and Prohibition — that repressively restricted basic life choices of immigrant groups.

The record of civil rights legislation compiled during the Progressive Era, therefore, is dramatically negative, in contrast to relatively positive state action on regulatory policies. Bills passed at the state and national levels evince an anti–civil rights cast in three ways. First, many laws were negative in content and therefore directly curtailed the civil liberties or civil rights of targeted groups. Second, there is evidence of the "unre-sponsive bystander" phenomenon, in which legislative bodies, through inaction, failed to correct widely recognized gross violations of the civil rights and liberties of some groups.[29] Third, legislation positive in civil rights content was undermined when its passage and/or implementa-tion was combined with anti-civil-rights rationales subverting its em-powerment of disadvantaged groups.

Hallmark legislation in the Progressive Era, therefore, is complex in the way it expands the scope and authority of government to solve social and economic problems even while holding back the ability of marginal groups to gain entry into the political system as fully participating voters and citizens. The scope of this mixture, in the early twentieth century, of progressive social and economic policies and repressive civil rights and civil liberty policies can be appreciated by examining the place of such marginalized groups in the Progressive Era as African Americans, immigrants, Native Americans, and women.[30]

Race

African American men had attained the formal right to vote as a result of the Fourteenth and Fifteenth Amendments passed in the aftermath of the Civil War. The late nineteenth-century populist movement had demonstrated the potential political power of African American men by stimulating their voting participation. In response, racist opponents suppressed the formal political participation of African American men beginning in the 1890s and culminating in the Progressive Era. By 1908 every southern state had passed legislation establishing voting requirements such as poll taxes and literacy and registration standards that made it impossible, or virtually impossible, for African American men and, in some cases poor whites, to qualify to vote.[31] The Fifteenth Amendment, of course, explicitly stated that "the rights of citizens of the United States to vote shall not be denied or abridged by the United States or by any State on account of race, color, or previous condition of servitude." Yet, though the federal government was fully aware of how state-level de facto disenfranchising laws successfully eliminated the formal political participation of most African American men, thereby violating the intent of the Fifteenth Amendment, no efforts were made in the Progressive Era by the national Congress, the president, or the courts to correct the South's success in subverting the Fifteenth Amendment.

President Wilson, for example, reintroduced race segregation in the Civil Service, thereby reversing decades of progress, and he failed to counteract initiatives by southern senators to promote passage of such racist legislation as laws against miscegenation in the District of Columbia. In general, the Progressive Era was a time, especially in the South, when racial segregation became "compelled by law," as legislation was passed to segregate recreational facilities, parks, ball fields, motion pictures, water fountains, toilets, theater entrances, and restaurants. In fact, "no detail was too minute to place on the statute books, even down to a provision for separate Bibles on which black and white witnesses could take their oaths in court."[32]

Even the Progressive Party, despite its commitment to principles of direct democracy, could not agree on whether that commitment should include support for the political participation of African Americans. As Sidney Milkis notes, the Progressive Party was hopelessly split over the issue of African American civil rights, which led to "bitter struggles at the Progressive party convention over delegate selection rules and the platform." Those pressing for inclusion of African Americans and for confronting Jim Crow policies lost the battles of the day, and, as a result, the Progressive Party in the end "accepted the right of the states and localities to resolve the matter of race relations,"[33] thereby leaving the fate of the civil rights of African Americans in the hands of those who had seriously undermined those rights in the first place.

Other groups identified in terms of racial and national origins also faced greater, rather than less, discrimination in the Progressive Era. Chinese and Japanese people were barred from citizenship, and the status of Asian residents remained a constant source of contestation. One of the most serious sources of conflict involved the right of Asians in the West to own property. In 1913 California passed the Webb-Heney Alien Land Law, which "prohibited aliens who were not (or could not be) citizens from owning land."[34] Despite significant protest from a wide range of groups and interests, progressive governor Hiram Johnson signed the bill into law.

In addition, the rights of Native Americans were all but obliterated in the Progressive Era. In the words of Morton Keller, the assault on tribal autonomy launched during the Progressive Era was devastating. Although Indians of the Five Civilized Tribes were granted American citizenship in 1901, and all Native Americans received American citizenship in 1924, this was coupled with the expectation that the "tribes would lose their identity, their laws would be abolished, [and] their lands divided."[35] The Supreme Court facilitated this process by ruling that the federal government had supremacy over both tribes and states. In 1903, in *Lone Wolf v. Hitchcock*,[36] the Court paved the way for Congress to allocate Indian reservation lands, thereby fatally undermining the autonomy of tribal sovereignty and authority.[37]

Yet, the intensification of racially oppressive policies in the Progressive Era is but part of a larger pattern of political exclusion, focused not only on African Americans, Asians, and Native Americans, but also on immigrants and women.

Immigrants

Immigrants in the Progressive Era also experienced the contraction, rather than expansion, of their access to the political system. Reducing formal political access for immigrants was accomplished in a variety of legislative ways, including legislation restricting initial entry into the United States and formal restrictions on personal lifestyle choices as well as de facto restrictions disenfranchising immigrants in large northern urban centers.

It is difficult to go back in time to recall the depth of hostility, suspicion, and control exerted over what are today's relatively assimilated groups, such as Jews, Italians, Greeks, Irish, Russians, Poles, and other European, but non-English-speaking, non-Protestant, non-Anglo-Saxon people. Yet, these groups were viewed literally and figuratively as alien to the American nation, if not as subhuman races portending the virtual destruction of the United States. What is more, this view of the inferiority of new immigrant groups was often shared by leading intellectuals of the day, such as sociologist Edward A. Ross, who supported immigration restriction in part because of his belief in hereditary causes of social pathology.[38]

Rather than expanding participation, the Progressive Era is marked by heightened legislative constrictions on the political status of immigrants. As Morton Keller notes, "immigration and Progressivism flourished together, and together they fed restrictionist sentiment." Though restrictive immigration legislation began in the late nineteenth century, it peaks in the Progressive Era with the 1917 Immigration Act requiring literacy as a qualification for entry. Despite arguments that a literacy test could not measure "good character" but would instead simply produce an immigration policy cutting off entry into America for those from the more disadvantaged populations of the world, Congress not only passed the immigration bill requiring a literacy test for entry into the United States, but successfully overrode President Wilson's veto of it. After World War I, restrictive immigration policies continued in the form of new nationality quotas, thereby ending, as Morton Keller argues, "a policy of receptivity to immigrants as old as the Republic."[39]

Denying immigrants entry is, of course, the fundamental way to restrict their political participation. Those immigrants who did reach

American shores, however, found aspects of their lifestyles severely constricted by legislation whose content, by today's standards, can only be termed "anti–civil liberties." Prime examples are miscegenation and eugenics laws, passed at the state level, infringing on marriage and/or reproductive choice. It was after 1900 that antimiscegenation laws flourished, such that by 1905 as many as twenty-six states prohibited marriage between whites and blacks, another six forbade marriage between whites and "Mongolians," and four states specifically banned marital unions between whites and Native Americans. In addition, by 1912, thirty-four states outlawed marriage between lunatics, in which the lunatic category sometimes included epileptics; and in so-called progressive states, such as Oregon, Wisconsin, and Pennsylvania, eugenic legislation to "prevent by law injury to the race" succeeded in 1912 and in 1913.[40]

Common eugenic remedies for social and political problems in the Progressive Era included forced sterilization. In 1907 in Indiana, for example, a law passed stating that, "since 'heredity plays a most important part in the transmission of crime, idiocy, and imbecility,' a board of two surgeons and the chief physician of a mental institution could authorize the involuntary sterilization of inmates." Between 1909 and 1912 as many as fourteen states followed suit. Morton Keller notes that, despite protests from some physicians, legal experts, and politicians, sterilization policies were accepted as practices, even in states known for their progressivism. In California, Keller found that three hundred sterilizations were conducted by 1915, while between 1909 and 1927 as many as one of every twelve mental patients was sterilized. By 1929 California had performed 5,800 such sterilizations, which was four times more than were performed in the rest of the world combined.[41]

While eugenics laws are commonly agreed to negate civil liberties, Prohibition laws have generally escaped criticism as a violation of civil liberty. Yet, Prohibition presents another example of restrictions on lifestyle choices in the Progressive Era, where the penchant grew for Prohibition legislation in the form of absolute bans on the production, sale, and manufacture of intoxicating beverages. The abuse of alcohol, to be sure, was a serious social ill then, as it is today, but the Prohibition Amendment was an absolutist formulation abrogating the civil liberties of millions of immigrant Americans, particularly the new immigrants from southern Europe, eastern Europe, and Russia. Among these new settlers, drinking was often part of their everyday lives, including their religious observances. Alcohol consumption, rather than representing a fall from some previous standards of abstinence, was integral to the cultural heritage they wished to preserve in the United States. In parts of eastern Europe, the founding of a township implied the founding of a brewery as well, and was regarded as necessary for a civilized life. For immigrants from southern Europe, such as Italy, their own regional identity of birth was associated with their native wine products.[42]

The absolute ban on all manufacture, sale, or transportation of alcoholic beverages, as provided by the Eighteenth Amendment passed in 1918 by Congress, stands in marked contrast to the careful regulatory experimentation that characterizes other areas of legislative concern in the early twentieth century. It is the absolutist character of the solution to the abuse of alcohol that is the clue that much more is operating here than is the case with other legislative responses to social and economic problems in the Progressive Era.

Thus, Prohibition was much more than a simple matter of "social control" or "status consistency," as some scholars have portrayed it.[43] It was, instead, part of a legislative pattern evident in the Progressive Era that contracted the participatory and lifestyle inclusion of marginalized groups in the American state. As Morton Keller contends, it was not at all clear at the turn of the century that Prohibition would be a policy to flourish so spectacularly at the national level. Only fifteen states had even experimented with Prohibition laws in the nineteenth century, and by 1900 all but three had completely abandoned the efforts. Yet, Prohibition policies in the Progressive Era succeeded, at least in part, because they linked a broad coalition of southern and northern interests, often united as much by their racism as by their Protestant and fundamentalist values. As prominent Texas progressive Thomas B. Love declared, "The Negro ought not to be permitted to vote on the question of whether or not liquor shall be sold in Texas any more than the Indian should be permitted to vote on the question of whether or not liquor shall be sold in the Indian country."[44]

The access of immigrants to the public sphere of political participation also was blocked by means of "good government" legislation, passed in the North, which had the effect of disenfranchising urban immigrants. Electoral reforms that reduced the patronage support for city machines by promulgating complicated registration procedures and ballots resulted in less, not more, immigrant voting. In fact, a total of

130 state laws were passed between 1903 and 1908 that regulated party, machine, and business interests, all of which increasingly restricted the participation of urban immigrants.[45]

Women

Not only did the marginalization of African Americans and immigrants increase in the Progressive Era, but so too, in a certain sense, did women's access to political participation decline as a result of Progressive Era policies. To be sure, the end of the Progressive Era marks a major accomplishment in the history of women's rights: a national guarantee of women's right to vote by virtue of passage of the Nineteenth Amendment in 1919 and its ratification by 1920. Yet, this milestone adds little to the Progressive Era record supporting the political participation of marginal groups, for four reasons. First, the Nineteenth Amendment was not a policy originally introduced at the behest of Progressive Era reformers, but rather was formally initiated as a goal in the mid–nineteenth century by the first group of feminist advocates when they convened the Seneca Falls Convention in 1848. Second, although woman suffrage eventually passed at the end of the Progressive Era, its rocky and fragile acceptance in this historical period attests to the generally hostile view for expanding women's voting rights characteristic of both grassroots citizens and political elites. Third, passage of woman suffrage was unaccompanied by congressional concern for — much less complementary passage of constitutional amendments to guarantee — a broader agenda of women's rights, in stark contrast to congressional attentiveness to such issues when passing the Fifteenth Amendment establishing the constitutional right of African Americans to vote. Fourth, Progressive Era reformers added the Nineteenth Amendment to the Constitution by using rationales valorizing women's traditional roles as wives and mothers, and hence women's "difference" from men, rather than women's "equality" with men; in the long run, this would prove to be a serious obstacle blocking expansion of women's access to participation in society, whatever might have been its utility for garnering the right to vote itself. Let us consider each in turn.

The woman suffrage amendment was introduced into Congress in 1868. However, both Houses of Congress had not voted on it until as late as 1915. Thus, not only did the woman suffrage amendment originate in Reconstruction rather than the Progressive Era, but it was well into the Progressive Era before there was even sufficient support among policy elites in Congress to vote on it in Congress. What is more, it is clear that general grassroots support for woman suffrage in the Progressive Era was all but nonexistent. With the exception of the West, prior to 1915, woman suffrage referenda characteristically failed at the state level. Ohio and Michigan voters, for example, defeated woman suffrage at the state level in 1912, as did New York, Pennsylvania, New Jersey, and Massachusetts voters in 1915.[46] Grassroots opposition to woman suffrage in the 1915–19 period meant that any gains made at the state level for women's right to vote were accomplished for the most part only on the basis of state legislators granting women "Presidential only" suffrage, as specified by Article 2, Section 2, of the federal Constitution.[47] Grassroots state-level constituents, however, steadfastly refused to endorse full woman suffrage, as table 7 indicates. State and national campaigns did not garner support from Woodrow Wilson until as late as 1916, when his own presidential ambitions could be affected by the growing number of votes cast by women, especially in western states that could be decisive in determining the electoral votes for Wilson's presidential candidacy. Thus, in all, it took seventy-two years to gain for women a national guarantee of the right to vote, starting with the 1848 Seneca Falls convention and ending with ratification of the Nineteenth Amendment in 1920.

Similarly, though the woman suffrage amendment in 1919 eventually mustered the two-thirds majorities required in both the House and Senate, it was barely ratified, even at the late date of 1920. Ratification literally hung on a thread in the form of one vote in the Tennessee state legislature. It took impassioned telephone pleas from prominent national leaders, including Woodrow Wilson himself, to convince the lone holdout to cast an affirmative vote for the suffrage amendment, without which the ratification process would have failed. Even after ratification, suffrage leaders feared the Supreme Court would rule it to be unconstitutional if given the opportunity. Thus, Carrie Chapman Catt, president of the National American Woman Suffrage Association, hired, at considerable expense, Charles Evans Hughes, a former presidential candidate and Supreme Court justice, as insurance against just such possibilities. The tireless political effort required to add woman suffrage to the Constitution, therefore, accomplished at the end of the Progressive Era, and then only in the context of continuing contestation, hardly supplies

Table 7*. Pattern of State Approval of Full Woman Suffrage and Presidential Suffrage, 1900–1920

	Constitutional Referenda: Full Suffrage	Statutory Action: Presidential Suffrage
Pre-1900	Wyoming, Idaho, Colorado, Utah	
1910	Washington	
1911	California	
1912	Oregon, Kansas, Arizona	
1913		Illinois
1914	Nevada, Montana	
1915		
1916		
1917	New York	Michigan,[a] Ohio,[b] N. Dakota, Rhode Island, Nebraska, Indiana[c]
1918	Michigan, S. Dakota, Oklahoma	
1919		Maine, Indiana, Tennessee, Iowa, Missouri, Ohio, Minnesota, Wisconsin
1920		Kentucky

*Table 7 adapted from Table 1, "Woman Suffrage in the Progressive Era," by Eileen L. McDonagh and H. Douglas Price, *American Political Science Review* 79 (1985): 417.
[a]Michigan referendum of 1918 superseded legislation of 1917.
[b]Ohio legislation of 1917 was repealed by popular initiative, but was reenacted in 1919.
[c]The Indiana law of 1917 was reenacted in 1919, owing to court challenge.

evidence of popular enthusiasm for expanding the electorate to include women. Rather, the woman suffrage campaign illustrates persistent restraint in the Progressive Era, if not hostility, toward formal expansion of the participatory base of the polity to include women as voters.

Adding women's right to vote to the Constitution without necessary complementary legislation guaranteeing women's equality in society at large also testifies to a lack of support in the Progressive Era for increasing women's access to the public sphere. The Nineteenth Amendment guaranteeing women's right to vote is identical in wording to the Fifteenth Amendment guaranteeing the right of African Americans to vote. The difference, however, is that the Fifteenth Amendment was added to the Constitution with two complementary amendments: the Thirteenth Amendment that made slavery unconstitutional and the Fourteenth Amendment that was intended by Congress to guarantee to African Americans equal legal protection and treatment.[48] Despite the failure of the Fourteenth Amendment initially to secure for African Americans equal protection and treatment under the law, it nevertheless eventually became the constitutional cornerstone of the dismantlement of race segregation in the United States. By contrast, no such constitutional amendment guaranteeing to women a more general constitutional right to equality with men was seriously considered by Congress in the Progressive Era, much less added to the Constitution, despite the fact that soon after passage of the Nineteenth Amendment, some women's rights reformers sought to add such an amendment. In 1923 suffrage leader Alice Paul proposed the Equal Rights Amendment (ERA) on the grounds that the right to vote in isolation from other guarantees of equality was certain to be insufficient to bring women into the polity as fully participant citizens.[49]

In addition, the woman suffrage amendment does not represent an increase in access to the public sphere for women in the early twentieth century because Progressive Era reformers characteristically attached women's right to vote to their traditional roles as wives and mothers, that is, women's "difference" to men, in contrast to nineteenth-century reformers who had stressed women's "equality" with men. When first initiated as a social reform in the nineteenth century, woman suffrage not only was part of a long agenda identifying a wide range of policy changes to secure women's equality with men, but suffrage itself was articulated as a "rights" issue. Women claimed the right to vote based on their equal standing as citizens with men and, thus, on the nontraditional claim that women were the "same" as men, not "different" from men.[50] By the turn of the century, however, the rationale for woman suffrage shifted. Those arguing for suffrage now emphasized women's "difference" from men, particularly women's distinct maternalist identities as wives and mothers and how women's maternal role would benefit society if women were to become voters. The shift from women's abstract "right" to vote to "utilitarian" arguments about how women's maternalist nature would infuse morality into the public sphere was viewed by those campaigning for woman suffrage in the Progressive Era as necessary to secure passage of the Nineteenth Amendment. Many went so far as to view the primary virtue of women's voting rights as a tool for women's continued contributions as maternalist feminists.

As Theda Skocpol observes, when major women's associations "endorsed female suffrage, they did so not simply for reasons of equality in the abstract, but as another tool that women might use to promote the home-protective, environmental, and child-centered reforms for which they had already been agitating for many years."[51] Similarly, the progressive municipal reformer Frederic Howe said in 1905, "To man the city is primarily a centre of industry. He measures it by commercial standards. . . . Woman, on the other hand, sees the city in the light of the home. The vice, the saloon, the schools, the libraries, the water, gas, and transportation questions are to her questions of the family, of the child, questions of comfort, of happiness, of safety." For these reasons, Howe and many other progressives assumed that satisfying the "demands of feminism" would improve social and economic conditions defining the public sphere.[52] Rheta Childe Dorr, for example, explained when asked in 1910 what women would do with the vote, "They will do, or try to do, precisely what they do, or try to do, without votes. . . . Social legislation alone interests women."[53]

The Progressive Era hallmark of founding women's right to vote in large part upon women's maternal identities had the effect of reinforcing the premise that "domestic and humanistic virtues (and obligations) were intrinsically female." As Jane Addams noted, "woman's traditional function [is] to make her dwelling-place both clean and fair," and this serves as an argument for the value of her enfranchisement.[54] Rogers Smith concurs. It was, in the end, "women's special domestic and maternal qualities and needs," he says, that won them "the vote via the Nineteenth Amendment in 1920."[55]

In retrospect, we can understand why women's maternal identities meshed well not only with their Progressive Era activities on behalf of maternalist programs, such as mothers' pensions, child labor, and consumer protection, but also with the argument for why they should have the vote. It was precisely because women were different from men, not equal to men, that their enfranchisement seemed to many to guarantee the introduction into the voting booth of hordes of new recruits that would back legislation establishing the emerging welfare state.[56] As Nancy Cott has shown, however, woman suffrage was supported by a diverse coalition of interests.[57] As part of that diversity, for some, the maternalist argument for enfranchising women became a major rationale and a persuasive argument. It was consistent with women's growing involvement in the public sphere in the Progressive Era as volunteers effectively transferring values associated with the home to the public sphere of politics and policies at the local, state, and national levels.[58]

Yet, even if women's maternalist identities can be credited in the short run as achieving for them the right to vote, in the long run women were to pay dearly for the use of a domestic rationale as a basis for claiming access to the public sphere of political participation. As was soon to be clear, basing the rationale for women's right to vote on traditional models of motherhood, rather than challenging those norms on the grounds of women's "sameness" and "equality" with men, reinforced the ideology of maternalism at the precise political moment when women gained the opportunity to claim new identities as formal participants in the public sphere possessing the right to vote. The effect of attaching the right to vote to women's maternalist identities was to prescribe for women norms derivative of "private conduct within the home, [even] while simultaneously legitimating women's public relationships to politics and the state, the workplace and the marketplace."[59] The significant aspect of this model of legitimation was to preserve women's *informal,* rather than *formal,* political status in the form of privileging women's private maternal roles as benefiting political society rather than women's formal political roles.

While some point to the profound indifference enfranchising women actually held for the political system,[60] the Progressive Era legacy of women's maternalist identities in relation to politics is anything but neutral. Whatever might have been their political utility to vote as a bloc (had it materialized), the enfranchisement of women as mothers, rather than as citizens, undermined their access to political power on the basis of an equal standing with others in society.[61] By emphasizing the political salience of women's maternal identities, they reinforced a social construction of motherhood as a rationale for political citizenship, a legacy that was to have continuing impact throughout ensuing decades, including contemporary debates about the appropriate domestic and political roles for women.[62] As late as 1961, for example, the Supreme Court ruled in *Hoyt v. Florida* that it was constitutional for a state to omit women systematically from jury duty on the grounds that it was of greater benefit to society to have women at home caring for the household and for children. As the Court stated in *Hoyt,* "Despite the enlightened emancipation of women from the restrictions and protections of bygone years, and their entry into many parts of community life formerly considered to be reserved to men, woman is still regarded as the center of home and family life. We cannot say that it is constitutionally impermiss-ible for a state acting in pursuit of the general welfare to conclude that a woman should be relieved from the civic duty of jury service."

The Supreme Court went on to say that even if women were not married and/or did not have children, it nevertheless was constitutional for a state to deny automatic eligibility for jury duty because, as the Court noted, "It is true, of course, that Florida could have limited the exemption [of jury duty], as some other states have done, only to women who have family responsibilities. But we cannot regard it as irrational for a state legislature to consider profitable a broad exemption [of all women]."[63]

The Court noted that three states at that time absolutely forbade women ever to be on jury duty at all, and eighteen states, as well as the District of Columbia, had an absolute exemption based on sex, which meant that women in those states had to file a petition to request eligibility for jury duty. Thus, rather than questioning the exclusion of women from jury duty based on women's identification with familial roles, the Court in *Hoyt* affirmed the breadth of women's exclusion from jury duty as evidence for sustaining the Florida statute in question.[64]

The liability of the Progressive Era formula using women's maternal identities to determine their access to the public sphere can be seen also in the impediments to women's more general right to choose the em-ployment occupation of their choice. As late as 1948, for example, in *Goesaert v. Cleary,* the Court declared a Michigan statute constitutional that prohibited women from serving alcoholic beverages as bartenders unless they were "the wife or daughter of the male owner" of a licensed liquor establishment. As Justice Frankfurter wrote when delivering the opinion of the Court:

> Michigan could, beyond question, forbid all women from working behind a bar. This is so despite the vast changes in the social and legal position of women. The fact that women may now have achieved the virtues that men have long claimed as their prerogatives and now indulge in vices that men have long practiced, does not preclude the States from drawing a sharp line between the sexes, certainly in such matters as the regulation of the liquor traffic . . . [s]ince bartending by women may . . . give rise to moral and social problems.[65]

While at first glance it may appear that family relationships gave women an employment advantage when choosing to be bartenders, it takes little reflection to recognize the disadvantage also entailed by a formula basing employment rights upon one's familial relationships. The Progressive Era emphasis, therefore, on women's "difference" from men rather than their "equality" with men, where the former is specifically defined in terms of women's maternal roles, while successful in securing women's formal right to vote, nevertheless resulted in blocking women's access to a broader set of basic civic duties and societal opportunities.

Policy Paradox

The goals of complex modern democracies, as Seyla Benhabib notes, are threefold: to secure political legitimacy, economic welfare, and "a viable sense of collective identity." Far from reinforcing each other, she adds, these "goods stand in a complex relation to one another: excessive realization of one such good may be in conflict with and may jeopardize the realization of others." Efforts needed to achieve policies improving economic welfare, she argues, may be possible to attain only at the cost of sacrificing other goals, such as political legitimacy or collective identity. In particular, she sees claims of political legitimacy as likely to conflict with the goal of collective identity, particularly when legitimacy claims take on a nationalist cast.[66]

When we examine the position of marginal groups in the Progressive Era, such as African Americans, Native Americans, immigrants, and women, we see how the difficulties in gaining their greater inclusion as participants in the political system coexists with the establishment of policies that introduce new forms of political legitimacy at the state and national level in order to activate the power of government to solve social and economic problems in new ways. The disjuncture, predicted by Benhabib, is evident in the Progressive Era use of government to achieve new regulatory welfare policies while at the same time establishing regressive civil rights and civil liberties policies that restrict the political participation of groups marginalized on the basis of race, class, and gender.[67]

Theda Skocpol's work, which uncovers the way reformers in the Progressive Era successfully established a maternalist state by securing passage of mothers' pensions legislation across a wide range of states, vividly

Table 8. Comparison of Passage by 1916 of Woman Suffrage with Child Labor Laws, by Region

Labor, Suffrage	Northeast	Central	South	West
Yes, Labor No, Suffrage	Connecticut Delaware Maine Massachusetts New Hampshire New Jersey New York Pennsylvania Rhode Island Vermont	Indiana Iowa Michigan Minnesota Missouri Nebraska N. Dakota Ohio S. Dakota Wisconsin	Alabama Arkansas Florida Georgia Kentucky Louisiana Maryland Mississippi N. Carolina Oklahoma S. Carolina Tennessee Texas Virginia W. Virginia	none
Yes, Labor Yes, Suffrage	none	Illinois Kansas	none	Arizona California Colorado Idaho Montana Nevada Oregon Utah Washington Wyoming
No, Labor No, Suffrage	none	none	none	New Mexico
No, Labor Yes, Suffrage	none	none	none	none

illustrates the policy paradox that characterizes the early twentieth century. While it may seem reasonable to think that social reform efforts directed toward gaining women's right to vote would reinforce efforts to pass mothers' pensions, Skocpol finds just the opposite. She sees no connection between state-level success in passing woman suffrage and success in passing mothers' pensions. Indeed, she finds that "exclusion from the suffrage for most American women (prior to the late 1910s and early 1920s) stimulated collective consciousness and counter-organization outside of the parties and regular electoral politics," leading to greater, rather than less, political mobilization by women.[68] What is more, as she argues, it was the "civic mobilization/agenda setting" by women's organizations activated prior to suffrage, rather than actual or anticipated "suffrage pressure," that accounts for the success in passing state-level mothers' pensions in the Progressive Era.[69]

So, too, with the exception of the West, regions that passed progressive regulatory welfare legislation, such as child labor, women's hours laws, and workmen's compensation, did not pass progressive civil rights legislation, such as woman suffrage. By 1916, for example, child labor laws are well established in all regions of the country, but, as table 8 indicates, only in the West do state legislators pass both child-labor statutes and woman suffrage laws. Similarly, by 1916 all but three states have passed women's hours laws, but as table 9 indicates, only ten states have passed both woman suffrage and women's hours laws. As table 10 demonstrates, workmen's compensation and minimum wage laws evidence the same pattern, where only a minority of states passing progressive regulatory statutes also pass woman suffrage.

With respect to American political development, the policy paradox so evident in the Progressive Era raises the question of the impact such a paradox has for subsequent periods of reform.

The Progressive Era Legacy

As we have seen, Progressives at the onset of the twentieth century succeeded in making government bigger in both the scope and centralization of public authority. State legislatures and the Congress enlarged the scope of state authority to cover new regulatory jurisdictions, such as the relationship between employers and employees and between business and consumers. State authority also expanded at the state and national levels through new mechanisms of fiscal management and the professionalization of government. In addition, state legislatures passed mothers' pension legislation to provide for the needs of women and children whose husbands were absent or incapacitated, thereby establishing a uniquely American maternalist welfare state.

These innovative reforms justify our crediting the Progressive Era as one in which the power of the state was successfully expanded, and in which a new regulatory power of government was not only established

Table 9. Comparison of Passage by 1916 of Woman Suffrage with Women's Hours Laws, by Region

Labor, Suffrage	Northeast	Central	South	West
Yes, Labor No, Suffrage	Connecticut Delaware Maine Massachusetts New Hampshire New Jersey New York Pennsylvania Rhode Island Vermont	Indiana Michigan Minnesota Missouri Nebraska N. Dakota Ohio S. Dakota Wisconsin	Arkansas Georgia Kentucky Louisiana Maryland Mississippi N. Carolina Oklahoma S. Carolina Tennessee Texas Virginia	none
Yes, Labor Yes, Suffrage	none	Illinois Kansas	none	Arizona California Colorado Idaho Nevada Oregon Utah Washington
No, Labor No, Suffrage	none	Iowa	Alabama Florida W. Virginia	New Mexico
No, Labor Yes, Suffrage	none	none	none	Montana Wyoming

at the state level, but was centralized as well. These innovations were to become the foundation for the subsequent social-spending welfare state of the New Deal. State-level mothers' pensions were nationalized in the form of Aid for Dependent Children policies, and the new regulatory power of the federal government was expanded to encompass social-spending policies, such as social security programs.

Yet, the very success in expanding state power and in reconfiguring the structure of democratic governance was combined in the Progressive Era with a set of policies that had the effect of further marginalizing individuals by their race, immigrant, and gender identities. Public policies that used government in new ways to solve social and economic problems and to return political power to the people were passed by state legislatures and the Congress in conjunction with policies that restricted the political participation and civil liberties of large segments of the populace. Rogers Smith attributes regressive civil rights policies to enduring ascriptive norms ever present in American political history, which he terms "centrist progressivism" in contrast to "left progressivism" that was an ideology more oriented toward civic ideals of rights and equality.[70] From a state-building perspective of American political development, the salient issue in the Progressive Era is the affirmation of

Table 10. Comparison of Passage by 1916 of Woman Suffrage with Workmen's Compensation and Minimum Wage Legislation

Labor, Suffrage	Northeast	Central	South	West
Yes, Labor	Connecticut	Indiana	Arkansas	none
	Maine	Iowa	Kentucky	
	Massachusetts	Michigan	Louisiana	
No, Suffrage	New Hampshire	Minnesota	Maryland	
	New Jersey	Nebraska	Oklahoma	
	New York	Ohio	Texas	
	Pennsylvania	Wisconsin	W. Virginia	
	Rhode Island			
	Vermont			
Yes, Labor	none	Illinois	none	Arizona
		Kansas		California
				Colorado
Yes, Suffrage				Montana
				Nevada
				Oregon
				Utah
				Washington
				Wyoming
No, Labor	Delaware	Missouri	Alabama	Idaho
	Pennsylvania	N. Dakota	Florida	New Mexico
		S. Dakota	Georgia	
No, Suffrage			Mississippi	
			N. Carolina	
			S. Carolina	
			Tennessee	
			Virginia	

ascriptive, regressive norms in the context of civil rights and civil liberties combined with democratic, progressive norms in regulatory policy domains. This policy paradox suggests that the dynamics of American political development can in some cases create an ongoing legacy of reform (subsequent reform periods building upon precedents set in an earlier one), while in other cases, later reform periods make corrections in the policies of earlier ones so as to reduce or eliminate inequalities embedded in preceding reform decades.

Impact for Subsequent Periods of Reform

Identification of this policy paradox raises questions about classic interpretations of the Progressive Era. The legacy of clashes between the historical greats, such as Gabriel Kolko and Richard Hofstadter, too often paints interpretive canvases in either pessimistic, conflictual tones that underscore the shortcomings of the Progressive Era, as in Kolko's work, or more optimistic ones, that argue for the constructive power of consensus in the age of reform, as in the case of Hofstadter. From a cross-policy perspective, however, it is evident that the Progressive Era was a period that combined positive initiatives in the area of welfare policies with negative ones in the area of civil rights. While many analyze the conflicts *within* the domain of welfare policies, the more dramatic contrast is *between* the domain of welfare and civil rights. The coexistence of a proactive welfare state and a regressive civil rights state defines the American state developing at this time as one based on a dual policy track that is evident at the state, regional, and national levels.[71] Correctly identifying the inverse policy pattern of the early modern American state, therefore, augments the range of ways that the continuities between the contemporary period and the policy legacies of the Progressive Era may be viewed.

Chief among these is that expansion of state power in the Progressive Era, manifested in a new regulatory state, became the foundation for the New Deal expansion of state power to provide for a social-spending welfare state in the 1930s. But as we have seen, the Progressive expansion of state power occurred in the context of policies constricting the political participation and lifestyle freedom of groups marginalized by their race, class, and gender identities. These constrictions, especially after World War II, have been challenged by the civil rights and other movements that have provided a corrective to the repressive civil rights and civil liberties policies of the early twentieth century. Thus, the very groups that were the target of increased discrimination in the Progressive Era — African Americans, immigrants, and women — are those that organized as social movements in the next social-reform period to claim their rights.

The Progressive Era, therefore, not only goes hand-in-hand with the New Deal as the period establishing the successful expansion and centralization of state power as a foundation for the subsequent establishment of a welfare spending state in the 1930s, but the very success in the Progressive Era of repressing the political rights of minority groups goes hand in hand with a complementary reform period, the sixties and seventies, reversing that repression. The sixties and seventies may therefore be seen as a period of expansion on the participatory axis of the state that complements the institution-building success of the Progressive Era.

Sixties and Seventies: A Corrective to the Progressive Era

Many cite the broad ways politics changed in the sixties and seventies, such as weakening the seniority system in Congress, increasing congressional control of the budget processes, and opening congressional committee hearings to the public.[72] These changes, however, focus on informal processes of how politics operates — not on major reformulations of institutional structural arrangements as embedded in law, nor on major new innovative conceptions of what the legitimate scope of government should be.[73] It is not the invention of presidential primaries, for example, that is the hallmark of the sixties and seventies, but rather their use, along with internal party regulations, to promote the participation of previously excluded groups. Focusing on the themes of protest, the impulse to explore and correct inequities, and the reassertion of democratic egalitarianism, far from identifying the sixties and seventies as a reform era harking back to Jacksonian democracy,[74] identifies it instead as the participation-expansion complement to the institution-building Progressive Era that preceded it.

We can see how complementary the sixties and seventies are to the Progressive Era by noting that it is exactly the groups whose participation and life styles were contracted during the earlier period who are successful in claiming greater access to the political system and to the political culture. While it is common to evaluate these civil rights decades in terms of race issues alone, it is the involvement of multiple

groups that best defines how the sixties and seventies decades complement and correct the Progressive Era.

As a reform era, the first efforts were aimed at gaining formal political
rights for African Americans. The focus on African American voting
rights directly addresses the very laws established in the Progressive Era.
It is the necessity to delegislate the disenfranchisement of African Americans on a de facto basis that establishes the participation agenda of the
sixties and seventies. Not only is the landmark 1965 Voting Rights Act
passed in Congress, but so too is the Twenty-fourth Amendment, ratified in 1964, which bars the use of any tax as a voting qualification,
thereby outlawing mechanisms put in place in the Progressive Era to
restrict the participation of African Americans.

The extent of the participation expansion for African Americans in the
recent reform era is also evident at the level of elite political leadership. In
the aftermath of these decades, Jesse Jackson's presidential campaign of
1988 stands as an example of the dramatic reversal of the exclusionary
political status accorded African Americans in the Progressive Era. His
presidential bid connects the more recent reform decades with the preceding state-building period of the Progressive years. In this view, the
chaos some see in the turbulent decades of the sixties and seventies
acquires a more positive valence.

Daniel Bell, for example, describes the sixties and seventies as an
almost dysfunctional response to cultural contradictions within postin-
dustrial America, marked by "a concern with violence and cruelty; a
preoccupation with the sexually perverse; a desire to make noise; an
anticognitive and anti-intellectual mood; an effort once and for all to
erase the boundary between 'art' and 'life'; and a fusion of art and politics."[75] Yet, it was these decades that successfully enlarged the participation base of the polity. It is by juxtaposing them with the earlier era of
reform that these decades may be seen as not merely a period of ferment
and change, but as one that corrects and thereby complements the Progressive Era.

It is common to chart the progress of the African American acquisi-
tion of formal political rights in the sixties and seventies, but there was
also a political revolution in the status of those immigrants most de-
spised in the Progressive Era. It is often noted, for example, that John F.
Kennedy's election to the presidency in 1960 is significant for overcoming prejudice about his Catholic background, if not his Irish ancestry.

The full significance of these characteristics, however, can be more fully appreciated in the context of the previous Progressive Era. Far from affirming the value of Prohibition legislation to control the lifestyle of such immigrants, the Kennedy family fortune was an object of public admiration and a source of political power, even though it was amassed at least in part by trade in liquor commodities.

The assimilation of exactly those groups of non-Protestant, even non-English-speaking and non-Anglo-Saxon, immigrants most excluded in the Progressive Era can be seen also at the level of political leadership in the 1980s. Michael Dukakis's success in winning the Democratic nomination for president in 1988, for example, rested for a moment in time upon a romantic view of the very immigrant groups most feared as subversive elements in the Progressive Era. Although George Bush eventually captured the White House in 1988, it was not his Anglo-Saxon, Yankee, family status that was the source of his appeal. Rather, it was exactly these characteristics that initially posed a political handicap for him and that only the Ronald Reagan coattails could assuage.

Participatory democracy was a rallying cry of the sixties and seventies, crystallizing the diverse goals and aspirations fueling the protest and demand for reform.[76] Women, who had also experienced difficulties in gaining full political participation in the Progressive Era, made some participatory progress in the sixties and seventies, but perhaps less than did African American and immigrant men. One reason, perhaps, was that women had two participatory battles to launch: one within the sixties and seventies social-reform movements themselves and the other in the social and political culture of the American nation at large.

Women's first participatory foray in recent decades was to gain equality within the very participatory organizations formed to garner greater civil rights for marginalized groups. The woman's movement in the sixties was launched in protest over the sex-stereotyping and relations of dominance experienced with regard to men in the southern civil rights organizations, such as the Student Nonviolent Coordinating Committee (SNCC), as well as northern, new-left organizations, such as Students for a Democratic Society (SDS). Women protested their systematic treatment as inferiors who were given menial secretarial tasks within civil rights organizations rather than leadership roles — sometimes they were even given custodial tasks, such as vacuuming the environs, in contrast to men who remained free of such chores.[77] Women's recognition of and confrontation with this patriarchal treatment within the very participatory democratic organizations designed to thwart such norms eventually led to a feminist awakening to the reality of the patriarchal principles that characterized American political culture as a whole.

The most important aspect of the political legacy of the woman's movement of the sixties and seventies, however, is the way reformers reinterpreted Progressive Era valorization of women's traditional roles to be the very obstacles blocking women's access to participation in both politics and society as a precursor to dismantlement of these roles. It was, indeed, the very hallmark of the Progressive Era formula for enfranchising women — the assumption that women's traditional roles as wives and mothers could be politically empowering — that became the first target of the feminist revolution in the sixties and seventies. Betty Friedan's rallying cry in 1963 caught the attention of millions when she proclaimed in her best selling book, *The Feminine Mystique,* that the realm of the home was a location of illness, not health, and was the reason for women's isolation from politics and society. As she put it, "I heard echoes of the problem . . . at PTA meetings and luncheons of the League of Women Voters. . . . Just what was this problem that has no name? What were the words women used when they tried to express it? Sometimes a woman would say, 'I feel empty somehow . . . incomplete. . . . I feel as if I don't exist.' . . . A Cleveland doctor called it 'the housewife's syndrome.'"[78]

Friedan called the "stagnating state of millions of American housewives a sickness" in which the strength of women was not the cause, but the cure. In her terms, not only could most women no longer use the roles of housewife to grow to their full human capacity, but there was something about the housewife state itself that was positively dangerous, even when combined with voluntary associations such as the PTA and League of Women Voters. She declared that "women who 'adjust' as housewives, who grow up wanting to be just a housewife, are in as much danger as the millions who walked to their own death in the [Nazi] concentration camps — and the millions more who refused to believe that the concentration camps existed." This is because to be just a housewife required surrendering one's human identity, individuality, and sense of self-determination.[79]

The sixties and seventies were a time when women defied traditional role norms associated with stay-at-home wives and mothers by entering the paid workforce (during peacetime rather than war) in larger numbers than ever before. The percentages are dramatic. In 1960 only 39 percent of women who had children between the ages of six and eighteen worked out of the home. By 1975 that number had jumped to 61 percent; and by 1993 three-quarters of women with children between six and eighteen were in the paid labor force. The influx of women into the labor force raised questions about women's equal treatment in terms of wages, employment opportunities, availability of credit, and workplace security from sexual harassment. In each of these dimensions of employment, the decades of the sixties and seventies offered crucial correctives to inequalities between men and women in the workplace, thereby in a piecemeal way correcting the failure of Progressive Era reformers to pass a constitutional amendment protecting women from sex discrimination as a complement to women's enfranchisement.

In 1963, for example, Congress passed the Equal Pay Act, which required employers to pay the same wage to employees of both sexes for equal work in the same establishment. In 1972 the provisions of the Equal Pay Act were extended to include state and local government employees as well as workers employed in management and professional occupations. In addition to the federal statute, all states today, except Alabama and Mississippi, have explicit state-level guarantees for equal pay for equal work.[80] In addition to securing equal pay for equal work, women also faced employment discrimination before the sixties, being barred from occupations solely on account of their sex, thereby reversing the policy upheld in 1948 in *Goesaert v. Cleary,* as noted above.[81] In 1964 sex was added to Title 7 of the Civil Rights Act barring discrimination in employment. Title VII provides that it shall be an "unlawful employment practice for an employer to fail or refuse to hire or to discharge any individual with respect to his compensation, terms, conditions, or privileges of employment, because of such individual's race, color, religion, sex, or national origin," and that it is also unlawful for an employer "to limit, segregate, or classify his employees or applicants for employment in any way which would deprive or tend to deprive any individual of employment opportunities or otherwise adversely affect his status as an employee, because of such individual's race, color, religion, sex, or national origin."[82]

In addition to equal pay and equal treatment when in an employment environment, Congress also addressed the issue of equal credit. By 1973 women not only had entered the labor force in great numbers, but were also the sole heads of household of six million families. Yet it was common for women to experience serious problems when attempting to open a line of credit in their own right. For a woman to obtain a credit card or bank loan routinely required the signature of her husband, if married, or of her father, if single. In 1972, for example, there is a documented case of a forty-three-year-old single woman who, though employed, was required to obtain the signature of her father as a co-signer for a bank loan.[83] Sarah Weddington, the pro-choice lawyer who argued *Roe v. Wade* before the Supreme Court, experienced similar difficulties in attempting to obtain a credit card in her own name. Although she was employed as a lawyer at the time, in contrast to her husband who was a student in law school, she was nevertheless asked to obtain the signature of her husband before she could be issued a line of credit.[84] In 1974 Congress passed the Equal Credit Act, which made it a federal crime to deny a person a credit line solely on the basis of gender.

When women entered the work force in the sixties and seventies, they also faced tremendous obstacles stemming from the Progressive Era valorization of women's traditional gender roles as wives and mothers. Many employers had discriminatory policies related to women's marital and maternal status. Employers often would not hire women if they were married, nor retain them if they were pregnant. A 1930–31 National Education Association (NEA) study found that 77 percent of the districts surveyed would not hire women if they were married, and 63 percent routinely fired women if they married. Similarly, in 1964 40 percent of all employers did not provide even unpaid maternity leave to women workers; rather, they simply fired women who became pregnant.[85] Of the 60 percent of employers who did provide maternity leave, over half required women to leave the work place on an unpaid leave by the second trimester of pregnancy. Of these employers, only six percent permitted women who were required to leave their jobs because of pregnancy to use sick leave for pregnancy-related illness or disability.

Feminist activists successfully dismantled the Progressive Era fusion of women's identities with maternalism by establishing new policies that secured for women their rights as both mothers and workers. In addition to Title 7 of the 1964 Civil Rights Act, Congress passed the Pregnancy Discrimination Act in 1978 that protected the job security of women workers who were also mothers. Due to the impact of Title 7, by 1973 the percentage of women workers guaranteed maternity leave and re-employment rights was 73 percent, and 26 percent could use sick leave for pregnancy-related disability or illness.[86] The passage by Congress of the Pregnancy Discrimination Act added language to Title 7 prohibiting discrimination against pregnant women in every aspect of employment, including hiring, firing, promotion, and fringe benefits. It also required employers who provide disability and health benefits to include pregnancy in that coverage. In the view of political scientist Dorothy Stetson, the Pregnancy Discrimination Act is particularly significant because its definition of pregnancy as a temporary disability "signaled the official acceptance of women as members of the work force."[87]

The Progressive Era assumption that women's gender identities and "difference" from men would always be a source of women's empowerment was also challenged in the seventies in the context of new policies barring sexual harassment, and in the inclusion of sexual harassment in Title 7, barring discrimination on the basis of sex. Prior to 1975 the problem of unwanted sexual advances in the context of one's employment environment had yet to be termed "sexual harassment." Without a name, it was all but impossible to define the problem as a policy issue. In the mid-seventies, judges refused to view sexual harassment as a violation of law, ruling instead that sexual encounters in the workplace were simply private matters, outside the purview of government, that were the inevitable result of women's "difference" from men. In 1980, however, the Equal Employment Opportunity Commission (EEOC) established regulations that defined sexual harassment as a form of sex discrimination prohibited by Title 7. In 1986, in *Meritor Savings Banks, FSB v. Vinson,* the Supreme Court ruled that Title 7 did cover sexual harassment, and hence, it was a federal crime for an employer to engage in either quid pro quo or hostile-environment types of sexual harassment.[88]

The sixties and seventies also mark another way the failure of Progressive Era reformers to pass constitutional amendments complementary to the Nineteenth Amendment was to some degree corrected. Although the Equal Rights Amendment was not ratified, the Supreme Court, in 1971, ruled for the first time that the Fourteenth Amendment applied to women, at least to some degree. In *Reed v. Reed,* the Court evaluated the constitutionality of an Idaho statute that gave automatic preference to the husband, rather than the wife, to be administrator of a deceased child's estate if other qualifications were equal. The Court ruled that such a statute was an arbitrary form of sex discrimination, and hence unconstitutional. The decision established that sex discrimination merited some level of scrutiny on the basis of the Equal Protection Clause of the Fourteenth Amendment, and that some forms of sex discrimination could be found unconstitutional on that basis.[89] The ruling effectively extended some of the protections of the Fourteenth Amendment to women. As such it has proven to be especially important as a substitute for passage of the ERA or other constitutional guarantees complementing the Nineteenth Amendment.

Thus, put in perspective, we can best understand the reform era of the sixties and seventies as the complement to the preceding state-building Progressive era. New mechanisms of direct democracy with the goal of returning power to the people make the institutional inventions of the early twentieth century reform decades, even while who constituted the people was even more narrowly defined than before. In the sixties and seventies, however, social reform activists succeeded in gaining participatory access for the claimants excluded in the preceding reform era. Consequently, those excluded in the Progressive Era—African Americans, immigrants, and women—became the participatory celebrants of the subsequent reform period of the sixties and seventies.

Axes of Democracy: Nonlinear Change

The Progressive Era was notable for expanding the institutional apparatus of government to provide for more democratic governance and to make more active use of government at both the state and national level for solving social and economic problems. Yet, at the same time, repressive policies diminished the political participation axis defining democratic governance. The paradoxical legacy of the Progressive Era, therefore, is that linear progress on one axis, the institutional arrangements and powers of the state, was combined with regression on the participatory axis. Examining the participatory status of those identified in terms of race, class, and gender, therefore, shows how patterns of political development can exemplify nonlinear complexities. Paul Pierson, for example, has shown how processes necessary for the institutionalization of policies, such as those of the welfare state, are asymmetric to processes entailed in the dismantlement of the welfare state.[90] The work of Karen Orren and Stephen Skowronek also demonstrates that it is a mistake to assume there must be linearly coordinated political development across all kinds of institutional arrangements. To the contrary, they argue that progress in one sector need not occur in conjunction with progress in another. Rather than development, they label this phenomenon "intercurrence."[91]

The identification here of the expansion of the *scope* of government with the simultaneous contraction in participatory *access* illustrates how the Orren and Skowronek layered model of political development can reveal an inverse relationship between citizen participation dimensions of society and institutional structures of the state. This finding reinforces conceptions of the relationship between society and the state in terms of porous boundaries.[92] It also shows how boundary negotiation can entail major contradictions between different domains of state-building. Surely, redrawing boundaries between society and the state was a major enterprise in the Progressive Era, necessary for expanding the authority of government to take on regulatory assignments responsive to the needs of those economically disadvantaged by the advent of rapid and brutal industrialization at the turn of the century.[93] Yet, as we have seen, development of progressive regulatory policies that strengthened the power of the state went hand in hand with regressive civil rights and civil liberties policies that dampened the participation of marginalized groups.

Thus identification of the paradoxical pattern operating in the Progressive Era links it as a period of reform not only to the expansion of state power in the New Deal, but also to the reforms of the sixties and seventies that corrected some of the more egregious negative civil rights and civil liberties policies of the Progressive Era. The uneven development along the two axes of democracy, institutional and participational, makes for interconnected moments of change that define and redefine the present in terms of the heritage of the past. This underscores the multidimensional complexity of democratic change in the Progressive Era and illustrates that periods of reform can simultaneously represent both progress and regression in different facets of democratic governance. It raises the question of whether the paradoxical pattern discerned in the Progressive Era is one that can also be found in periods of reform predating the twentieth century. As such, a focus on race, class, and gender in the Progressive Era not only reveals important dynamics underlying the legacy of this era for the subsequent development of civil rights and civil liberties in the twentieth century, but also suggests new ways to frame questions for future study encompassing earlier periods of reform, thereby promising to link the study of the Progressive Era not only to ensuing periods of change, but also to its antecedents.

Notes

The author thanks Richard Harris, Jerome Mileur, Sidney Milkis, and Dan Tichenor for their helpful advice.

1. Robert D. Putnam, *The Beliefs of Politicians: Ideology, Conflict, and Democracy in Britain and Italy* (New Haven: Yale University Press, 1973), 168, 169–70.

2. For an analysis of how state-level referenda votes and congressional roll call votes reveal a policy paradox along these two axes in the Progressive Era, see Eileen L. McDonagh, "The 'Welfare Rights State' and the 'Civil Rights State': Policy Paradox and State Building in the Progressive Era," *Studies in American Political Development* 7, 2 (Fall 1993): 225–74.

3. Jürgen Habermas, "Three Normative Models of Democracy," in *Democracy and Difference: Contesting the Boundaries of the Political,* ed. Seyla Benhabib (Princeton: Princeton University Press, 1996), 21.

4. Ibid.

5. As Seyla Benhabib argues, Habermas contrasts liberal and republican models of democracy with what he terms the "discourse theory of democracy," also known as the "deliberative model of politics," which avoids centering a democratic model on the state. Benhabib, "Introduction to Habermas," *Democracy and Difference,* 6. For a comprehensive analysis of the importance of political participation and what accounts for it, see Sidney Verba, Kay Lehman Schlozman, and Henry E. Brady, *Voice and Equality: Civic Voluntarism in American Politics* (Cambridge: Harvard University Press, 1995).

6. Sidney Milkis, "Introduction—The Critical Year of 1912," chap. 1 of *The 1912 Election and the Birth of Modern American Politics* (forthcoming), 5.

7. Stephen Skowronek, *Building a New American State: The Expansion of National Administrative Capacities, 1877–1920* (New York: Cambridge University Press, 1982).

8. Milkis, "The Critical Year," 1–2.

9. Quoted in E. J. Dionne Jr., *They Only Look Dead: Why Progressives Will Dominate the Next Political Era* (New York: Simon and Schuster, 1996), 36.

10. Ibid., 15, emphasis added.

11. Robert D. Putnam and William B. Parent, "The Dawn of an Old Age? Why America May Be Ready for a New Progressive Era," *Washington Post,* 23 June 1991, B5, emphasis added.

12. Morton Keller, *Regulating a New Society: Public Policy and Social Change in America, 1900–1933* (Cambridge: Harvard University Press, 1994), 1.

13. Arthur Link and Richard L. McCormick, *Progressivism* (Arlington Heights, Ill.: Harlan Davidson, 1983), 36; Ann Orloff, "The Political Origins of America's Belated Welfare State," in *The Politics of Social Policy in the United States,* ed. Margaret Weir, Ann Shola Orloff, and Theda Skocpol (Princeton: Princeton University Press, 1988).

14. Keller, *Regulating a New Economy,* 2.

15. The exaggeration of laissez-faire principles of individualism as a cause of social distress is more coterminous with late nineteenth-century Spencerian notions linking Adam Smith with Darwin than it is with initial principles of liberalism per se, Dorothy Ross, *The Origins of American Social Science* (Cambridge: Cambridge University Press, 1991), 15, 18.

16. John D. Buenker, *Urban Liberalism and Progressive Reform* (New York: W. W. Norton and Company, 1978), chap. 2.

17. Richard C. McCormick, *The Party Period and Public Policy: American Politics from the Age of Jackson to the Progressive Era* (Oxford: Oxford University Press, 1986), 269; Eric Goldman, *Rendezvous with Destiny* (New York: Alfred Knopf, 1953), 75. Debates continue to rage, of course, about whether enough welfare legislation was passed in the Progressive Era and whether it was passed as an attempt to assist, co-opt, or socially control the disadvantaged. See Gabriel Kolko, *The Triumph of Conservatism: A Reinterpretation of American History, 1900–1916* (New York: The Free Press, 1963). Yet, given the tenacity of the American laissez-faire context, there is reason to credit these early achievements as marking a conspicuous departure from previous norms restricting the use of government as an instrument for advancing welfare policies.

18. James Weinstein, *The Corporate Ideal in the Liberal State* (Westport, Conn.: Greenwood Press, 1981), x.

19. Richard Hofstadter, *The Age of Reform: From Bryan to FDR* (New York: Vintage Books, 1955), 15.

20. McCormick, *The Party Period and Public Policy;* Thomas K. McCraw, ed., *Regulation in Perspective: Historical Essays* (Cambridge: Harvard University Press, 1981); Thomas K. McCraw, *Prophets of Regulation: Charles Francis Adams, Louis D. Brandeis, James M. Landis, Alfred E. Kahn* (Cambridge: Harvard University Press, 1984); Keller, *Regulating a New Economy;* Robert H. Wiebe, *The Search for Order, 1877–1920* (New York: Hill and Wang, 1967).

21. State-level mothers' pensions legislation and passage by Congress of the Sheppard-Towner Act are exceptions. Theda Skocpol, *Protecting Soldiers and Mothers: The Political Origins of Social Policy in the United States* (Cambridge, Mass.: Harvard University Press, 1992), 10.

22. Samuel P. Huntington, *American Politics: The Promise of Disharmony* (Cambridge: Harvard University Press, 1981); Wiebe, *The Search for Order.*

23. Skocpol, *Protecting Soldiers and Mothers.*

24. Ann Vanderpol, "Dependent Children, Child Custody, and the Mothers' Pensions: The Transformation of State-Family Relations in the Early Twentieth Century," *Social Problems* 29, 3 (1982): 229–30. Eugene Tobin identifies the

combination of a "concern for positive government intervention and a sensitivity for reform" as the nexus between the Progressive Era and subsequent achievements in the New Deal. *Organize or Perish: America's Independent Progressives, 1913–1933* (Westport, Conn.: Greenwood Press, 1986), 8.

25. *Erie R. Co. v N.Y.*, 233 US 671 (1914); Don D. Lescohier and Elizabeth Brandeis, *History of Labor in the United States, 1896–1932,* vol. 3 (New York: Macmillan Co., 1935), 549.

26. Roger Lubove, *The Struggle for Social Security, 1900–1935* (Pittsburgh, Penn.: University of Pittsburgh Press, 1986), 54.

27. U.S. Dept. of Labor, 1914, Bulletin: 123. James Weinstein notes that labor unionists often opposed workmen's compensation legislation, believing that it would only "pension off the worker during his period of disablement at something less than his regular wages," in contrast to what might be won by employees in court, *The Corporate Ideal*, 43.

28. Scholars caution us also to recognize the complexity and limitations of mothers' pensions legislation. For example, Linda Gordon, "The New Feminist Scholarship on the Welfare State" in *Women, the State, and Welfare,* ed. Linda Gordon (Madison: University of Wisconsin Press, 1990); Linda Gordon, "Black and White Visions of Welfare: Women's Welfare Activism, 1890–1945," *The Journal of American History* 78, 2 (1991): 559–90.

According to Barbara Nelson and Gwendolyn Mink, policies within the welfare domain contained anti–civil rights principles adversarial to the interests of the very groups they were meant to benefit. See Barbara Nelson, "The Origins of the Two-Channel Welfare State: Workmen's Compensation and Mothers' Aid," in Gordon, *Women, the State, and Welfare;* Nelson, "The Gender, Race, and Class Origins of Early Welfare Policy and the Welfare State: A Comparison of Workmen's Compensation and Mothers' Aid," in *Women, Politics, and Change,* ed. Louise A. Tilly and Patricia Gurin (New York: Russell Sage Foundation, 1990). Also see Gwendolyn Mink, *The Wages of Motherhood: Inequality in the Welfare State, 1917–1942* (Ithaca, N.Y.: Cornell University Press, 1995).

As Nelson points out in "Origins of the Two-Channel Welfare State," in some states at the turn of the century, women receiving mothers' pensions benefits were susceptible to civil restrictions on paupers, limiting where they could live and their rights to marry and vote. Such anti–civil rights elements embedded in welfare policies are a preview of what this research identifies as the defining feature of Progressive Era reform: the institutionalization of an anti–civil rights state in conjunction with a pro–welfare state.

29. Social psychology defines "unresponsive bystander" as one or more bystanders, who though obviously curious and attentive, offer no assistance to an individual in obviously desperate trouble. A notorious example occurred in 1964 when thirty-eight "unresponsive bystanders" witnessed the murder of Kitty Genovese without aiding her in any way whatsoever. See Eileen L. McDonagh, "Social Exchange and Moral Development: Two Dimensions of Traumatic Human Interaction," *Human Relations* 35 (1982):666.

The explanation offered by most social psychologists for this phenomenon is that the behavioral "costs" for involvement are too great. Roger W. Brown and Richard J. Hernstein, *Psychology* (Boston: Little, Brown, 1975), 300. Analyses of individuals, groups, and institutions adjudicating civil rights policies suggest ideological orientations as well. Five states, for example, have legislated "good samaritan" statutes, requiring individuals to come to the aid of victims of crimes or accidents if they can do so without endangering themselves, thereby rendering in those instances "unresponsive bystander" behavior to be criminal.

30. For an extensive analysis of the Progressive Era policies targeted toward African Americans, immigrants, and women in conjunction with regulatory policies, including data analysis showing comparative voting patterns on these issues at the state and national level, see Eileen L. McDonagh, "The 'Welfare Rights State' and 'Civil Rights State': Policy Paradox and State Building in the Progressive Era." Discussion of political participation policies here draws upon this earlier published work.

31. J. Morgan Kousser, *The Shaping of Southern Politics: Suffrage Restriction and the Establishment of the One-Party South* (New Haven: Yale University Press, 1974).

32. Arthur Link and Richard L. McCormick, *Progressivism*, 96, 98.

33. Milkis, "The Critical Year of 1912," 17.

34. Keller, *Regulating a New Society*, 245–47.

35. Ibid., 283–86.

36. *Lone Wolf v Hitchcock*, 187 US 553 (1903).

37. Keller, *Regulating a New Society*, 285.

38. Ibid., 3.

39. Ibid., 225, 227.

40. Ibid., 14.

41. Ibid., 34–35.

42. See McDonagh, "The 'Welfare Rights State'" 244–45.

43. Joseph R. Gusfield, *Symbolic Crusade: Status Politics and the American Temperance Movement* (Urbana, Ill.: University of Illinois Press, 1963); Hofstadter, *The Age of Reform*.

44. Keller, *Regulating a New Society*, 125, 131.

45. Frances Fox Piven and Richard A. Cloward, *Why Americans Don't Vote* (New York: Pantheon Books, 1988), 76–77, 90.

46. New York voters later passed woman suffrage at the state level in 1917.

47. Article 2, Section 2 specifies that "Each state shall appoint, *in such manner as the Legislature thereof may direct*, a Number of Electors, equal to the whole Number of Senators and Representatives to which the State may be entitled in Congress" (italics added).

48. Eileen L. McDonagh, "The Nineteenth and Fifteenth Amendments: What's the Difference?" Paper delivered at the Connecticut Women's Education and Legal Fund, "Celebrating Woman Suffrage," Trinity College, Conference on Woman Suffrage, October 1995.

For a discussion of the relationship between gender and American political development, including an analysis of woman suffrage, see Eileen McDonagh,

Carole Pateman, Gretchen Ritter, Wendy Sarvasy, Panel Discussion on "Gender and American Political Development," *Clio: Newsletter of the Politics and History Section, American Political Science Association* (forthcoming). On this panel, political scientist Gretchen Ritter refers to the view that the Nineteenth Amendment was necessary but not sufficient for establishing women's political inclusion, as the "incompleteness thesis."

49. As historian Nancy Cott notes, feminist activists at the time were divided as to the utility of the ERA. Although some members of the National Woman's Party had begun to survey state legal codes for sex discriminations that could be addressed by the ERA, others were concerned that the ERA would undermine gains women had made to obtain protective labor legislation in the Progressive Era on the basis of women's reproductive difference from men rather than women's equality with men. As Cott explains, now feminist leaders "had to grapple with the question whether such legislation was sex 'discrimination,' hampering women workers in the labor market, or a form of necessary 'affirmative action.'" Cott, *The Grounding of Modern Feminism* (New Haven: Yale University Press, 1987), 120.

50. Aileen S. Kraditor, *The Ideas of the Woman Suffrage Movement, 1890–1920* (New York: Columbia University Press, 1965).

51. Skocpol, *Protecting Soldiers and Mothers*, 340.

52. Goldman, *Rendezvous With Destiny*, 76.

53. Quoted in Skocpol, *Protecting Soldiers and Mothers*, 340.

54. Adolph Reed Jr., "DuBois's 'Double Consciousness': Race and Gender in Progressive Era American Thought," *Studies in American Political Development* 6, 1 (1992): 124–25.

55. Rogers M. Smith, "One United People: Second Class Female Citizenship and the American Quest for Community," *Yale Journal of Law and Humanities* 1 (1988): 274.

56. For an analysis of the long-term effect on policy networks of the assumption that woman suffrage would increase women's political influence, see Anna L. Harvey, "Women, Policy, and Party, 1920–1970: A Rational Choice Approach," *Studies in American Political Development* 11, 2 (1997): 292–324.

57. Cott, *Modern Feminism*.

58. Skocpol, *Protecting Soldiers and Mothers;* Paula Baker, "The Domestication of Politics: Women and American Political Society, 1780–1920," *American Historical Review* (1984): 620–47.

59. Koven and Michel, *Mothers of a New World*.

60. Goldman, *Rendezvous With Destiny*, 292; Skocpol, *Protecting Soldiers and Mothers*, 506.

61. The maternal albatross hung round the Nineteenth Amendment exemplifies the dangers Joan Scott sees as inherent for women positioned in a democratic system founded upon both a principle of equality and the reality of inequality between groups. The dilemma posed for women becomes "[h]ow to recognize and refuse terms of discrimination, [and] how to act collectively on behalf of women without confirming the 'reality' of a separate female sphere,"

Joan Wallach Scott, *Gender and the Politics of History* (New York: Columbia University Press, 1988), 196.

This "difference and sameness" argument is a point of ongoing contention in feminist scholarship, not to mention historical interpretation. As Harriet Burton Laidlaw put it in 1912, "insofar as women were like men they ought to have the same rights; insofar as they were different they must represent themselves," as paraphrased in Aileen S. Kraditor, *The Ideas of the Woman Suffrage Movement, 1890–1920*, 1965), 111.

62. See Nelson, "Origins of the Two-Channel Welfare State" and "Women's Poverty and Women's Citizenship: Some Political Consequences of Economic Marginality," in *Women and Poverty*, ed. Barbara C. Gelpi, et al. (Chicago: University of Chicago Press, 1986).

Some saw clearly the liability of the underlying materialism justifying woman suffrage. Consequently, they immediately pushed for an Equal Rights Amendment, as a corrective. Though the ERA was proposed in 1923, it failed the ratification process after passage in Congress. Most point to the residual assumptions of differences between men and women as the reason. See Jane J. Mansbridge, *Why We Lost the ERA* (Chicago: Chicago University Press, 1986). As Barbara Nelson put it so succinctly, in the development of the American state, motherhood remains a reason "both for the political inclusion of some women and the political exclusion of others," "The Origin of the Two-Channel Welfare State," 3.

63. *Hoyt v Florida*, 368 US 57 (1961), 61–62, 163.

64. The Court reversed this decision in 1975 in *Taylor v Louisiana*, 419 US 522 (1975).

65. *Goesaert v Cleary*, 335 US 464 (1948), 465–66.

66. Benhabib, "Toward a Deliberative Model of Democracy Legitimacy," in *Democracy and Difference*, 67.

67. See McDonagh, "The 'Welfare Rights State.'"

68. Skocpol, *Protecting Soldiers and Mothers*, 52.

69. Theda Skocpol et al., "Women's Associations and the Enactment of Mothers' Pensions in the United States," *American Political Science Review* 87 (1993): 686–99; Theda Skocpol, "Response," *American Political Science Review* 89 (1995): 721.

70. Rogers M. Smith, *Civic Ideals: Conflicting Views of Citizenship in U.S. History*, The Yale IMPS Series. (New Haven: Yale University Press, 1997), 412–24.

71. For a more complete analysis of state, regional, and national patterns characterizing a policy paradox in the Progressive Era, see McDonagh, "'The Welfare Rights State.'"

72. Samuel P. Huntington, *American Politics: The Promise of Disharmony*, 201.

73. Many scholars, such as Sidney Milkis and Richard Harris, identify the sixties and the seventies in terms of institutional administrative reforms, Richard A. Harris and Sidney M. Milkis, *Remaking American Politics* (Boulder, Colo.: Westview Press, 1989). Though ultimately such analyses depend upon agreement of what defines "new," the view advanced here is that the expanded use of

institutions is to be distinguished from the new use of institutions or from new institutions per se. Although there was a tremendous expansion of the national agenda in the sixties and seventies, I do not see a fundamental alteration of the scope and centralization of the state comparable to that which occurred in the Progressive Era.

74. Samuel P. Huntington, *American Politics: The Promise of Disharmony*, 174.

75. Daniel Bell, *The Cultural Contradictions of Capitalism* (New York: Basic Books, 1976), 121.

76. James Miller, *"Democracy Is in the Streets": From Port Huron to the Siege of Chicago* (New York: Simon and Schuster, 1987), 152–53.

77. Sara Evans, *Personal Politics: The Roots of Women's Liberation in the Civil Rights Movement and the New Left* (New York: Vintage Books, 1980).

78. Betty Friedan, *The Feminine Mystique* (New York: Dell, 1963), 20.

79. Ibid., 305–6. In the view of historian Daniel Horowitz, the power of Friedan's critique was that she was able to locate her feminist analysis of the suburban housewife as part of a growing number of books registering distress with middle-class American life in the 1950s, such as Vance Packard's *The Hidden Persuaders* (New York: D. McKay Co., 1957); David Riesman's *The Lonely Crowd* (New Haven: Yale University Press, 1950); William W. Whyte's, *The Organization Man* (New York: Simon and Schuster, 1956); and Rachel Carson's *The Sea Around Us* (New York: Oxford University Press, 1951) and *Silent Spring* (New York: Fawcett Crest, 1962).

This is particularly significant, given that Friedan's own background was as a labor journalist who sympathetically reported on the United Electrical, Radio, and Machine Workers of America (UE), which many consider to have been the "most radical American union in the postwar period . . . and 'the largest communist-led institution of any kind in the United States.'"

In 1952 Friedan published a pamphlet, *UE Fights for Women Workers,* arguing for better wage and working conditions for women, including a "gender-blind" workplace. By the mid-fifties, however, Friedan turned away from the plight of working women, eventually bringing her critical gaze to that of economically privileged, suburban women who nonetheless were caught in a meaningless morass. Daniel Horowitz, "Rethinking Betty Friedan and *The Feminine Mystique:* Labor Union Radicalism and Feminism in Cold War America," *American Quarterly* 48, 1 (1996): 15, 22–23, 1.

80. Stetson, *Women's Rights,* 227.

81. *Goesaert v Cleary,* 335 US 464 (1948).

82. Stetson, *Women's Rights,* 231.

83. Joyce Gelb and Marian Lief Palley, *Women and Public Policies* 2d ed. (Princeton: Princeton University Press, 1987), 65, 66.

84. Sarah Weddington, *A Question of Choice* (New York: G. P. Putnam's Sons, 1992), 24.

85. Gelb and Palley, *Women and Public Policies,* 163, 164.

86. Ibid., 164–65.

87. Stetson, *Women's Rights,* 267.

88. Ibid., 316–18.

89. The level of scrutiny the Court uses for sex discrimination is an "intermediate" level in distinction to the level of "strict" scrutiny the Court uses to evaluate race discrimination.

90. Paul Pierson, *Dismantling the Welfare State? Reagan, Thatcher, and the Politics of Retrenchment* (New York: Cambridge University Press, 1994).

91. Karen Orren and Stephen Skowronek, "Institutions and Intercurrence: Theory Building in the Fullness of Time," *Nomos 38, Political Order,* ed. Ian Shapiro and Russell Hardin (New York: New York University Press, 1996); Karen Orren, "Ideas and Institutions," *Polity* 8, 1 (1995): 97; Stephen Skowronek, "Order and Change," *Polity* 28, 1 (1995): 91.

92. See John Bendix, "Comment: Going Beyond the State?," *American Political Science Review* 86, 4 (1992): 1010.

93. See Walter Dean Burnham, *The Current Crisis in American Politics* (Oxford: Oxford University Press, 1982), 42; and Wiebe, *Search for Order.*

The Metropolis and Multicultural Ethics

Direct Democracy versus Deliberative Democracy in the Progressive Era

Philip J. Ethington

Among the many ironies of the so-called Progressive Era (circa 1890s–1920s), the saddest perhaps is the deep and enduring damage done to democracy by her closest friends. The chief features of this damage are well known. Today, one century after the reform movement calling itself "progressivism" began, very few Americans participate in any aspect of self-government. Voter participation, even in the highest-turnout presidential elections, decreased steadily during the second half of the twentieth century, so that by 1996 only about 50 percent of eligible voters went to the polls. Turnout in off-year and local elections (for jurisdictions that touch citizens most directly) has been far lower.[1]

That which is called participation consists of multi-million-dollar media advertising campaigns in which the spirit of negation reigns (against welfare, against immigration, against liberalism, against abortion, against taxes, against incumbency of office, against affirmative action, etc.). In California, the state in which the progressive attack on organizational party politics was the most successful, the political process is clearly driven now by plebiscitary initiatives, which in turn have practically set the national political agenda since Proposition 13 in 1978. The anti-immigrant Proposition 187 (1994), the anti–affirmative action Proposition 209 (1996), and most recently, the anti–bilingual education Proposition 227 (1998) have all sparked campaigns in other states and directly influenced federal legislation.

Initiatives, referendums, and recalls, along with direct primaries and the direct election of U.S. senators, were the core achievements of "direct democracy" by the Progressive generation during the first two decades of the twentieth century. A related achievement was the assault on political parties. Weak party institutions and strong direct democracy institutions have also supported waves of independent millionaire candidacies, epitomized by Ross Perot's 1992 presidential bid. Software millionaires now impose themselves on our republic directly, rather than needing to seek party sponsorships, and even mainstream politicians spend an inordinate amount of their terms of office squeezing money from the wealthy, merely to finance voracious campaign consulting firms and the media tools of their trade.[2]

The United States, I shall argue, missed an opportunity to realize a very different kind of democracy than the plebiscitary advertising campaign that reigns supreme today. It is no accident, this essay suggests, that many if not most of the agenda-setting direct democracy measures pose questions of distributive justice regarding the relative privileges of ethnoracial groups. The "direct democracy" reforms of the Progressive Era institutionally empowered a theory of representation that virtually guaranteed an ethically barren public discourse. The tragedy of the Progressive Era is that what began as a movement to save democracy from industrial capitalism and its many social transformations actually impoverished democracy by mishandling the core question of diversity so that the marketplace could capitalize on the politics of difference.

The great metropolises of the United States in the industrial North, especially New York City and Chicago, were the decisive settings for a drastic recasting of normative thinking about democratic representation and an equally drastic reshaping of participatory institutions. The overall challenge was to reinvent American democracy in the face of emergent "multiculturalism," defined here as the recognition that the public sphere would be fragmented by many different definitions of the good life. These different understandings arose in strikingly different ethnocultural communities: of Yiddish-speaking Russian Jews; of Baptist African American migrants from the rural South; of Roman Catholic Poles and Italians. Just as striking were the contrasts between middle- and upper-class advocates of laissez-faire capitalism and working-class socialists, or between evangelical-fundamentalist Anglo-Saxon Protestants and Anglo-Saxon liberal Protestants.

As the twentieth century began, the mainstream political culture of the United States had already adjusted to accept the presence of multiple definitions of the public good: something of which Abraham Lincoln in the 1850s could not conceive (the nation had to be "all one thing" or "all the other.")[3] But it was up to the Progressive generation to recast institutions such that plural publics could engage productively with one another in a single political system. The best outcome would have been to make the political system benefit from the diversity of voices and perspectives. The worst outcome would have been to make the political system work against that diversity by creating institutions that encouraged stimulus-response politics in which mobilization of fear could become a dominant mode of discourse. The worst outcome came to pass. That outcome was not inevitable, even though, as we shall see, the forces arrayed against genuine democracy were formidable.[4]

Democracy, Representation, and the Problem of Multicultural Ethics

The meaning of democracy is not self-evident. It requires every generation to "represent" it in the form of careful propositions. There were afoot during the 1890s–1920s period several contrasting representations of democracy. This essay redacts from the broad discourse of the Progressive Era two rival representations of democracy and connects them to the institutions of practice that came to dominate U.S. political culture in the twentieth century. Neither was promoted as a pure type except in the writings of a very few, exceptionally rigid thinkers.

On the "left" (within liberalism in general) was the first modern theory of "deliberative democracy" designed to deal constructively with a sociocultural diversity of value orientations. This was the intersubjective procedural theory of the Chicago Pragmatists: principally Jane Addams, John Dewey, and George Herbert Mead. In parallel and as a mirror image, W.E.B. Du Bois also elaborated an intersubjective democratic ethics much more aware of the hard questions about "otherness" and progress than that of his mainstream colleagues. But neither of these variants survived the Progressive Era to generate further offspring.

The other, triumphant theory — that of group behavioral liberalism — was most clearly adumbrated by Arthur Bentley and John B. Watson, but it was also an organic practice in the sociopolitical field regardless of the intellectual influence of its exponents. This theory was almost completely cynical as regards the ethical, value-oriented content of democratic debate. Instead, it stressed purportedly nonideological (material) interests, a blunt view of human action that enshrined stimuli and responses, and an open embrace of the capitalist market model for the mobilization of political will. I shall argue that the triumphant group-behavioral theory exacerbated racism, mortgaged American democracy to the logic of the capitalist marketplace, and foreclosed participation in debates about the relationship between justice and the good life.

Contrasting *just* two representations of democracy entails some risk, given the large literature on the diversity of social and political thought during the 1890s–1920s period. It is worthwhile, therefore, to navigate the thicket of Progressive Era democracy in low gear for a few pages in order to clarify my argument. The principal questions here are: Why focus on the metropolitan milieu? Why were different representations of democracy so momentous? What is so important about intellectuals and their ideas?

There were many "progressivisms" — certainly no single "Progressive Movement" as Richard Hofstadter once claimed; nor was there a single Progressive "public doctrine" as Eldon Eisenach argues.[5] Eisenach has, however, convincingly established the case that Progressive intellectuals had a "regime-founding" role in the transformation of American political institutions for this century. "The academic Progressives were not only at home in urban industrial America," Eisenach correctly observes, "they were among its first inhabitants and surely the first to seek a systematic understanding of its wealth and power."[6]

But the significance of the urban milieu goes considerably further. Urban-based intellectuals were deeply engaged in political and social change, both directly and indirectly. Directly, men and women like John Dewey, George Herbert Mead, Albion Small, William I. Thomas, Grace and Edith Abbott, Charles Merriam at the University of Chicago; Samuel Lindsay, Mary K. Simkhovitch, Charles and Mary Beard at Columbia; Edward A. Ross and Amos Warner at Stanford — these people and many more constituted what could be called an "interlocking progressive directorate." They frequently took major policy-making or political public roles themselves. Professor Charles Merriam was a Chicago city councilman and two-time mayoral candidate by 1919. He went on in the 1920s to head the Social Science Research Council, launching the

President's Committee on Social Trends for Herbert Hoover, and became an architect of Franklin Roosevelt's later, unrealized welfare state.
Indeed, the list of intellectuals or at least college-trained activists in the
cities during the 1890s–1920s period who would become New Dealers
is very long. Harold Ickes was a Merriam protégé; Social Security Act
coauthor Grace Abbott was an Addams protégé; Harry Hopkins cut his
social welfare teeth in the settlement houses of New York City.[7]

Indirectly, the academics at Johns Hopkins, Columbia, Stanford,
Wellesley, Bryn Mawr, the Universities of Chicago, Wisconsin, Michigan, and Nebraska produced thousands of young graduates who went
directly into public service. These people became the law writers, lobbyists, litigants, corporate liberals, officeholders, bureaucrats, and social
workers in the new, reconstructed American state.[8]

Next, why should we focus on "democracy"? Why not other progressive fixations such as "efficiency" or "control"? My answer is that nearly
all other concerns during the Progressive Era can be subsumed under the
more general crisis of self-rule. The last fin de siècle may even be seen as
one of those rare moments in modern history when truly fateful paths
where chosen regarding human emancipation. Let us take the common
sense definition as a starting point, that "democracy" is a condition in
which *all segments* of the people of a sovereign polity take a role in the
exercise of power over themselves. Genuinely democratic government,
as Sheldon Wolin reminds us, is extremely rare in human history. Moments when all or even most segments of a society have really engaged in
something approaching self-rule have only appeared during rare revolutionary movements (1777–87 in the United States, 1789–94 in France,
1917–24 in Russia/the Soviet Union). So frightening have these moments been to the ruling classes, that they have imposed constitutions
specifically designed to contain and constrain unmediated expressions of
popular power. These constitutional forms, Wolin argues, were not
"representative democracy" so much as "representations of democracy,"
ensuring legitimacy for regimes that are in fact mediating rather than
distributing power — the interests of the wealthy, the corporations, and
the dominant race-ethnic groups.[9] It is not unfair to characterize the
United States of America in this way.[10]

Suppressing the voices of diversity within U.S. political discourse was
a consuming project prior to the Progressive Era — and during it. States
and the federal government had taken positive action to limit the politi-

cal participation of the poor, African Americans, women, and immigrants. As C. Vann Woodward, J. Morgan Kousser, and others have shown, the limitations on black voting after Reconstruction were a decisive response by the Bourbon ruling class to the threat of a black-white coalition — especially in the People's Party movement. The final defeat of the Populists in 1896 only ended a rural democratic threat for the time being. That decade also marked the shift of American society from a predominantly rural to a predominantly urban nation, and therein lies the key to understanding how the Progressives played a decisive role in the redefinition of democracy in the United States.[11]

Upon enactment of the Charter of Greater New York in 1897, New York became the second largest city in the world (after London) and larger (at a population of 3.5 million) than any of the Atlantic seaboard states. The metropolis (as a magnification of urbanism in general) is the seat of class formation, of revolutions in gender roles, and the forge of publicly constructed group identities. As nodes in global migration streams, the great metropolises of the United States focused and magnified questions of diversity. In 1915 New York City had more than twenty-seven English-language dailies and an equal number of dailies or weeklies in at least sixteen other languages: Arabic, Chinese, Croatian, Czech, French, German, Greek, Hungarian, Italian, Polish, Russian, Serbian, Slovak, Slovenian, Spanish, Yiddish.[12] This magnitude of difference reframed the debates about representation that had been ongoing since the adoption of the Constitution.

A crisis concerning multicultural ethics arose, then, in the metropolitan centers of the United States during the late nineteenth century, and the Progressive generation stood at a crossroads of two major alternative pathways to deal with it. The crisis consisted of the realization that (a) there can be more than one "true" value orientation; (b) political power was maldistributed to benefit elites with inordinate money-power; and (c) any downward redistribution of political power would empower multiple, mutually conflicting value orientations and immensely complicate the problem of achieving just settlements.

Now we are in a position to see the significance of the two rival representations of democracy I have briefly introduced, and it is time to examine them more carefully. Two major received traditions about the meaning of democracy were available to the Progressive generation as the principal pathways toward democratic reconstruction. Since ideas do not exist in a vacuum, nor have a force of their own, it is most useful to see these received traditions as institutional structures, historical patterns of discourse and practice with great normative weight at the beginning of the twentieth century. Each tradition was constantly in the process of reformulation in the context of public political practice.[13]

The two major traditions can be most recognizably denoted as "republican" and "liberal." The republican tradition portrays political participation as "a process of citizen self-creation," constitutive of social well-being by any criterion. This is why periods of U.S. history characterized by republicanist movements are thick with a discourse of "virtue." Republicanism, from the U.S. and French Revolutionary periods through the U.S. Workingmen's parties and the People's party movements of the 1880s–1890s, saw the practice of democracy as a debate about the values the society as a whole *ought* to pursue.

The "liberal" tradition of representing democracy asserts a very different norm, one rooted unmistakably in the norms of capitalism itself. Participation by this tradition is the work of individuals with generic "interests." The content of those interests is not specified, nor even relevant to the liberal model of democracy. This liberal or Lockean view, in the words of Jürgen Habermas, portrays "politics (in the sense of the citizen's political will-formation)" as having the "function of bundling together and pushing private interests against a government apparatus specializing in the administrative employment of political power for collective goals."[14] For most of the nineteenth century, the United States political culture could be characterized as an atomistic, individual-based understanding of this model. Near the end of the nineteenth century, however, a recognizably "pluralist" variation emerged, in which the work of "bundling" the private interests of millions of individual voters was henceforth to be performed by institutional leaders who created these bundles as interest *groups,* through successful marketing strategies. Unfortunately, this model leaves a huge ethical void, as Iris Marion Young observes: "Each citizen may reason about the best means for achieving his or her own privately defined ends, but the aggregate outcome has no necessary rationality and itself has not been arrived at by the process of reasoning."[15]

Inheriting and working within these two traditions, the first generation of Ph.D.-holding social scientists and their academic associates operating as "public intellectuals" had a complicated problem at hand. The elements of their crisis, summarized above, had formed a one-way door blocking return to past models. First, they had to think of a way to accommodate plural value orientations among the citizenry. The republican tradition, as we have seen, considers democracy a matter of the formation of values. But earlier republicanism had not contemplated the permanent existence of multiple, even conflicting, values. Instead, it had always been consensual: projecting a nation with a single cultural norm. Second, the Progressive generation had to think of ways to rectify the maldistribution of power that enabled the "interests" to injure the "people" in so many ways: in public health, in taxation and spending, in unsafe working conditions and consumer products, and so on. But opening the political process to the masses, as in the assault on political parties and in favor of various mechanisms of direct democracy, also risked opening that process to the very interests whose power seemed over-represented, if that opening was conducted solely within the liberal tradition's model of democracy—which is patently market modeled.

We turn next to a detailed examination of how intellectuals attempted to resolve these difficulties. In the following section I will argue that the Chicago Pragmatists reformulated the republican tradition in a very promising way, but failed: (a) to overcome key contradictions in their own theory, and (b) to recognize the perils of a commercialized public sphere.

The Chicago Pragmatists and Intersubjective Democracy

For a brief and shining moment there throve in Chicago a remarkable reformulation of democracy, generated by a community of intellectual-activists who took as their primary challenge the continued viability of democracy within the metropolitan condition of capitalist exploitation and intercultural conflict. The central, senior figures in this community were Jane Addams and John Dewey. With Ellen Gates Starr, Addams founded Hull House, the nation's preeminent social settlement and headquarters for urban social research, in 1889. Hull House rapidly became the most dynamic staging site in Chicago for social research, labor organizing, feminist thinking and policy formation, and reform politics in general.[16] Addams recruited and collaborated with innovative activist-public intellectuals such as Florence Kelly, Julia Lathrop, Grace and Edith Abbott, and many others in her forty-six years in residence at

Hull House. John Dewey left the University of Michigan to become the founding chair of the philosophy department at the new University of Chicago in 1892. Dewey recruited and collaborated with an equally impressive group of philosophers, including James R. Angell, Edward S. Ames, and George Herbert Mead. Mead, working closely with Dewey, developed a highly original, intersubjective theory of the self and society, and threw himself into political policy movements at the same time. Their best student was William I. Thomas, who would synthesize their ideas and produce, with Florian Znaniecki, the sociological masterwork of the period, *The Polish Peasant in Europe and America,* five volumes (1918–20).

Addams, Dewey, Mead, and Thomas often worked together and were deeply influenced by one another, meeting frequently at Hull House. Their collaboration was both political and intellectual. While Dewey spent his political energies primarily on the famous laboratory school, his closest colleague, George Herbert Mead, marched with workers to demand the eight-hour day and published more widely, in fact, on political policy issues than he did on philosophic ones. Both Addams and Dewey wrote prolifically during the critical decade of the 1890s: Addams formulating her theory of Social Ethics; Dewey formulating his naturalistic, nonfoundational pragmatism. Addams summarized her theory in *Democracy and Social Ethics* in 1902; Dewey and his colleagues summarized their "Chicago School" of pragmatism in their *Studies in Logical Theory* in 1903. Upon reading this volume, an awestruck William James called Dewey "a real hero" and proclaimed the appearance of a "Chicago School" of philosophy.[17]

What was so heroic about the work of this circle? Only during the past several years have their contributions come not only to be recognized, but also to take a central place in the philosophical-political debates of our own day. For many years Dewey's pragmatism was misunderstood as a sort of naive faith in the application of scientific methods to philosophical, social, and political questions. European theorists, beginning with Weber, either barely noticed American pragmatism or did not care to learn about it. Beginning in the 1980s, writers such as Jürgen Habermas, Axel Honneth, Hans Joas, James Kloppenberg, Richard Rorty, and Robert Westbrook corrected these misconceptions and this neglect.[18] They have shown that Dewey and Mead, especially, forged a real solution to the crisis of "objectivity" in the foundationless world since Nietzsche; that they were not mere apologists for a technocratic culture but, quite the contrary, had a clear program for participatory democracy; and that they developed a viable solution to the problem in social theory of connecting the actions of individuals in everyday life with the large structures we call social systems. Their solution was an intersubjective communications theory of mind, self, and society.

The Chicago Pragmatists were centrally concerned with ethical pluralism in the context of metropolitan multiculturalism. In concert with William James, Dewey and his colleagues constructed a critique of Kantian universal ethics and convincingly pluralized the understanding of truth.

Among the core features of Dewey's pragmatism is his lifelong assertion that Western philosophy had taken a wrong turn from Plato through his own time, in what he called the "spectator theory of knowledge." By showing in hundreds of writings how the cognitive inquiries of the self mediate from experience to experience, with an orientation to the future based on assessments of the "situation" of the present and past, he denied the dualities of mind/body, means/end, fact/value. This was nonfoundationalism with a thorough vengeance, but it was not ethical nihilism. Ideas are formed in action, which is usually social action. What is true is not revealed from God or from nature's law, but in the formulation of "warranted assertability," which had to be built from elements of the present situation.

Implicit in this was a republican model of democracy. Since individuals need a structure of value referents in order to guide their actions in specific situations of daily interaction, and since those situations of daily interaction are public ones in a crisis of capitalist exploitation, ethnic conflict, and gender domination, and since there are no eternal guides to the ethics of a situation outside of the community of humanity in which these conflicts occur, then the modern self must be a democratic self if it is to thrive. Our solutions to problems must entail a discussion of the values on which we base our actions.

As is well known and much lamented, however, Dewey never applied his model of pragmatic democracy in a sustained way, but rather forged ahead from one project to another, leaving a huge but nevertheless vague opus. Jane Addams and George Herbert Mead were more engaged in Chicago politics (Dewey left for Columbia in 1904) and were responsible for filling in the pragmatic solution to multicultural ethics.

Possibly the single most unifying theme in Jane Addams's long career was the crossing of the cultural divides between class and ethnic groups. The spatial logic of Hull House was for modern women and men to take up residence in the neighborhoods that contained value orientations alien to the bourgeois Protestant ones of her ruling-class milieu. Her theory of "social ethics" required a very radical step: the relativization of her own ethical standards. The writings of Jane Addams are the first deliberate attempt to define what is now called "multiculturalism." Addams, along with James and Dewey, literally pluralized ethical truth, claiming that the "ought" in modern society must emerge from the "new knowledge" (experience) discovered from engaging in sociality among the groups that are now interdependent, and not from the received standards of the dominant group.[19]

Addams first fully developed this theory in an essay published simultaneously in two different forums. The longer one appeared as "Ethical Survivals in Municipal Corruption," in the April 1898 number of the *International Journal of Ethics;* a version about half as long appeared as "Why the Ward Boss Rules," in the 2 April 1898 issue of the middle-class opinion magazine *Outlook.* The longer version, clearly addressed to intellectuals, such as its editors Josiah Royce, Felix Adler, and Henry Carter Adams, contains a fuller elaboration of the theory at work.[20]

"Ethical Survivals" contains Addams's thesis in the title. The empirical case is the corrupt rule of the most powerful alderman in Chicago, Johnny Powers, elected from the Nineteenth Ward, in which Hull House was located. Addams has three objectives in this essay: (1) to explain not only "why the ward boss rules," but also why reformers have been so unsuccessful in voting them out of office; (2) to show the constitutive relationship between local political institutions and popular ethics, what Addams calls "plastic morals"; and (3) to make a pragmatic case for bourgeois Protestant reformers to relativize their own beliefs and work toward new, unknown ethical standards through synthesis with those of the unfamiliar communities around them. This last point is the revolutionary one, because it leaves ethical truth groundless and uncertain, and yet, as in Dewey's and James's pragmatism, locatable through democratic action/dialogue with others.

"Primitive people," Addams writes, "such as the South Italian peasants who live in the Nineteenth Ward, deep down in their hearts admire nothing so much as the good man."[21] As this language clearly indicates, Addams reaches her pluralistic, social theory of ethics by way of deep-time evolutionary thinking. The *other* ethics she seeks to interpret to her Anglo-Protestant bourgeois audience is not simply different in ethics, it is an "earlier" stage of "moral evolution," on the road to "moral progress." Drawing on the folk psychology of Wilhelm Wundt, Addams adopts a theory of moral evolution in which primitive societies have only attained a sense of interpersonal reciprocal obligation, ("moral fact") and modern societies have attained a "higher form of moral ideas," serving to benefit the community in some abstract way. Johnny Powers ruled the Nineteenth Ward, because he played into the perfectly valid, yet "more primitive" standard of personal deeds. In the experience of Addams, her primitive neighbors had been helped many a time by Powers — at funerals, when their sons were arrested and in need of bail, and when a few dollars per vote was being offered.[22]

Many historians have interpreted the seemingly bigoted language of Addams as a case of ruling-class or anti-immigrant condescension.[23] There is a great fault in Addams's moral evolutionism, which holds the different cultures of the metropolis to occupy lower and higher positions on a very long historical ladder. That conceit ultimately cost Addams and most of the Chicago Pragmatists their seat at the postmodern table, where cultural otherness cannot be held as lower or higher on any metric. But it is vitally important to understand that Addams did not hold the values of the South Italian peasant lower in *value*.

Her courage and vision consists in this: She is *not* saying that the South Italian peasants, or the fifty thousand who were "Latin, Celt, Teuton, Jew, and Slav" in her neighborhood, *ought not* to emulate Johnny Powers and value his magnanimity. They were perfectly justified in doing so, Addams writes, and also pointedly criticizes her own culturally insensitive actions at Hull House, especially during past, failed reform campaigns. There is, in this "primitive" life-world, a set of values that the bourgeois Protestant women from the suburbs like Evanston ought to emulate.

During the Hull House residents' attempts to unseat Powers and to fight the power of his saloon-based connections with the streetcar magnate Yerkes, Addams had learned several crucial lessons. The first was that winning popular elections requires moral authority. The Hull House candidates were not winning because they were not communicating in a decipherable moral language with their neighbors. She gives the example of a reform speaker denouncing an allegedly corrupt, but now deceased, politician. Speaking ill of the dead, however, appalled the listeners, and insulted them as well, because they had once supported the deceased: "He certainly succeeded in irrevocably injuring the chances of the candidate for whom he was speaking. The speaker's standard of ethics was upright dealing in positions of public trust. The standard of ethics held by his audience was, being good to the poor and speaking gently of the dead. If he considered them corrupt and illiterate voters, they quite honestly held him a blackguard."[24] Elsewhere, Addams proliferated like examples, as in the case of the anonymous dead baby deposited at the door of Hull House. Addams and associates disgusted their neighbors by putting it in a public pauper's grave rather than raising money for a proper funeral and headstone.[25]

Addams learned another, larger lesson in her battles with Johnny Powers. He was not simply playing on the "simple minds," he was actively *shaping* those minds by example. This was all the more so because of the "primitive" stage of moral evolution occupied by the peasants in the Nineteenth Ward. Their moral sense, by Wundt's model, was based on emulation (Addams illustrates this inheritance with the role of saints in Christian moral teaching). Powers exemplified not only the right moral conduct for a peasant, but also reinforced undemocratic practices by showing that a man can become rich and powerful by owning saloons, springing criminals from jail, taking kickbacks from corporations, and buying votes. Therefore, "no greater mistake could be made than to assume that politics is something off by itself which does not affect the common lot."[26] This assertion should be read as an evocation of the republican tradition of democracy: politics shapes the moral sense and self-identities of its participants.

"If we discover," she concluded the *Outlook* version of this essay, "that men of low ideas and corrupt practice are forming popular political standards simply because such men stand by and for and with the people, then nothing remains but to obtain a like sense of identification before we can hope to modify ethical standards."[27] It would be hard to overstate the innovation contained in Addams's "Ethical Survivals." She was operating in a political culture far removed from that of her idol Abraham Lincoln, to whose Gettysburg Address the passage above alludes. Lincoln's conception of "the people" was not plural; Addams's was. Whereas U.S. political culture had come to turn on this plural understanding of the people, as politicians openly mobilized the interests of "groups," Addams was now going a step further to suggest that a political leader could adopt enough of the moral views of the "other" in order to achieve public authority, and then take her/his own group to some as yet unknown ethical plane. Doing this would require that "we . . . dramatize 'public spirit'" and "learn to trust our huge and uncouth democracy."[28]

While Addams took the ideas of the Chicago Pragmatist circle far and wide, George Herbert Mead developed them deeply. He laid the groundwork for a multicultural ethics, more so than Addams, by specifying the social-psychological process of intersubjectivity. Mead's contributions have been classified as both sociological and philosophical—with good reason. According to Mead, "the self . . . is essentially a social structure, and it arises in social experience." Mead's elaboration of his basic thesis has taken the label "symbolic interactionism." The simple form of the argument is that the human organism, interacting symbolically, must at every turn "take the attitude of the other" with whom it interacts. An individual emits signs with an already-formed anticipation of how those signs will be received by another organism. In Mead's theory, one's self is formed in the intersubjective process. This process, which becomes unreflexive in adults, must be learned, through "play" and "games," terms with technical significance for Mead. In *play,* children take the roles of others, but at first *just* the singular other. The child at first "plays that he is, for instance, offering himself something, and buys it; he gives a letter to himself and takes it away; he addresses himself as a parent, as a teacher; he arrests himself as a policeman. He has a set of stimuli which call out in himself the sort of responses they call out in others." *Games* come at a later stage, when the child learns to adopt a third-person attitude to the interactions: "The fundamental difference between game and play is that in the latter the child must have the attitude of all the others involved in the game." This is taking the "attitude of the generalized other," the ability to see the whole set of interactions of which the self is a part.[29]

We can readily see the importance of this pragmatic theory of mind to the "social ethics" of Addams, who consistently stressed the "subjective necessity" of putting one's self into what she called "the wider world." To Mead, the "generalized other" is the locus of normative ethics: "It is in the form of the generalized other that the social process influences the behavior of the individuals involved in it and carrying it on, i.e., that the community exercises control over the conduct of its individual members; for it is in this form that the social process or community enters as a determining factor into the individual's thinking."[30]

Mead formulated this theory simultaneously with his political writings and activities. Marching with garment workers for union recognition and the eight-hour day is possibly what kept Mead from writing major treatises. Neither Mead nor Dewey nor Addams was interested in democracy for its own sake. The whole point of rethinking democracy was to solve the problem of exploitation. This could not be done within the liberal tradition of democracy because that tradition is inherently contentless: it simply aggregates individual preferences on the market model, but does not address the quality of the preferences.

Industrial capitalism transcends individual choice, Mead argued. It requires a collective reassessment. "The [industrial] machine is a social product for which no individual can claim complete responsibility," Mead wrote in 1907. "But the group morality under which the community suffers, recognizes no responsibility of the exploiter to the laborer, but leaves him free to exhaust and even maim the operator, as if the community had placed a sword in his hand with which to subjugate."[31] Mead denies here the validity of the "group morality" of natural rights ethical law. The "generalized other" assumed by the attitude of the industrial capitalist is clearly wanting; it fails as a group morality to correspond to the actual interdependency of the factors of production.

Similarly, Mead thought that the employers' treatment of immigrant labor failed to recognize the international interdependencies. The Chicago businessmen "had absolutely no feeling of responsibility to the immigrant," who "comes ignorant and helpless before the system of exploitation which enwraps him before he leaves the old country and may last for two generations after he enters our gates."[32]

Since, in Mead's view, "the self . . . is a social structure," any democracy that detached individual values from social deliberation was not democratic. Merely to outvote the capitalist, leaving his values unaddressed, leaves the cultural hegemony of his values in place, poised to exploit the next generation of laborers. Democratic action needs to create a dialogue about the ends we ought to pursue: moral values (which are also, Dewey would remind us, empirical social facts, and therefore not invisible feelings but visible objects available for public discussion).[33]

To realize this potential requires active participation with one another, in mutual recognition of the "different universes of discourse." Here Mead clearly anticipated Ludwig Wittgenstein's "language games," not to mention Gramsci's "cultural hegemony." That participation must of course be democratic, but the content of the "universal" will always be contingent upon the quality and extent of participation. "The question whether we belong to a larger community is answered in terms of whether our own action calls out a response in this wider community." Mead meant a *favorable* response, of course, and he needed to be optimistic to mean that.[34]

Du Bois, Difference, and Democracy

I have emphasized the most promising features of the Chicago Pragmatists' theory of deliberative democracy in order to establish their record of achievement. Their theory was also fraught with serious shortcomings, however. A major problem with many versions of deliberative democracy, writes Iris Marion Young, is an assumption that sociocultural difference needs to be *overcome*. Some accounts assume that "common culture" is a precondition for debates about ethical values; others assume that a common culture is the desirable outcome of deliberative communication between members of different groups. Addams and her colleagues clearly assumed that a single, national culture was the desired end of the "melting pot." Most damaging was her assumption that the work of intersubjectivity would result in a higher form of civilization than that brought by the *other:* "primitive" Italian peasants or black migrants from the rural South. In the last analysis, Addams and her colleagues in Chicago expected too much consensus,[35] and the limits of their vision was shown by their own contemporary, W.E.B. Du Bois.

Du Bois, onetime student of William James, can be seen as the mirror image of Mead. Mead stated scientifically and abstractly how the self is formed in relation to the generalized other; Du Bois named the content of that self, and named the "generalized other" as a coercive moral force, as in this famous passage from *The Souls of Black Folk:* "[T]he Negro is a sort of seventh son, born with a veil, and gifted with second-sight in this American world, — a world which yields him no true self-consciousness, but only lets him see himself through the revelation of the other world. It is a peculiar sensation, this double-consciousness, this sense of always looking at one's self through the eyes of others, of measuring one's soul by the tape of a world that looks on in amused contempt and pity."[36] Dewey and Addams and Mead could have learned a great deal from Du Bois about the relations of cultural power in the "universe of discourse" they otherwise so brilliantly theorized. The Chicago Pragmatists told us that democracy needed to engage the citizen at the level of values, but rarely told us what values were best to pursue. They could aim the gun of democracy at injustice, but they could not pull the trigger, because the bullet they prescribed was another process: that of working together on values. The real tragedy is that they theorized about, but did not themselves take part in, a communication across the divide of otherness: ignoring Du Bois and other potential collaborators cost the very life of their best ideas.

As Carey McWilliams argues in this volume, Du Bois stood possibly alone among the Progressives as a direct critic of the "progress" that was not immediately inclusive. Far too much of the Dewey-Addams-Mead paradigm assumed that the burden of progress in the modern metropolis rests on the shoulders of the immigrants from "primitive" locales. Addams's advocacy of Americanization programs was symptomatic. Du Bois bravely followed in the tradition of the Freedman's Bureau and spent two years tutoring hungry minds in a rude shack, only to return ten years later to see that no amount of education could pierce the deadly veil of unjust institutions: "How many heartfuls of sorrow will balance a bushel of wheat? . . . And all this life and love and strife and failure — is it the twilight of nightfall or the flush of some faint-dawning day?"[37] As a theory, deliberative democracy can be rectified of these shortcomings. Young proposes a model that is neither predicated on consensus nor seeks to abolish difference: "A richer understanding of processes of democratic discussion results if we assume that differences of social position and identity perspective function as a resource for public reason rather than as divisions that public reason transcends."[38] But neither the Chicago Pragmatist nor our own contemporary theories of deliberative democracy will stand a chance of success in the face of institutional practices that are diametrically opposed to discussions of ethical value. Those practices empowered a very different theory, one that answered Du Bois as he rode to Nashville on that Jim Crow car: he was witnessing the "twilight of nightfall."

With Open Arms: The Commercialized Public Sphere's Reception of Direct Democracy Reforms

Direct democracy may be seen as the hallmark element in the progressives' reconstruction of U.S. political institutions. Arthur Link and Richard McCormick see in the four-way presidential contest of 1912 the first mature appearance of late twentieth-century U.S. political culture, the elements of which are: "the use of direct primaries, the challenge to traditional party loyalties, the candidate's issue orientation, and the prevalence of interest-group activities." Sidney Milkis and Daniel Tichenor go beyond this to argue that the Progressive Party itself was the vehicle for mainstreaming these myriad institutional reforms. Significantly, all varieties of progressives threw their support behind Theodore Roosevelt and Hiram Johnson and their remarkable Progressive Party platform authored in Chicago by the likes of Jane Addams.[39] This illustrates, I believe, the broad consensus that direct democracy was simply a good end in itself. But it is, after all, merely an empty institutional vessel, into which can be loaded any conceivable ethical cargo.

No sooner were the direct democracy reforms in place than we witness the rise of intolerance politics. The "tribal twenties" were typified by a victorious anti-immigrant movement (culminating in the Restriction Acts of 1921 and 1924, and the Anti-Japanese Alien Land Laws of California); race riots; the rise of the Ku Klux Klan in the urban North; big-city mayors who waged openly ethnoracial campaigns (James Michael Curley in Boston and William Hale Thompson in Chicago); the intensification of race segregation in the urban North. Dewey, Mead, and Addams were certainly not hoping to achieve such a political atmosphere, but they were not thinking ahead very well either.[40]

Direct democracy's advocates were thinking primarily in terms of thwarting the influence of the corrupt political parties and the giant corporate "interests." They did not pause long enough to reflect on how easily those same interests could colonize the public sphere on which "direct democracy" depends. Their sad failure lies in the fact that nearly all Progressives gleefully embraced the emergent mass media in a mistaken belief that it would represent "public opinion" and supplant the corrupt mechanisms of governmental power.[41] The newspaper, Mead wrote in 1899, "is effecting changes that are assumed to be those which follow governmental action." Thus: "If only it becomes possible to focus public sentiment upon an issue in the delicate organism of the modern civilized community, it is as effective as if the mandate came from legislative halls, and frequently more so."[42] But not all "public sentiment" is alike. Mead also decried the "sensationalism [that] is the expression of a fundamental social conflict which the community feels but which [it] is not willing to come to terms with."[43] Although at times they managed to warn themselves about the perils of the new sensational media industry pioneered by Hearst and Pulitzer, they were more concerned to defeat the chief enemy of the age: undemocratic political parties.

The crowning blow to deliberative democratic practice came not directly from the political reformers, however, but from Madison Avenue. The rise of a consumer culture and a political economy to match it is one of the most important large-scale stories of the early twentieth century. No valid assessment of the impact of Progressive Era political reforms can afford to ignore the commercial reconstruction of public communications and the colonization of that new public sphere by values oriented only toward increasing consumption, appearances, and lifestyle.

The Progressive Era coincided with a massive shift in American culture, characterized as the rise of a consumer culture. The new "captains of consciousness," in Stewart Ewen's phrase, were the advertising agencies. Thorough scholarship (primarily from the cultural studies field of American Studies) has given us a very complete picture of the broad transformation of public discourse under the influence of commercial advertising during the first half of the twentieth century.[44]

In concert with the sensational press that disseminated their messages, advertisers switched from appeals to reason to appeals to emotion, and they did so just as the nation became majority urban, with consumption choices becoming paramount for people who were now working shorter workdays and, increasingly, in the costume of the white-collar worker. This reorientation of mass attitudes was mirrored by the captains of industry, facing now the problem of finding markets for the phenomenal outputs of the second industrial revolution. "The chief economic problem today," observed Stanley Resor, head of the J. Walter Thompson advertising agency, "is no longer the production of goods but rather their distribution."[45]

Advertising and social science crossed paths with the publication of a landmark study by Walter Dill Scott, *The Psychology of Advertising*

(1903), in which Scott introduced the concept of "suggestion." Based on experimental research, Scott concluded that the mere association of a product with symbolic phenomena was much more powerful psychologically than a fact-by-fact comparison of the relative merits of competing brand products that, in the end, were not very different in any case.[46]

Based on this new received wisdom and, ironically, on concerns about lawsuits arising from Progressive Era regulation of truthfulness in advertising, firms stopped using what they called "reason-why" appeals in their advertisements and made a decisive move toward irrational, suggestive appeals through images and poetic discourse to some favorable or unfavorable association.[47] With access to readers growing more concentrated in great newspaper chains, and the newspaper chains using advertising logic to sell ever more papers, the most potent force in the traffic of public discourse was effectively dethroning reason from the Age of Enlightenment.

With this brief overview of the commercialized public sphere in mind, let us return to the earnest Progressive reformers and their project of establishing direct democracy. It is most instructive to consider the hopes and fears of another leading Progressive intellect. Herbert Croly in *Progressive Democracy* (1915) made an effusive and urgent case for the initiative, recall, and referendum, the direct election of senators, and other measures cutting out the middleman of American political representation.

His first job was to answer the august argument against direct democracy in large nations. Such a scale, it was argued throughout the Revolutionary period, obviated the possibility of each person representing him/her self in government. But Croly cleverly reversed this standard argument about large, complex societies needing representative government. Representation, he thought, had only been necessary in the early republic, "imposed by the physical and technical conditions under which government had to be conducted." Since it took days merely to travel between each of the new united states circa 1800, communication was clearly too slow to keep several million citizens in a common "town meeting." But the modern, metropolitan nation had an advantage:

> In the twentieth century, however, these practical conditions of political association have again changed, and have changed in a manner which enables the mass of people to assume some immediate control of their political destinies. While it is more impossible than ever for the

citizens of a modern industrial and agricultural state actually to assemble after the manner of a New England town-meeting, it is no longer necessary for them to so assemble. They have abundant opportunities of communication and consultation without any actual meeting at one time and place.

Here Croly too fell prey to the promising novelty of mass communications. The citizens circa 1915, he claimed, "are kept in constant touch with one another by means of the complicated agencies of publicity and intercourse which are afforded by the magazines, the press and the like."[48] Given the *relative* independence of the mass media at the time Croly wrote, his optimism was not wholly misplaced. But today, circa 2000, in the age of the powerful television networks, one can only groan at the mistake he made to believe that anything close to deliberation is possible in commercial capitalist media markets. Although Croly was fatefully naive about the media, he knew that the experiment in direct democracy might yield the wrong results:

> The American experiment in direct democracy is still in its early youth. Its meaning and its tendencies cannot be demonstrated from experience. If the active political responsibilities which it grants to the electorate are redeemed in the negative and suspicious spirit which characterizes the attitude of the American democracy towards its official organization during its long and barren alliance with legalism, direct democracy will merely become a source of additional confusion and disorganization.[49]

Sadly, the bulk of our direct initiatives (California's Proposition 13, Massachusetts's Prop 2½, limiting property taxes, term limitation amendments, anti-immigration amendments, anti–affirmative action amendments, and so on) *are* "in the negative and suspicious spirit" that Croly associated with the nineteenth century. But that spirit was not embedded particularly in the nineteenth century, as Croly believed. It can easily be mobilized in any era if the structures of political practice favor simple numerical mobilization within a public sphere whose managers are skilled in the sale of products through emotional rather than rational discourse.

The line of march in the advertising industry's capture of the most important apparatus of American participatory institutions is easy enough to trace. Michael McGerr has shown that politicians began using advertisers as early as the 1896 presidential campaign, and that "advertised politics" became very common during the Progressive Era. Advertisers received a much welcomed legitimation during the Great War as George Creel brought them into the propaganda effort. Thereafter, as direct democracy measures took hold, advertisers were simply needed, whether or not they were admired or respected.[50] The now formidable campaign consulting industry was first perfected in prototype form in California by Clem Whitaker and Leone Baxter in their 1934 media campaign against Upton Sinclair. By the 1940s Whitaker and Baxter were retained by the California Medical Association to defeat the California state health plan and then by the American Medical Association to defeat Harry Truman's national health plan in 1949.[51] Thus were the "Interests" empowered by the Progressives. By the late 1940s Hollywood dilettante Joe Kennedy would say, "We're going to sell Jack [John F. Kennedy] like soap flakes." Ronald Reagan's 1980s Great Communicator presidency sealed the merger of advertising, entertainment, and the participatory institutions of the American state.[52]

In many respects in parallel with these developments in commercial culture, was a critical development for the triumph of a plebiscitary politics of intergroup antagonism: the legitimation of the antidemocratic tendencies by intellectuals in the social sciences. Their skillful surrender, through the formulation of group behaviorism, to the instrumental spirit of capitalism put the nail in the coffin of deliberative democracy.

The Group Behavioral Theory

The great task in the study of any form of social life is the analysis of . . . groups. . . . When the groups are adequately stated, everything is stated. When I say everything I mean everything.

—Arthur F. Bentley, *The Process of Government* (1908)

We turn now to the winning representation of democracy, that of group-behavioral liberalism. My treatment of this model differs from my treatment of the Chicago Pragmatists' model of deliberative democracy primarily because the latter ran counter to the great structures of institutional practice — which is to say: it ran against history. The group behavioral model, on the other hand, was more like a certification than a prescription. Its advocates redacted from the practices of the contemporary marketplace and electoral politics lawlike rules for an allegedly scientific approach to democracy.

The "advocates" of which I write were the political scientist Arthur F. Bentley and the psychologist John B. Watson.[53] Both launched, in particularly clear fashion, the essential features of the group-behavior model of democracy. Neither, I hasten to add, was a mainstream academic, and I do not suggest that their influence was a function of having trained graduate students or political leaders over several decades. Instead, I argue here that their work crystallized programmatically the most effective tools for managing and manipulating "direct democracy." Their work was diametrically opposed to the ideas of the Chicago Pragmatists, and so, it turned out, was the institutional legacy of progressive political reform. The theories of Bentley and Watson fitted the institutional reforms of direct democracy as a fist fits a glove. But that is not to claim that direct democracy reforms were inspired by the writings of these two intellectuals.

Arthur F. Bentley was among the most brilliant of the intellectuals engaged in the revision of the liberal model during the Progressive Era.[54] Dewey, Addams, and Mead encountered a political culture headed in the direction of a thoroughgoing adoption of the market model as a representation of democracy, and attempted to fight that model with a different one—partially drawn from indigenous republican institutions and partially innovated in their pragmatism. Bentley faced the other direction, seizing upon these tendencies toward a market liberal model and shoving them forward in the form of political science.

I have argued at length elsewhere that by 1900 the United States had adopted as its dominant political culture a "social-group paradigm," or a social conception of politics. According to this conception, the *political* is the outcome of *social*. The widespread recognition that social groups had plural yet legitimately different interests contrasted profoundly and diametrically with the widespread assumption circa 1850 that there could be only one public interest. This new political culture was the product of the actions of politicians and journalists who worked to mobilize groups in the social revolution that was the outcome of the Civil War. By 1900 the Progressive generation saw plural group interests as a natural condition of modern society, and saw their problem as weaving them together, in the formation of policy.[55]

We have seen how the Chicago Pragmatists approached this problem. They emphasized the values that served to give each subcommunity its solidarity and self-recognition, and yet argued that these subcommunities could and must communicate with one another, and in the process actually adopt the "role of the other," in effect participating in one another's value orientation, if only for the purpose of reaching a mutual understanding. This was not at all the commonsense view of the matter, however. The commonsense view of the matter was simply that different groups had interests that could be represented, misrepresented, or ignored. "We must recognize the fact that, aside from their general interests as citizens, special groups of citizens have special interests," Theodore Roosevelt crisply observed.[56] Woodrow Wilson was not less observant, but stated the same commonsense view from the obverse: "It is the business of government to organize the common interest against the special interests."[57]

Bentley adumbrated a scientific account of how such raw interests lie at the heart of group difference. He did so in direct opposition to the communicative theory of Dewey and Mead: "I readily admit that the point I am trying to make is utterly indifferent so far as the processes of ordinary speech are concerned."[58] But it would be a mistake to exaggerate the contrast between Bentley, Dewey, and Mead. Bentley was one of the products of a discourse on social institutions that grew from the Johns Hopkins Seminary of Historical and Political Science.[59] He worked very well with many of the same concepts as Dewey and Mead and had been influenced directly by attending Dewey's lectures. But he took them in a different direction. The point of overlap was this: they were all fierce critics of liberal individualism. Dewey and Mead saw democratic ethics arising from the intersubjective processes of group life. Politics should be about the formation of common values.

According to Bentley, those values are merely fig leaves for deeper group interests (by which he meant economic interests) and a scientific politics would hasten to ignore the distractions of "speech forms."[60] Thus, individual choice for Bentley was a chimera. Individuals were really agents of their groups. Bentley's longer-term contribution was to have founded "liberal pluralism," but that founding required another element: behaviorism.

Along with Bentley, the ideas of John B. Watson crystallized what would become by the 1920s the hegemonic discourse of American political culture. Watson completed his Ph.D. in 1903 in the exciting environment of the University of Chicago. At the age of twenty-five, he was the youngest Ph.D. Chicago had yet produced, and his dissertation,

"Animal Education," contained the seeds of a striking revolution in psychology. Through experiments on rats and monkeys, Watson constructed the outlines of "behaviorism," which promoted the central (but unlikely) axiom that consciousness should not be a concern to psychology. Only the observable phenomena of stimuli and responses matter, and all aspects of thinking can be explained by reference to the stimuli that shaped them in the human being's early developmental years. In 1913, now a star member of the faculty at Johns Hopkins University, he published the manifesto of the new movement: "Psychology as the Behaviorist Views It." The theoretical goal of psychology, Watson claimed, "is the prediction and control of behavior . . . nor is the scientific value of its data dependent upon the readiness with which they lend themselves to interpretation in terms of consciousness."[61]

The abruptness of Watson's revolution is all the more striking when we consider that his advisers were none other than James Angell and John Dewey. They were clearly unhappy with his conclusions, and only in recognition of his rigorous methodology and brilliance did they confer the Ph.D. Indeed, Angell even told Watson that his ideas were inappropriate for humans and belonged confined to animal subjects.[62] The contrast between Dewey and Watson, in fact, represents the most fundamental difference between the deliberative and group-behavioral models of democracy. Dewey had made, in 1898, a landmark critique of the stimulus-response model of the mind. In that essay, "The Reflex Arc Concept in Psychology," Dewey argued that the mind guides the individual proactively to each new stimulus, and so it cannot be considered just a reactive phenomenon.[63] Watson not only defied this viewpoint, but authored a mountain of essays and popular books claiming exactly the reverse. In his 1928 bestseller, *Behaviorism,* Watson wrote: "We feel quite sure now . . . that the simple process of conditioning is quite sufficient to account for the genesis and growth of all emotional complexity."[64]

The similarities and differences between Bentley and Watson are instructive. Both adopted a nearly absolute cynicism about ethics, meaning, and language. All that mattered to Bentley was the interests of the group; all that mattered to Watson was the response to a stimulus. Meaning was explicitly banished from their models. The chief difference between these two thinkers lay in the fact that Bentley was also cynical about individuals: he saw them simply as products of their groups. To

Watson, the individual was the basic unit of analysis. Although substantial, these differences did not preclude a neat merger of the two viewpoints in the emerging practice of direct democracy. Since mobilizing groups to vote in certain ways would become the chief goal of politics, then Watson's theory of finding appropriate stimuli to produce that behavior would be the ideal practical tool. Since the ethical content of the stimulus is irrelevant to its effectiveness, "direct democracy" could be taken in any possible direction, including away from genuine democracy (understood as self-determination).

It is quite fitting that after John Watson was forced (because of an extramarital affair) in 1920 to leave his academic position at Johns Hopkins, he landed a job at the J. Walter Thompson Advertising Agency, the nation's leading agency by total billings from the 1920s until the 1970s. There he became a vice president and directed such ad campaigns as that for Pond's Skin Freshener and Cleansing Tissues. He did so, moreover, while publishing widely on behaviorism and enjoying the height of his fame, his name now becoming a veritable household word through a torrent of popular magazine articles on child-rearing and other subjects. Watson, in his own words, writing to his admirer Bertrand Russell, had "begun to learn that it can be just as thrilling to watch the growth of a sales curve of a new product as to watch the learning curve of animals or men."[65]

A fascinating debate has been conducted by scholars of both advertising and psychology about Watson's relative influence on commercial practices. He himself denied in an interview conducted in the 1950s that he had had much impact.[66] A former Thompson Agency colleague agreed, and summed the relationship this way: "Advertising absorbed John . . . without absorbing much of his psychology."[67] I think this view of the matter is most appropriate. The more interesting aspect of this crossover between social and commercial science is the alacrity with which Stanley Resor, the president of J. Walter Thompson (Yale graduate and lifelong disciple of his favorite teacher, the Social Darwinist William Graham Sumner), recruited Watson.[68]

What really matters is not the impact of Watson or Bentley, per se, but rather the wholesale accommodation by social scientists of the market model to the problem of social leadership. By the end of the Great War, social science was increasingly receptive to "scientism," an overwrought faith in the value-free objectivity of the disciplines. Dorothy Ross and others have made a convincing case that the turn toward scientism became hegemonic during the 1920s. Even figures close to the Addams/Dewey/Mead circle like Charles Merriam made this transformation, according to Ross: "Whereas in the progressive mode he had offered a science that was part of history and encouraged reform by informing the people about the interdependence of society, he now proposed a science defined by 'method,' oriented to 'control,' and sustained by organized professional structures to promote research."[69] "Control," in fact, was fast becoming a central keyword in the 1920s, appearing ominously in many titles.[70] When we consider the axioms of Bentley ("when the group is stated, everything is stated") and Watson (the goal of psychology "is the prediction and control of behavior"), it appears that all the ingredients were in place by the 1920s for an instrumental approach to democracy — one that completely abandoned the deliberative approach of the Chicago Pragmatists.[71]

What I am calling the group behavioral theory of democratic justice was never formally codified as such during the Progressive Era, but its elements did evolve into the theory of Liberal Pluralism associated with the work of David Truman, Robert Dahl, Seymour Martin Lipset, and Richard Hofstadter in the 1950s.[72] How to combine Watson's ideas with those of Bentley was something that practicing politicians and the sensational media titans like William Randolph Hearst and Joseph Pulitzer did not need to learn in graduate school.

This group behavioral approach to multicultural ethics was far less cumbersome to implement than that of the Chicago Pragmatists. Indeed, it was quantifiable and subject to scientific principles, consonant with the scientistic methods that evolved at the University of Chicago's National Opinion Research Center (NORC) by the 1920s. The difference was between an intersubjective dialogue about value orientations and an objectifying manipulation of targetable group characteristics. In short, multiculturalism was reduced to the instrumental rationality that Weber warned us about in his famous outline of the "iron cage." The rationality of means was used to replace a rationality about the ends we ought to pursue.

Conclusion

Progressives were usually animated by overtly ethical goals: what kind of society we all should live within was their primary concern. Progressives like Jane Addams wanted a society in which immigrant cultural values were shared with those of native Protestants in an ongoing process of seeing the connections we all have with one another. They wanted to simplify the institutional apparatus so that these ethical goals could be achieved. Ironically, however, they inadvertently implemented structures of practice that empowered cynical methods of manipulation that promote precisely the nightmare opposite of the society they hoped to achieve. A multicultural society is now one in which group can be pitted against group with remarkable efficiency, rather than one in which members of diverse groups deliberate with each other about the contrasts between their alternative views of the good life.

Advocates of deliberative democracy never developed a sufficient institutional program to make their goals viable. If democracy was to be realized in the process of intersubjective communication, as Dewey, Mead, and Addams consistently claimed, then they needed to assure that some structure for this kind of action guarded against the manipulations promoted by their colleagues Bentley and Watson. As it happened, their ideas could not thrive because they failed to see how their own institutional goals worked against their ethical goals. Bentley and Watson did not make this mistake.

Deliberative democracy of the type that Dewey, Addams, and Mead began to invent and which many today hope to revive requires a firewall between the capitalist marketplace and the structures of participation. But how to pry our politics free from the gears of the money machines is not at all clear. The Chicago Pragmatists provide no help on this question: long on complaints about the abuses of individual capitalists, they never developed a sufficient critique of capitalism itself. Fixated on the benefits of modernity, they never appreciated the extent to which capitalism could fasten its own moral void on the contents of political participation. Any attempt to revive the promise of deliberative democracy today will need to extricate our metropolitan multicultural publics from this thralldom of the marketplace, and to dethrone the hegemony of Bentley's dictum, "when the group is stated, everything is stated."

Undoing the institutional wreckage of the Progressive reformers will require emulating them in their fearless immersion into constitutional change. Whether the intellectuals of today can muster the courage to battle interests far more entrenched today (ironically, in the name of direct democracy), as their forebears did circa 1900, however, remains to be seen.

Notes

This essay is adapted from *The Metropolitan Crisis of Modernity in the United States, 1890s–1920s.* Forthcoming from the University of North Carolina Press. Used with permission of the publisher. It was presented at the conference entitled "Progressivism, Then and Now," organized by the editors of this volume, Sidney Milkis and Jerome Mileur. I want to thank the organizers and participants of that conference for their helpful remarks. I also wish to thank Sidney Milkis, Jerome Mileur, Steven Ross, and the members of the Los Angeles Social History Study Group, for their incisive criticism of earlier drafts.

1. Warren E. Miller and J. Merrill Shanks, *The New American Voter* (Cambridge: Harvard University Press, 1996), 39–69.

2. See Ronald Dworkin, "The Curse of American Politics," *New York Review of Books,* 17 October 1996, 19–24. Even the self-nominating millionaires like Ron Unz are switching to more direct methods. " 'For a politician you spend a lot of money and you probably lose,' Unz said while crowing about his initiative's victory." "With the initiative process, you can have a lot more direct impact, and if you can get your thing on the ballot [*sic*], there's a good chance you'll win." "Direct" is the keyword here. Unz spent $700,000 of his own cash to pay workers to gather the necessary 430,000 signatures to qualify a measure of his own authorship for an initiative vote by the electors of the ninth largest economy in the world. It passed handily, prodding the voters' chronic fears about the perils of a diverse society. Frank Bruni, "The California Entrepreneur Who Beat Bilingual Teaching," *New York Times,* 14 June 1998, A1.

3. Philip J. Ethington, *The Public City: The Political Construction of Urban Life in San Francisco, 1850–1900* (New York: Cambridge University Press, 1994).

4. R. Jeffrey Lustig writes: "Even the emergence of identity politics—the inclination to cast one's interests as identity interests—is a historically shaped occurrence. One of the limitations of identity politics is that it tends to discourage recognition of this fact." From "Race, Class and Politics: Universalism in the Shadow of Identity," paper presented to the Western Political Science Association, Tucson, Arizona, 13–15 March 1997. Copy in possession of author.

5. Richard Hofstadter, *The Age of Reform: From Bryan to FDR* (New York: Alfred A. Knopf, 1955); Eldon Eisenach, *The Lost Promise of Progressivism* (Lawrence: University Press of Kansas, 1994). Eisenach achieves a singular definition of "Progressive" only at the cost of excluding such figures as Woodrow Wilson and Louis Brandeis. Most unaccountably, he excludes the most prominent political scientists and historians: John W. Burgess, J. Franklin Jameson (explicitly), Frank Goodnow, and Charles Beard (by omission). Further, within his "Progressive" group he glosses over the stark differences between such figures as the antiracist Jane Addams and the virulent racist E. A. Ross.

6. Eisenach, *Lost Promise,* 72.

7. Barry D. Karl, *Charles E. Merriam and the Study of Politics* (Chicago: University of Chicago Press, 1974), 210–11, and passim.

8. The sources for my claims in the previous two paragraphs are numerous,

but see, in addition to Eisenach, *The Lost Promise,* James T. Kloppenberg, *Uncertain Victory: Social Democracy and Progressivism in European and American Thought, 1870–1920* (New York: Oxford University Press, 1986); Dorothy Ross, *The Origins of American Social Science* (New York: Cambridge University Press, 1991); Robyn Muncy, *Creating a Female Dominion in American Reform, 1890–1930* (New York: Oxford University Press, 1991); Kenneth Finegold, *Experts and Politicians: Reform Challenges to Machine Politics in New York, Cleveland, and Chicago* (Princeton: Princeton University Press, 1995).

9. Sheldon S. Wolin, "Fugitive Democracy," in Benhabib, *Democracy and Difference,* 31–45, quotation at p. 34.

10. Generations of constitutional scholarship have confirmed the profound conservatism of the Founders at Philadelphia: first boldly detailed by the Progressive historian Charles Beard. In comparative perspective, an impressive array of scholars has demonstrated a familiar pattern in the Euro-American revolutionary process: elites unleashing real popular sovereignty and then quashing it again with either constitutional or authoritarian representational regimes. Lester Langley, *The Americas in the Age of Revolution, 1750–1850* (New Haven: Yale University Press, 1996); Eric Hobsbawm, *The Age of Revolution, 1789–1848* (New York: New American Library, 1962); Jackson Turner Main, *The Anti-Federalists: Critics of the Constitution, 1781–1788* (Chicago: Quadrangle, 1964); Gordon Wood, *The Creation of the American Republic, 1776–1787* (New York: Norton, 1972).

11. C. Vann Woodward, *The Strange Career of Jim Crow* 2d. rev. ed. (New York: Oxford University Press, 1966); J. Morgan Kousser, *The Shaping of Southern Politics: Suffrage Restriction and the Establishment of the One-Party South, 1880–1910* (New Haven: Yale University Press, 1974).

12. Based on a list compiled by Erica Judge, in *The Encyclopedia of New York City,* ed. Kenneth B. Jackson (New Haven: Yale University Press, 1995), 819–20.

13. Ethington, *The Public City.*

14. Jürgen Habermas, "Three Normative Models of Democracy," in Benhabib, *Democracy and Difference,* 21. Most of Habermas's very large opus is a case for deliberative democracy in some way, but see his recent work in *Moral Consciousness and Communicative Action,* trans. Christian Lenhardt and Shierry Weber Nicholsen (Cambridge: MIT Press, 1995). An excellent introduction is Stephen K. White, *The Recent Work of Jürgen Habermas: Reason, Justice, and Modernity* (New York: Cambridge University Press, 1988).

15. Iris Marion Young, "Communication and the Other: Beyond Deliberative Democracy," in Benhabib, *Democracy and Difference,* 121.

16. Kathryn Kish Sklar, "Hull House in the 1890s: A Community of Women Reformers," *Signs* 10, 4 (1985): 658–77; Allen Davis, *Spearheads for Reform: The Social Settlements and the Progressive Movement, 1890–1914* (New York: Oxford University Press, 1967).

17. Dewey's circle was dubbed the "Chicago School" by an admiring William James in 1904. "A real school and real thought," James wrote concerning

Studies in Logical Theory. "At Harvard we have plenty of thought, but no school. At Yale and Cornell, the other way about." Quoted in Robert B. Westbrook, *John Dewey and American Democracy* (Ithaca: Cornell University Press, 1991), 72, 77.

18. Jürgen Habermas, *The Theory of Communicative Action, Volume 2: Lifeworld and System: A Critique of Functionalist Reason,* trans. Thomas McCarthy (Boston: Beacon Press, 1987), 1–113; Axel Honneth, *The Fragmented World of the Social: Essays in Social and Political Philosophy,* ed. Charles W. Wright (Albany: State University of New York Press, 1995); Hans Joas, *Pragmatism and Social Theory* (Chicago: University of Chicago Press, 1993); James T. Kloppenberg, *Uncertain Victory;* Westbrook, *John Dewey.*

19. The standard works are Allen Davis, *The American Heroine: The Life and Legend of Jane Addams* (New York: Oxford University Press, 1973); and Christopher Lasch, "Jane Addams: The College Woman and the Family Claim," in *The New Radicalism in America, 1889–1963: The Intellectual as a Social Type* (New York: Chatto and Windus, 1966), 3–37; but see especially Jean Bethke Elshtain, "Jane Addams," in *A Companion to American Thought,* ed. Richard Wightman Fox and James T. Kloppenberg (Cambridge, Mass.: Basil Blackwell, 1995), 14–16.

20. I am indebted to Terrence McDonald for making me aware of the radical implications of these essays. His own interpretation of the way Addams and her colleagues reformulated liberalism is partially stated in his introduction to William L. Riordan, *Plunkitt of Tammany Hall* (Boston: St. Martins, 1994), 1–41. Jane Addams, "Ethical Survivals in Municipal Corruption," *International Journal of Ethics* 8, 3 (April 1898): 273–89; Addams, "Why the Ward Boss Rules," *Outlook* 58 (2 April 1898): 879–89; reprinted in Christopher Lasch, *The Social Thought of Jane Addams* (Indianapolis: Bobbs-Merrill, 1965), 124–33. Quotations and citations will be from the longer *International Journal of Ethics* version when material is exclusive to that version. When I quote material common to both, I will cite the *Outlook* version, with the pagination from the reprint in Lasch, *Social Thought.*

21. Addams, "Why the Ward Boss Rules," 126.

22. Addams, "Ethical Survivals," 274, 279, 285.

23. Elisabeth Lasch-Quinn, *Black Neighbors: Race and the Limits of Reform in the American Settlement House Movement, 1890–1945* (Chapel Hill: University of North Carolina Press, 1993); Rivka Shpak Lissak, *Pluralism and Progressives: Hull House and the New Immigrants, 1890–1919* (Chicago: University of Chicago Press, 1989).

24. Addams, "Why the Ward Boss Rules," 133.

25. Jane Addams, *Democracy and Social Ethics* (New York: Macmillan, 1902), 240–42.

26. Addams, "Ethical Survivals," 285, 274.

27. Addams, "Why the Ward Boss Rules," 133.

28. Addams, "Ethical Survivals," 291.

29. Mead, *Mind, Self, and Society,* 140, 150–51, 153–54, 152–64, 155.

30. Mead, "Review of Jane Addams's *The Newer Ideals of Peace,*" *American*

Journal of Sociology 13 (1907): 127, quoted in Shalin, "G. H. Mead, Socialism, and the Progressive Agenda," 928.

31. Mead quoted in Shalin, "G. H. Mead, Socialism, and the Progressive Agenda," 929.

32. Ibid.

33. Mead, *Mind, Self, and Society,* 140.

34. These ideas were developed in Mead, "Natural Rights and the Theory of Political Institutions," *Journal of Philosophy* 12 (1915): 141–55, and reprinted in Mead, *Mind, Self, and Society.* Quotations at 269, 271.

35. See especially Lissak, *Pluralism and Progressives;* Lasch-Quinn, *Black Neighbors.*

36. W.E.B. Du Bois, *The Souls of Black Folk* (New York: Signet, 1995), 45.

37. Ibid., 108.

38. Young, "Communication and the Other," 127.

39. Sidney M. Milkis and Daniel J. Tichenor, "'Direct Democracy' and Social Justice: The Progressive Party Campaign of 1912," *Studies in American Political Development* 8, 2 (1994): 262–340.

40. James Connolly, *The Triumph of Ethnic Progressivism: Political Culture in Boston, 1900–1925* (Cambridge: Harvard University Press, 1998); William Leuchtenberg, *The Perils of Prosperity, 1914–1932* (Chicago: University of Chicago Press, 1958); Kenneth T. Jackson, *The Ku Klux Klan in the City, 1915–1930* (New York: Oxford University Press, 1967); William R. Tuttle Jr., *Race Riot: Chicago in the Red Summer of 1919* (New York: Atheneum, 1970).

41. The Progressives (of all stripes), as Eisenach rightly argues, had an almost mystical faith in the power of "public opinion" to overwhelm private interests, if those interests could just be separated from the levers of power they held in parties and bureaucracies. See Eisenach, *Lost Promise,* 74–103.

42. Mead, "Working Hypothesis in Social Reform," *American Journal of Sociology* 5, 3 (Nov. 1899), 368.

43. Quoted in Shalin, "G. H. Mead, Socialism, and the Progressive Agenda," 933.

44. The literature on this development is vast, but see especially Richard Wightman Fox and T. J. Jackson Lears, eds., *The Culture of Consumption: Critical Essays in American History, 1880–1980* (New York: Pantheon Books, 1983); Stuart Ewen, *Captains of Consciousness: Advertising and the Social Roots of the Consumer Culture* (New York: McGraw Hill, 1976); Roland Marchand, *Advertising the American Dream: Making Way for Modernity, 1920–1940* (Berkeley: University of California Press, 1985); Lary May, *Screening Out the Past: The Birth of Mass Culture and the Motion Picture Industry* (Chicago: University of Chicago Press, 1983); Roy Rosenzweig, *Eight Hours for What We Will: Workers and Leisure in an Industrial City, 1870–1920* (New York: Cambridge University Press, 1983).

45. Quoted in Kerry W. Buckley, *Mechanical Man: John Broadus Watson and the Beginnings of Behaviorism* (New York: Guilford Press, 1989), 136.

46. Deborah J. Coon, "'Not a Creature of Reason': The Alleged Impact of

Watsonian Behaviorism on Advertising in the 1920s," in *Modern Perspectives on John B. Watson and Classical Behaviorism,* ed. James T. Todd and Edward K. Morris (Westport, Conn.: Greenwood Press, 1994), 61, 379.

47. The general trends are treated by Jackson Lears, *Fables of Abundance: A Cultural History of Advertising in America* (New York: Basic Books, 1994). The ironic connection between truth-in-advertising laws and the shift to nonrational appeals is made by Coon, " 'Not a Creature of Reason,' " 61.

48. Herbert Croly, *Progressive Democracy* (New York: Macmillan, 1915), 263–64.

49. Ibid., 268.

50. Lears, *Fables of Abundance,* 218–21.

51. Carey McWilliams, "Government by Whitaker and Baxter," *The Nation,* 14, 21 April, 5 May 1951.

52. Joe Kennedy quoted in Garry Wills, *The Kennedy Imprisonment: A Meditation on Power* (Boston: Little, Brown, 1982); Michael Paul Rogin, *Ronald Reagan, The Movie and Other Episodes in Political Demonology* (Berkeley: University of California Press, 1987).

53. Arthur F. Bentley, *The Process of Government: A Study of Social Pressures* (Chicago: University of Chicago Press, 1908), 208–9.

54. Bentley was also one of the most idiosyncratic intellectuals, and not the kind of person to build a "school" with lots of adherents. He was an irascible, ruthless thinker. "The most immediately striking feature of his book, *The Process of Government: A Study of Social Pressures,*" Dorothy Ross observes, "was its attack on just about everyone." Dorothy Ross, *The Origins of American Social Science,* 330.

55. "It was not the *discovery* of groups in society that marked the breakthrough of the 1890s, but the *legitimation* of groups in a pluralist ethics." Ethington, *The Public City,* 11.

56. Quoted in Richard L. McCormick, *The Party Period and Public Policy: American Politics from the Age of Jackson to the Progressive Era* (New York: Oxford University Press, 1986), 303.

57. Quoted in Richard Hofstadter, *The American Political Tradition and the Men Who Made It* (New York: Vintage, 1973), 330.

58. Bentley, *Process of Government,* 16.

59. I treat this discourse at greater length in the forthcoming book from which this essay is drawn: *The Metropolitan Crisis of Modernity in the United States, 1890s–1920s* (Chapel Hill: University of North Carolina Press).

60. Bentley, *Process of Government,* 15–16.

61. Buckley, *Mechanical Man,* 33–58; David Cohen, *J. B. Watson: The Founder of Behaviorism, A Biography* (London: Routledge and Kegan Paul, 1979), 5–50; John B. Watson, "Psychology as the Behaviorist Views It," *Psychological Review* 20 (1913): 158–77, quotation at 158.

62. Cohen, *J. B. Watson,* 34–35.

63. Alan Ryan, *John Dewey and the High Tide of American Liberalism* (New York: W. W. Norton, 1995), 124–26.

64. Quoted in Coon, "'Not a Creature of Reason,'" 47.

65. Buckley, *Mechanical Man,* 148–76; Cohen, *J. B. Watson,* 113–95; Watson to Russell quoted in Buckley, 136.

66. Otis Pease, *The Responsibilities of American Advertising: Private Control and Public Influence, 1920–1940* (1958) (New York: Arno Reprint, 1976). Pease argues that Watson was influential, while Stephen R. Fox, *The Mirror Makers: A History of Modern Advertising and Its Creators* (New York: Morrow, 1984), argues the opposite.

67. Quoted in Fox, *Mirror Makers,* 86.

68. Buckley, *Mechanical Man,* 135–36.

69. Dorothy Ross, *The Origins of American Social Science,* 396. Ross cites here Charles E. Merriam, "The Present State of the Study of Politics," *American Political Science Review* 15 (May 1921): 174, 177, 176.

70. Robert Park wrote *The Immigrant Press and Its Control* (New York: Harper and Brothers, 1922), a study concerned with the possibility of "Americanizing" immigrants within the constraints of mass-circulation newspapers in foreign languages. Merriam and Harold F. Gosnell published *Non-Voting: Causes and Methods of Control* (Chicago: University of Chicago Press, 1924), a landmark study using quantitative methods.

71. See notes 53 and 61.

72. See R. Jeffrey Lustig, *Corporate Liberalism: The Origins of Modern American Political Theory, 1890–1920* (Berkeley: University of California Press, 1982); Paul F. Kress, *Social Science and the Idea of Process: The Ambiguous Legacy of Arthur F. Bentley* (Urbana: University of Illinois Press, 1970); David Truman, *The Governmental Process* (New York: Knopf, 1951); Michael P. Rogin, *The Intellectuals and McCarthy: The Radical Specter* (Cambridge: MIT Press, 1967).

Progressive Internationalism

Eldon J. Eisenach

Progressive internationalism is an integral part of Progressive nationalism in that the Progressive view of the future of America as a national community is inseparable from its view of America as the dominant force for justice in the world community. This is not to repeat the commonplace that "foreign policy" expresses the imperatives of "domestic policy" and is therefore dependent upon those imperatives, but rather that both domestic and foreign policy flow from a common source of ideas and institutional values.

This view of Progressive internationalism is more clearly seen when one steps back from partisan-electoral politics and looks instead to the deeper intellectual and cultural currents that increasingly held sway in American public life from the 1890s onward. From here we can see two features that, on the surface at least, seem in some tension. The first is a resurgence of the ideal of America as the covenant nation with a world-redemptive calling. This resurgence was most clearly and convincingly expressed, however, not by Protestant "churchmen," but by philosophers, sociologists, and political economists in the new universities, and their counterparts and followers in the national journalistic and organizational complex that came into being at the same time. It is this second feature that warrants our attention because it at once redescribes a long-standing component of American identity and transforms that identity into a set of highly sophisticated ideas and explanations that integrated local, national, and international events, issues, and politics.

A good illustration of this conflation is the publication of *The New Encyclopedia of Social Reform,* edited by William D. P. Bliss and published in 1908. Successor to a less ambitious version published eleven years earlier, this new edition promises in its subtitle to be a compendium of "all social-reform movements and activities, and the economic, industrial, and sociological facts and statistics of all countries and all social subjects." The articles, statistical tables, reform organization listings and, especially, the biographies portray social reform as the common enterprise of the civilized world, flowing inexorably from the lives and thoughts of its most intellectually and morally advanced citizens. Every major heading views the status and progress of reform in a comparative perspective. While prominence is given to America and Americans, Great Britain and Germany are always featured and statistical data from every region of the world are presented in superabundance.

Article contributors to the *New Encyclopedia* are overwhelmingly American Progressives, with a sprinkling of British Fabians and Liberal M.P.s and a few German Social Democrats and academics. American contributors include social workers Edward Devine and Florence Kelley, economists John R. Commons and Arthur Twining Hadley, sociologists Franklin Giddings and Charles Ellwood, labor leaders Samuel Gompers and Morris Hilquit, clergymen reformers Graham Taylor and J. Cardinal Gibbons, and celebrity reformers and war horses such as Booker T. Washington and William Lloyd Garrison. Billed also as "contributing," but only because their writings are extensively quoted, are Jane Addams, Richard Ely, Josiah Strong, Sidney Webb, and President Theodore Roosevelt.

Bliss (1856–1926), like so many of the founding generation of Progressives, had a New England and clergyman background.[1] Indeed, his parents were serving as Congregational missionaries in Turkey when he was born. After a degree at Amherst College, Bliss himself studied divinity at Hartford Seminary. While Bliss devoted his life to reform organizations and journalism and developed close ties to American academics through his encyclopedia ventures, his religious background permeated his reform activities and constituted an important source of his internationalism.[2] The *New Encyclopedia* reflects this combination: its headings "Christ and Social Reform," "Christian Socialism," "Christianity and Social Reform," and "Church and Social Reform" rival in extent and scope such seemingly more central topics as "Child Labor" and "Factory Legislation." The *New Encyclopedia,* one of the most sophisticated and cosmopolitan compilations of social data and legislation in its day, can be read as a handbook for a Social Gospel Internationale. Encoded in this handbook is a sort of Church invisible, headquartered in America but with powerful centers throughout the English-speaking world and in the advanced states in Europe, especially Germany. Its leading lights are academic social scientists and reform leaders whose ideas and spirit radiate throughout many hundreds of reform organizations, many thousands of periodicals, books, and pamphlets, and many millions of enthusiastic followers. America is the leading national actor, Bliss's *New Encyclopedia* seems to say, and its stage is the whole world.

This essay proceeds by examining two frameworks through which Progressive internationalism was shaped and expressed: the intellectual/institutional and the political/economic. It moves then to the mobilization for and entry into World War I, seen as both an apotheosis of Progressivism and the moment of its sudden fragmentation. Nevertheless, Progressive internationalism was institutionalized and persisted in the 1920s and 1930s, and became resurgent during World War II and the Cold War, often driving domestic policy away from some of its Democratic Party and New Deal directions and into earlier nationalist Progressive (and Republican) pathways. Following an examination of this period, the essay concludes by examining current struggles over the meaning and legacy of Progressivism as indicators of the alternative paths that seem available for any future restoration of national reform liberalism in America.

The Intellectual/Institutional Framework

We wish, fully and entirely, TO NATIONALIZE THE INSTITUTIONS OF OUR LAND AND TO IDENTIFY OURSELVES WITH OUR COUNTRY; to become a single great people, separate and distinct in national character, political interest, social and civil affinities from any and all other nations, kindred and people on the earth.

—*American Republican,* 7 November 1844

Here is a "Progressive" call to arms — but one voiced in 1844 in a Whig Party newspaper. My point is a simple one. The intellectual founders of Progressive internationalism were Whig-Republican, enthusiastically Protestant, of New England ancestry, and shared a biblical-historicist and social-evolutionary view of America. In their view, the American nation was from the start a "world-historical" people whose political and institutional history was only the overt expression of the unfolding of a covenantal and prefigured destiny. Rooted in the Calvinist and Puritan hermeneutic of Israel and its promised rebirth and victory, it was the rebirth of the American nation under Abraham Lincoln that was, for the Progressives, the defining moment in American/biblical history and prophecy. Perhaps the greatest literary expressions of this idea are Lincoln's second inaugural address and Julia Ward Howe's "Battle Hymn of the Republic."

This "nationalist" intellectual background to Progressive internationalism has an institutional counterpart. Prior to the Civil War there were very few "national" institutions in America. The federal government as defined by constitutional law encoded separate sovereignties, limited national power, and individual and states' rights. The mass-based and electorally oriented political parties were local in the extreme, both in their organization and in their coalitional function. While there were national "movement" parties (e.g., anti-Masonic league, Liberty Party) prior to the Republican Party, the dominant electoral parties reinforced federalism and provided the patronage conduit for the mobilization of local interests and loyalties. There was, however, one set of antebellum institutional structures that was national in intent, organization, and reach — religion, especially its "parachurch" reform and philanthropic offshoots. This complex of ecumenical reform and missionary organizations existing before the Civil War, has been aptly termed "the benevolent empire" or "the evangelical united front."[3] When one includes the individual churches and their local societies, as well as the colleges and seminaries that supplied trained personnel and intellectual leadership, this complex was indeed a potential competitor to political parties for the dominance of our politics and public opinion at the national level. But until the slavery issue emerged in the 1850s, this national complex was more a "voluntarist" alternative than a direct challenge to electoral and party politics. Because of their British connections, the prominence of women and clergymen, and the stress on moral and religious regeneration, these institutions, including the academic ones, symbolized deep estrangement from the increasingly tough, masculine, violent, and interest-dominated universe of party-electoral politics in the Jacksonian era.[4] The Civil War and Lincoln changed all that — at least for one shining moment. When this set of national counterinstitutions did mobilize politically and electorally in the 1850s, the Whig Party disintegrated, the Democratic Party fractured, and the Republican Party was born.[5] It was this memory and model and this institutional setting that formed the organizational and ancestral-cultural nidus from which Progressive national-internationalism was born. Indeed, the parents of almost the entire first generation of Progressive intellectuals were active abolitionists and Republican leaders.[6]

It was American churchmen, moreover, who taught the early Progressive philosophers, sociologists, and political economists to think in historical-national ways. In the decades prior to the Civil War, American churchmen went to German universities to study the ways in which German scholars had translated narrowly theological and evangelical ideas into a more philosophical and sociological language. This romanticized and historicized translation also transformed theology and moral philosophy into the more political and reformist ideas of national development and the world-historical role of advanced nations. While the Unitarians of Harvard could be said to have played an important role — five of the six Divinity School faculty under its dean, Charles Everett (1878–1900), had studied in Germany — it was Yale and liberal evangelical theology that carried the day after the Civil War, and it was this transposed liberal-evangelical image of America that served as the template of Progressive nationalism and internationalism. Not surprisingly, from this Yale milieu emerged the founding presidents of the three new leading graduate universities: Daniel Coit Gilman at Johns Hopkins, Andrew Dickson White at Cornell, and William Rainey Harper at Chicago. Presidents of two other leading graduate centers, Henry P. Tappan at Michigan and John Bascom at Wisconsin, began their careers as churchmen. Along with Harvard, Columbia, and Yale, these new institutions quickly became powerful intellectual centers for the Progressive critique of American political life and its prevailing moral-political culture.[7]

The academic journals and professional associations established by faculty in these new universities are all listed in Bliss's *New Encyclopedia* as part of the world movement for social reform, and properly so, for these associations and journals, along with the universities that housed them, were profoundly at odds with the dominant public philosophies and party-ruled politics of their day. Their shared historical-evolutionary perspective, their analysis of political, economic, and social institutions and practices as parts of larger organic relationships, and their stress on interdependence, cooperation, and the socially formed self were far removed from the hyperindividualism built into America's Gilded Age constitutional, legal, and party-political culture. In their view, America could only be understood as a national culture, a national economy, and increasingly, a powerful national state with major interests to project and to protect in a world of powerful nation states. Taking their cue from the sudden political and economic emergence of Germany, where most of them had studied, they saw our localized party and patronage system, the protection of local monopolies and small producer capitalism, and prevailing constitutional doctrine as deep-seated barriers to American development and to the achievement of social justice.[8] Paradoxically — and this cannot be stressed too much — one of the *greatest* barriers to the achievement of national responsibility, national purpose, and national citizenship was the federal government itself. Ruled by an interest-dominated Congress, bereft of a talented and energetic civil service, and profligate and wasteful to a degree that put the powerful European nation states to shame, the national government was less reliable as a vehicle for nation building than were many state governments, advanced municipalities, and, of course, the emerging national universities, professional associations, and reform societies.[9] These latter "parastates" — like the institutions of the "benevolent empire" and "evangelical united front" that preceded them — were emerging as a powerful intellectual, moral, and political counterculture to the dominant one and became increasingly linked through the new mass circulation magazines of the day.[10]

The books, articles, and lectures by philosophers like John Dewey and James Tufts, sociologists like Thomas Horton Cooley and Albion Small, and political economists like Simon Patten and Richard Ely at once articulated this new social and historical philosophy and mobilized a new nationally oriented citizenship dedicated to consciously formulated ideals of social justice. Because this philosophy flowed so seamlessly from a common evangelical and biblical-historical background, these writers found a ready-made and rapidly growing audience and used familiar styles and models for reaching that audience. This complex of Progressive institutions, connected by the new journalism and animated by a shared spirit, represented not only a powerful rebirth of the older ecumenical united front, it now directly and successfully challenged the political parties as the primary engine driving the political agenda and the national mobilization of public opinion.[11] The political reforms it inspired defunded, demoralized, and demobilized the political parties, placing the (now considerably diminished) electorate increasingly in the hands of the "nonpartisan" reform press and the intellectuals and activists of the Progressive movement.[12]

This connection may now be restated directly in terms of internationalism. Protestant theology in America was always "internationalist" in the way in which the American Church cum American nation was seen as the critical actor in the fulfillment of a universal sacred history and prophecy.[13] By the turn of the century, this national theology had been relocated in the universities and into the new historical-evolutionary social sciences and philosophy — sciences and philosophies with international sources and audiences.[14] This relocation and redirection tended to deepen its intellectual power, broaden its reach, and tie it more directly to the state — not least because it had already become severed from an ever smaller and narrower denominational church base. It was this transformed and relocated vision of America that provided the animating political spirit opposed to the dominant party-electoral and court system.

The internationalist side of this organizational complex was most manifest in the foreign missionary societies and in the cross-national movements against child labor and drunkenness, and for compulsory schooling, women's rights, workmen's compensation, and factory legislation. On college and university campuses at the turn of the century, organizations like the Student Volunteer Movement to recruit candidates for foreign missions complemented the huge international programming and presence of the YMCA and the World Student Christian Federation.[15] The organizers of women's clubs, settlement houses, and the emerging profession of social work also saw their institutions as part of an international crusade for justice and developed many international ties and alliances. In marked contrast to national political parties, these national reform institutions were international and cosmopolitan as well. This internationalism was strongly reflected in and encouraged by the new higher journalism, especially in successful periodicals like Albert Shaw's *Review of Reviews* and Walter Hines Page's *World's Work,* journals that in turn influenced more popular mass-circulation magazines.

Symbolically, the meeting point between the older evangelical theology and the new social science was the same as that between the older institutional churches and the new university: it was the "social gospel." Always the province of lay leaders and ecumenical reform organizations, social Christianity became increasingly "post-Protestant" as it became institutionalized in graduate departments, the settlement movement, the new journalism, and the institutions comprising the women's movement. To these "ministers of reform," the terms "to democratize," "to Christianize," "to Americanize," "to nationalize," and "to internationalize" were largely interchangeable: they all meant to be animated by the moral ideals of personal responsibility, social justice, and a democratic community.[16] If "Christianize" necessarily pointed both to the nation-people and beyond it to the larger world, so too did "nationalize" and even "Americanize." This "people" must have a self-conscious identity and shared purpose, constituting, in the words of the Whig editorialist in 1844, a "race" distinct from "all other nations, kindred, and people on the earth," whose spirit and purposes are destined to rule the world.

The Political/Economic Framework

The civilized nations of the old world will yet do homage to the wisdom and learning, the science and arts of our people, and the combined powers of all Europe shall bow before the majesty of our power.

—*American Republican,* 7 November 1844

Among all the agencies for the shaping of the future of the human race, none seems so potent now, and still more, hereafter, than the English-speaking man. Already he begins to dominate the world. . . . Their citizens, with all their faults, are leading the van of civilization.

—William Thomas Stead, *Review of Reviews* (British), 1890

Given this intellectual and institutional background, it is not surprising that the earliest and most sophisticated American political economists were quick to shape their writings within these larger contours. The social evolutionary perspective posited both increasing integration of economic units and their increasing interdependence — all pointing to a coming era where individualist competition is increasingly supplanted by cooperation and mutual responsibility. When these phenomena are accompanied by vast improvements in productivity, lower costs, and high wages, a higher morality and a higher standard of living necessarily follow. In the words of Columbia Professor Edwin Seligman, "with every improvement in the material conditions of the great mass of the population there will be an opportunity for the unfolding of a higher moral life."[17]

For the Progressive professorate the development of capital-intensive industry, the mechanization of agriculture, and the integration of national and international markets were marks of moral and spiritual progress. Some, like Wharton Professor Simon Patten, saw this as a displacement of a "pain" economy premised on scarcity by a "pleasure" economy resting on abundance. With abundance, competitive motives necessary to insure survival in the older economy of scarcity come increasingly into conflict with the social bonds created by the increasingly interdependent economic networks. Thus, even individual utilities depend on the development of stronger social bonds as expressed in higher conceptions of morality and religion. The virtues demanded in this new age of abundance are "intelligence and self-control."[18] As both an ethical and a social science, political economy describes this new reality and reveals its inner ethical and moral meanings. For Patten, as for Arthur Hadley at Yale, Henry Carter Adams at Michigan, John Bates Clark at Columbia, Richard Ely at Wisconsin, and Albion Small at Chicago, the new industrial economy constitutes a kind of "voluntary socialism," in that wealth production becomes separated from individual ownership of property. As early as 1887, economists like Adams recognized that because "the source of the increment of product is the new [social] relations that men enter into," we can no longer function as "a society whose moral code is expressed in the language of rights" but must instead see ourselves as "a society whose moral code is expressed in the language of duty."[19]

The hostility of these economists to "laissez-faire" was not hostility to markets as such but rather to certain forms of small-producer capitalism that were barriers to economic and moral progress — and were also the mainsprings powering the current party-electoral system. Not only did this earlier form of capitalism necessarily rest on individual ownership and rights claims opposed to the obligations to the larger national community, many of its benefits to individuals flowed not from deserved "profits" but from undeserved monopoly "rents." This rent increment is necessarily entailed in land ownership, but it is also an element wherever local or "main street" advantage prevails. Unlike temporary advantages of successful large scale corporations, the rents of small-producer capitalism are permanently built into local economies and small markets. The coming of national and international markets and the emergence of large-scale business not only dislodges many of these local monopoly rents, it releases these resources into the community in the form of lower prices — even while earning temporary "super-profits" for the entrepreneurs in the process. Local monopoly rent, small producer capitalism, and an ethic of individualism are as inseparably connected as was the new technology, the new industrial economy, and an emerging social ethic. For the founding generation of Progressive political economists — early presidents of the American Economics Association and authors of the first textbooks — "the present struggle is not between the rich and the poor but between centralized and localized wealth."[20] The entire material and moral future of America rested on preventing the forces of the latter from plundering and disabling the former.

The material and moral promise of the new industrial economy was the Progressive answer to the moral and material limits of the older small-producer or "yeoman" economy. That older economy was trapped in individualism and isolated ownership and the often ruthless struggles over scarcity. The new industrial economy promised a future in which stewardship, mutual responsibility, and ever-increasing abundance and leisure would prevail. With every increase in the scale and scope of these enterprises and their connecting links, there would be corresponding opportunities and motivations for individual development of skills and talents.[21]

When Richard Ely declared that "mutual dependence is not slavery" but an invitation to a larger freedom, he was writing an academic epitaph to the American yeoman and small-producer ideal of independence as freedom. The American economy, along with that of England and Germany, was the leading engine in "the evolution of industrial society" and a major factor in the emerging world civilization. Indeed, the very rise of modern industrial society mandated that political economy be a historical and an ethical science because man's spirit was increasingly being revealed in and through these new material forces and institutions. The older science of economics must yield to the new science of political economy because the nation state, not the individual firm, was now the primary economic unit and mechanism of coordination. This also meant that it increasingly fell to the state to underwrite the conditions of future moral progress. In the words of Ely's proposal for founding the American Economics Association: "We regard the state as an educational and ethical agency whose positive aid is an indispensable condition of human progress."[22] This was necessarily true in the case for establishing new standards for industrial relations and in regulating competition among oligopolistic firms. But there were many other reasons as well, reasons that directly tied national economies to international ones. During this period, international capital markets played an increasing role, first in funding American railroads and industry and later in American overseas investments. The mechanization of American agriculture, the development of mass food processing and marketing, and the creation of commodities markets and standards first nationalized and then internationalized agriculture. Indeed, as agriculture in much of the South was becoming increasingly decapitalized and even feudalized, that in the Midwest was literally swamping world markets with its products, making Chicago first the national and then the world center of agricultural commodities.[23]

While many of these changes were taking place as early as the 1870s and 1880s, it was the election of 1896 that marked a decisive shift in policy and practice across many fronts. As a "realigning election," the Republican victory condemned both the Democratic Party and competitive partisanship itself to the margins of national political life.[24] Over the next twelve years, waves of anti-party legislation and values swept the country, especially its more advanced regions, effectively displacing localized and patronage-based parties from their primacy in setting agendas, articulating policy choices, and leading public opinion.[25] This displacement had the effect of suddenly empowering those nationally oriented "parastates" and social forces most determined to "Americanize" (democratize, Christianize) both the country and the world.

Given this freedom from prior electoral (and therefore constitutional) constraints, the major policy changes that followed had the combined effect of committing the national government to an activist international role on a permanent basis. Without recounting this history, its first element was the guarantee of the gold standard, releasing large capital inflows into the American industrial economy and triggering a wave of industrial consolidations and rationalizations.[26] This had the side effect of committing America to a permanent regime of trade and tariff diplomacy premised on reciprocity and international cooperation rather than on a confluence of domestic interests. A second element was the rapprochement with Great Britain, initially occasioned by the need to abrogate the 1850 Clayton-Bulwer Treaty that prevented the United States from constructing the Panama Canal. This new era of cooperation with Britain was strengthened by our sudden naval and colonial expansion into a universe dominated by the British empire. Finally, the remarkable success of our trade expansion abroad and industrial profits at home quickly transformed America from a debtor to a creditor nation. The new need to invest large amounts of capital abroad in order to maintain profits, employment, and financial stability at home only intensified the earlier shifts toward internationalization of our political, economic, and institutional culture.[27]

These shifts in policy and direction may also be stated in spatial terms. From 1896 until the New Deal, national policy reflected the geographical distribution of economic, cultural, and intellectual energies and powers more than it did constitutional separations and distributions of power. This de facto "core" dominance over the periphery — a dominance precluded de jure by our constitutional arrangements — could only prevail if power shifted from locally based political parties to nationally constituted "parastates" and from Congress and the courts to the executive and its allies in the larger society.[28] So long as reform journalism, the new universities and professions, and the myriad reform organizations supported by social gospel values and the organizational network of the ecumenical Protestant establishment kept the "antiparty," or national elements in the Republican Party, dominant, this "core" dominance along the Chicago–New York economic and cultural axis was assured.[29]

Progressive academics, journalists, and reformers were aware of these changes in all of their economic, political, and cultural dimensions. Their writings not only helped to bring these changes about, they integrated these political and economic changes into the cultural-religious meanings of the place of America and Americans in world history. In anti-party reforms, in the increasing divorce of management from owners in corporations, and in the rapid expansion of American products, power, and money abroad, these Progressives and their ever-growing and increasingly self-confident audience saw signs of the spirit revealed. But appropriately, perhaps, it was an Englishman — the liberal reformer, evangelical, and journalist William Stead — who combines the intellectual-institutional and the political-economic sides of Progressive internationalism and who most clearly captures this moment of America on the verge of triumph.

William Thomas Stead, a Gladstonian social reformer and editor of the *Pall Mall Gazette,* is noteworthy in three respects: as founder of both the British and the Americn *Review of Reviews* (1890), as author of a best-selling book, *If Christ Came to Chicago: A Plea for the Union of All Who Love in Service of All Who Suffer* (1894), and as director of a journalistic project tracing America's rise as the world's most dynamic industrial power, compiled and published as *The Americanization of the World* (1902).

The purpose of the two *Reviews* is made clear in the first British issue:

> There exists at this moment no institution which even aspires to be to the English-speaking world what the Catholic Church in its prime was to the intelligence of Christendom. To call attention to the need for such an institution, to enlist the cooperation of all those who will work towards the creation of some such common centre . . . are the ultimate objects for which this review has been established. . . . Already [the English-speaking man] begins to dominate the world. The [British] Empire and the [American] Republic comprise within their limits almost all the territory that remains empty for the overflow of the world. Their citizens, with all their faults, are leading the van of civilization.[30]

While the British *Review* was moderately successful, the American one, taken over by Albert Shaw in 1892, quickly established itself as the leading organ of Progressive internationalism in America.

The series of reports on American economic expansion first appeared in the British *Review of Reviews* in 1901. These reports stressed how American economic growth was coming to dominate world markets, citing as examples the fact that in 1900 the United States was supplying the United Kingdom with over half of its salt pork, more than 70 percent of its live cattle and fresh beef, and almost 90 percent of its bacon and ham.[31] The Steel Trust in America brought in ore by rail to its furnaces at one-fifth the British cost per ton mile; railroad shipping costs for heavy goods were one-half of Germany's and one-fourth of Britain's. This material success, Stead writes, only reflects a deeper cultural and political success: America is forging all the nationalities within her borders "into one dominant American type . . . [creating] one uniform texture of American civilization." Conceding America's dominance and Britain's secondary role, the book concludes with a quotation from Gladstone: "Will it make us, the children of the senior race, living together under [the American's] action, better or worse? Not the manner of producer, but what manner of man is the American of the future to be? How is the majestic figure, who is to become the largest and most powerful on the stage of the world's history, to make use of his power?"[32]

In a sense, Stead had already answered Gladstone's question. *If Christ Came to Chicago* was an impressive piece of investigative journalism into the economic, social, and moral conditions of Chicago.[33] Following a long tribute to Jane Addams and Hull House, Stead concludes his book with a prophecy: having already achieved first rank as an ocean port and as the nation's transport, commercial, and financial center, Chicago is soon to be made the capital of the United States and thus become the "imperial city" of the world. Every Progressive's dream has come true: prosperity, religious unity, housing cooperatives, popular education and culture, free medical care, and municipally owned utilities, stores, banks, gymnasiums, parks — even pawn shops and neighborhood saloons (Stead *was* British) — have made Chicago every reformer's model city. To crown its achievements, the city holds a great festival. The high point is the arrival of the emperor of Germany who has come to pay homage to "the ideal city of the world." At the City Hall he is received by the mayor, Mrs. Potter Palmer.

The Great War and Progressivism

By 1900 most Progressives shared the view expressed by Lyman Abbott: "We are a world power; we are likely to be a leader among the world powers. We could not help ourselves if we would; we would not help ourselves if we could."[34] As close followers of European events and long-time participants in international reform and charitable and disaster-relief causes, the first response of Progressive political and cultural leaders to the war in Europe was to urge "preparedness." While preparedness included governmental plans for military mobilization, its initial thrust was moral and voluntarist — a call for all Americans to prepare themselves for a momentous test of resolve and will. Without question it was Progressives who led the way.[35] Their very willingness to "prepare" for some as yet unknown collective sacrifice was itself proof that republican virtue was more important than individual material comfort — proof that, in the words of Theodore Roosevelt some years earlier, we are not a nation of "well to do hucksters . . . sunk in a scrambling commercialism."[36] Once the struggle in Europe was framed in terms of the fate of democracy in the world, Progressives did not doubt that America would be called to take the leading role in its defense. Herbert Croly, the founding editor of *The New Republic,* had long believed that no European nation or group of nations could be committed unreservedly to the cause of democracy: "A European nation . . . cannot afford to become too complete a democracy all at once, because it would thereby be uprooting traditions upon which its national cohesion depends. . . . " In America, however, "we can trust its interest to the national interest, because American national cohesion is dependent . . . upon fidelity to a democratic principle."[37]

When defense of democracy at home and abroad is also a defense of a certain kind of post-Protestant American national identity, the call for preparedness takes on the ideal of national regeneration through atonement — the selfless sacrifice by the "innocent" and "righteous" for the evils of others. As preparedness turned to mobilization, and mobilization to war, it was almost as if four decades of cultural and political preparation by the Progressives had at last found an object worthy of its impulses. Indeed, Lyman Abbott's *The Twentieth Century Crusade* (1918) stands as a sort of "proof text" for the flood of books and articles written by Progressive intellectuals in that same year.

American civic virtue, according to Abbott, is best embodied in her mothers and their sons: the mothers by the sacrifice of their sons to the larger cause of justice and democracy, the sons by their physical courage and risk of life to atone for the sins of others.[38] Despite their sentimentality Abbott's nine "letters" to mothers are a robust call to arms. The first letter recalls Lincoln and the Civil War, telling the mother that her son "has joined the noble army of patriots." By the fifth letter, he is contrasting the "glory in tribulation" to the sordid ends of personal happiness. The sixth and seventh letters remind the reader that democracy is not a form of government but a way of life, a faith in human brotherhood that informs the character of all American institutions — religious, industrial, educational, and political. Our democratic republic is the modern Israel, a holy nation opposing Rome in all its forms. Lincoln and Wilson stand for Hegel and Christianity; Germany and the kaiser represent materialism, paganism, and power. The concluding letters are triumphal. Democracy and social justice are marching to victory. They "who have offered their lives, not merely for their country, but for an unknown people, of a different land, a different language and often of a different religious faith" will be crowned with immortality "not as a hope for the future [but] as a present possession, . . . the consciousness that I am more than the body which I inhabit."[39]

This understanding of American civic virtue gave early preparedness campaigns and later war mobilization a decidedly voluntarist cast. While this was most evident in the thousands of Americans who served in expeditionary units prior to the declaration of war, it was also manifest in the way in which small federal-governmental units functioned largely through unofficial voluntary organizations and efforts. From George Creel's Committee on Public Information, with its volunteer army of 150,000 intellectuals, writers, and speakers, to Herbert Hoover's Food Administration with a paid staff of 1,400 directing 750,000 volunteer housewives allocating and rationing the nation's food supply, it appeared that "official" action was only the final procedural act, not the substantive animating source, of the war effort. Even the initial funding for allied loans was raised voluntarily. In June 1917 four million Americans joined in offering the government $3 billion in "Liberty Loans" — an amount that increased to more than $25 billion within two years. The crowning achievement of this style of mobilization, however, was military conscription itself. Almost the entire apparatus of the draft functioned outside of the official federal government. Of the 192,000 workers administering the draft, just 429 were salaried federal employees. Only a nation already integrated and mobilized in spirit for many decades could have accomplished what still appears almost miraculous today. Two weeks to the day after Congress passed the Conscription Act, nine and a half million men presented themselves to local draft boards. With only the most rudimentary federal administrative apparatus, the American nation did what the most powerful and centralized European states could barely imagine.

Progressive Internationalism in the 1920s

The period immediately following the war maintained this heady sense of shared purpose. Returning from the peace conference in 1919, Woodrow Wilson's rhetoric summarized these preparedness and mobilization themes:

> Our participation in the war established our position among the nations. . . . the whole world saw at last . . . a Nation they had deemed material and now found to be compact of the spiritual forces that must free men of every nation of every unworthy bondage. . . . The stage is set, the destiny is disclosed. It has come about by no plan of our conceiving, but by the hand of God who led us into this way. We cannot turn back. We can only go forward following the vision. It was of this that we dreamed at our birth.[40]

While Progressive political leaders were soon disabused of their hope that the spirit and unity of preparedness and mobilization would continue to animate national government policy after the war, Progressive leadership in other sectors of American society remained optimistic. This was especially the case with leaders of "parachurch" ecumenical organizations who enjoyed unprecedented prestige and support during the war. In the words of one prominent religious publication, "War drives for world freedom [were] passing into Christian drives for world redemption. . . . Christian churches mobilize when armies demobilize."[41] And mobilize they did. The most ambitious of these plans was to create and fund a gargantuan umbrella organization called the Interchurch World Movement. This organization would embrace not only all churches in America, but would call on the support of leaders in government, labor, and industry to help underwrite a sort of national voluntarist parastate to spearhead the drive for democracy and justice at home and abroad.[42] Motivation for the success of this venture was all the stronger after America's rejection of membership in the League of Nations. By 1920, Interchurch, with a paid staff of 2,600 in New York City and expenditures exceeding a million dollars a month, began its drive to raise more than a third of a billion dollars over a five-year period. With the support of prominent Progressive wartime leaders from all sectors of American society and help from major national advertising agencies, the campaign to conquer disease, poverty, oppression, and injustice at home and abroad was finally launched. While the campaign within most of the thirty individual church denominations was quite successful, support for the post-Protestant ecumenical organization itself was a colossal failure. Not even 10 percent of the goal was met. The mainline Protestant underwriters of the venture (Methodist, Baptist, Presbyterian, Congregational, Disciples of Christ) bailed out quickly, and Interchurch simply disappeared. This failure paralleled a precipitous decline in the major ecumenical and student organizations as well.[43]

While there are many explanations for this sudden shift in religious and political culture, the long and gradual theological movement from liberal evangelicalism to "modernism" and the sudden rise of a strident and angry fundamentalism in the 1920s surely played a major part.[44] The immediate result was that Progressivism as a political culture, especially its internationalist side, was now located in institutions that had fewer and less salient connections to a popular base. Its moral and intellectual redoubts were the liberal ecumenical associations and the national universities with their allied colleges and professional associations. And while it may be true that many Progressive intellectual and cultural elites suddenly appeared as secular technocrats in bureaucratic alliance with the new industrial state, this outcome seems more inevitable than chosen. The popular base in churches, journalism, labor, and enlightened small business was so reduced that only the more abstract and secular language of an emerging liberal cosmopolitanism could hold the Progressive remnant together.[45] This remnant, however strong at the national heights of our organizational culture, could no longer command a popular electoral following and therefore had very little leverage in the national political parties. In 1912 each of the three leading presidential candidates had some impressive Progressive credentials; in 1924 the Republicans nominated Calvin Coolidge and the Democrats, John W. Davies, a Wall Street lawyer from West Virginia who ended his career defending state segregation of schools before the Supreme Court in *Brown v. Topeka.*

John Dewey wrote a sort of epitaph to popular Progressivism in a 1922 article in *The New Republic:*

> What we call the middle classes are for the most part the church-going classes, those who have come under the influence of evangelical Christianity. These persons form the backbone of philanthropic social interest, of social reform through political action, of pacifism, of popular education. They embody and express the spirit of kindly goodwill toward classes

which are at an economic disadvantage and toward other nations, especially when the latter show any disposition toward a republican form of government. . . . [This middle class] followed Lincoln in the abolition of slavery, and it followed Roosevelt in his denunciation of "bad" corporations and aggregation of wealth.

But in marked contrast to all of his prewar writings, Dewey here seems to dismiss this constituency as a source of future reform. Reflecting the rupture in Protestantism between modernism and fundamentalism, he now declares that this evangelical middle class "has never had an interest in ideas as ideas, nor in science and art for what they may do in liberating and elevating the human spirit."[46]

Despite Dewey's pessimism — understandable in the period of the Scopes trial and the Red Scare — Progressive values remained the defining ones in the mainline churches through the Federal Council of Churches, in the thriving academic professional organizations and research universities, in the higher journalism, in the higher reaches of a now increasingly competent and self-confident federal civil service, and in the labor, business, and financial sectors organized earlier through the National Civic Federation and permeated with the ideals of welfare capitalism.[47]

At the same time, Progressive values were becoming increasingly powerful in the nation's premier law schools. Long the object of contempt by Progressive intellectuals for their legal formalism, a fixation on abstract rights, and an antidemocratic animus, both law schools and courts were thought constitutionally incapable of understanding the new industrial order and shaping the law to its imperatives. It was almost an article of faith among Progressive academics and intellectuals that the Constitution and its high priests were more a barrier to overcome than a source of social and political direction.[48] In the 1920s, however, major law schools more and more reflected the teachings of the Progressive political economists, sociologists, and philosophers, first under the banner of "sociological jurisprudence" and then "legal realism." Critical of an abstract and mechanical jurisprudence and accepting of both administrative law and the administrative-regulatory state, these new legal cadres were becoming equally capable of serving government, international finance, and large business corporations in managing and coordinating the larger economic and legal framework of America.

Hoover's election and the responsible role that the United States played in sustaining the international economy in the 1920s also testify to the enduring power of Progressive political values.[49] But this popular electoral strength was somewhat illusory: the demobilization of the electorate and the dramatic decline in voting in this period assured that Progressive values most attuned to new industrial values would remain powerful while more popular (and populist) ones would not. Investment bankers, large oligopolistic business and its labor beneficiaries, scientific proponents of efficiency and rationalization in government, and the foundations, universities, and national publications that propounded these values were especially advantaged. Those Progressive followers and values more heavily influenced by an earlier populism and by ideals of Christian socialism were not.

Progressive Internationalism from the New Deal through the Cold War

The long fall in agricultural commodity prices, the stock market crash, the collapse of international trade, and the defeat and discrediting of Hoover almost reversed the electoral equation and therefore the fortunes of Progressivism in the 1930s. Its financial and industrial redoubts collapsed from the inside, while its educational, professional, and philanthropic allies were in moral and intellectual disarray. Combined with its earlier fragmentation, this collapse set the stage for a new public philosophy of New Deal liberalism very different in intellectual origins and constituencies from Progressivism. Without reopening the debate about the relationship of Progressivism to the New Deal in its domestic relief, welfare, and regulatory policies, it is surely the case that the simultaneous rise of the New Deal lawyer and the Washington law firm was both a link to and a major subversion of Progressive values. The New Deal, especially after the election of 1936, was partly a victory of the marginals and of a politics of patronage, party, and elections necessarily subjecting policy to localism and policy-making to elaborate coalitional games. None of this maneuvering, of course, had much to do with sustained economic recovery. It is clear, however, that Progressive internationalism as a national policy collapsed along with international investment and trade and was implicitly repudiated by the autarkic economic policies of both Hoover and Roosevelt in response to the depression.

If the depression destroyed Progressive economic internationalism and discredited both international finance and large industrial corporations, the war restored the centrality of both sectors — and revitalized the other centers of 1920s Progressivism as well. Unlike the First World War, mobilization for World War II was much more extensive, "state-centered," and legal-bureaucratic. Nevertheless, because of its scale and duration, mobilization drew even more heavily upon the energies and talents of those "parastates" utilized in the earlier war, especially the universities, professional and trade associations, and the national media.

This presidentially centered relationship between nationally minded (and often liberal Republican or nonpartisan) political leaders and leaders of universities, foundations, corporate law, finance and business, and labor continued and grew stronger in the Cold War. The "national security state" was much more than a system of anti-Soviet military alliances abroad and a military-industrial complex at home. Abroad, the national government managed postwar European and Asian economic and political reconstruction, presided over the decolonization of much of Africa and Asia, and dominated international monetary and trade policies. It was precisely this American identity abroad — its "mission to the world" — that was the engine for sustaining Progressive visions of reform at home.

Given international economic policies, those policies of the New Deal undertaken in the spirit of Wilsonian "New Freedom" and the older small-producer capitalism were consistently subordinated to the demands of large-scale industrial and financial capitalism. The demands of labor were met selectively according to these same criteria. Even the persistent impulses in Democratic Party ideology for acknowledging (and exploiting) religious, regional, cultural, ethnic, and racial "difference" were subordinated to the demands of American internationalism. This was also true at the level of political beliefs. The first demands to purge suspected Communists and "fellow travelers" came from New Deal liberals — loyalty screening began under Truman — and was widely supported by the liberal establishment in all of its major locations from national universities and foundations, through mainline churches, to the American Civil Liberties Union, the National Association for the Advancement of Colored People, and Americans for Democratic Action.[50]

But there is another side to this demand for national unity for international ends; that is the demand to dismantle racial segregation in the South. As anticommunism abroad drove anticommunism at home so too anticolonialism and leadership of the "third world" abroad impelled integration at home, even if it meant repudiating the last vestige of constitutional federalism. These projects were initiated, led, and driven by liberal national elites and institutions — elites and institutions that had the most direct connection to earlier Progressive ones.[51]

Another sign of a postwar Progressive restoration was the emerging norm of "bipartisanship" in foreign policy and its domestic requirements. By common elite consensus lasting more than a quarter of a century, American foreign policy, i.e., internationalism as a dominant value, was removed from the normal tug of domestic interests and party-electoral politics. So long as this consensus prevailed and so long as foreign policy imperatives could prevail over domestic interests, the newly institutionalized presidency standing above party became the official repository of American identity and purpose in the world. Through these presidential institutions the spirits of anti-party Republican Progressivism still provided the limiting conditions within which both New Deal domestic liberals and Republican domestic conservatives could function.

This postwar condition can be restated in two other ways. The first is by James MacGregor Burns, whose books codified and rationalized a Progressive ideological, political, and constitutional perspective between the New Deal and the Vietnam War. Burns postulated a "four-party" system in America wherein each party had a responsible, presidentially led nationalist/internationalist wing and an irresponsible, interest-dominated congressional/localist wing.[52] The most important institutional locations of Progressive internationalism were associated with the presidency, as Burns describes, but its power and reach was often hidden. From the antifascist Office of Strategic Services to the anticolonial and anticommunist Central Intelligence Agency, strong but secret ties were established between the national security apparatus and most of the liberal establishment, ranging from national labor, student, and youth organizations through universities, foundations, publishing houses, the national media, and ecumenical church organizations. These connections and forms of informal cooperation were willingly entered into by the leaders of these national institutions because they all shared the same liberal cosmopolitan political and cultural values — and shared the same set of enemies on the left (largely abroad) and on the right (largely at home).

This "internationalist" restoration of Progressivism in midcentury differed in significant ways from its earlier period of glory at the beginning of the century. Because of the continued electoral dominance of the

New Deal coalition, domestic policy was largely in the hands of locally oriented congressional leaders and not national elites, and thus there was little "fit," rhetorically or socioculturally, between domestic and foreign policy.[53] The justifications and practices of "interest-group liberalism" at home were often incommensurate with the justifications and practices (not to speak of the economic needs) of our policies abroad. The former was both "populist" and "constitutional," while the latter was neither but tended to dominate important policy areas — as in extracting domestic resources to support defense and foreign aid spending and trade policies. Liberal internationalism lacked full constitutional legitimacy because neither the "intelligence community" and its clandestine allies nor presidential powers could be contained within any formalist reading of the Constitution. They were permitted to exist outside the Constitution simply because Congress and the courts permitted it. Liberal internationalism lacked a coherent popular electoral base because domestic interests were neither intellectually nor economically integrated into international policies except insofar as some foreign aid and defense-related spending became pork and thus held hostage to powerful congressional leaders and interest groups.

The only post–New Deal domestic policies that were at once national in purpose, clearly within constitutional understandings, and possessed of a powerful electoral base were the attempts to address persistent and grinding poverty and to achieve some measure of racial integration. What has been termed the "nationalization of rights" associated with the Warren Court could never have come from the New Deal electoral coalition. But given World War II and the Cold War, it bore many of the marks of an earlier Progressive vision translated into a new form of an organic and nationalist constitutional law. This nationalization of rights paralleled in purpose and support the "internationalization of rights" as the foundation for our anticommunist foreign policy. With some exceptions, however, this nationalization of rights still lacks a truly popular base and appears increasingly removed from any recognizable constitutional foundations.

The Historiography of Progressivism

The preceding analysis incorporates a reading of Progressivism that is, to say the least, not without controversy. Because contemporary attempts to reorient and restore American liberalism necessitate a rethinking of Progressivism, the controversy about the identity and history of Progressivism is also a controversy about the identity and future of American liberalism.[54] It may be useful to conclude, therefore, by sketching the dimensions and import of my reading both to clarify its understanding of Progressivism and to contrast it to alternative readings.[55]

My starting point is that Progressivism began as a movement to restore the American *nation,* to inculcate a substantive idea of public good and infuse its purposes into all areas of American life from family government to national government, from academic culture and religion to public education, from small businesses to international investment banks. Readings of Progressivism that slight or subordinate this nationalist orientation will miss the only intellectual and organizational framework that brought together and connected its leading figures, institutions, and practices over many decades. This nationalist orientation forces attention on ideas and social theories, on institutions, civil society, and culture, and at least initially, away from "interests," their interplay, and events in party-electoral politics.[56]

This cultural/intellectual orientation is a powerful way of understanding and of explanation because it is authentically historical; it assumes that actions and behaviors are deeply embedded in self understandings and systems of social meaning. Only as and until these are significantly altered is it possible, literally, to conceive of new political and social institutions and practices. Because these new self and social understandings can only be forged from materials already at hand—another explicitly historical perspective—this reading of Progressivism is able to connect with earlier languages and practices in American culture that were reformulated and relocated into coherent and powerful social and political forces. It necessarily follows that this nationalist reading restores the role of religious ideas and institutions to a central place in our political culture precisely because religious language was the most compelling and powerful language of national identity within a framework of universal (world) history. When this language is directly infused into social movements and politics, as it was during the American Revolution and the American Civil War, it can become a hegemonic national culture and even a "civil religion." Progressivism in the hands of its most articulate philosophers and social theorists both aspired to that goal and, in most national institutions, achieved it, i.e., achieved an intellectual/cultural dominance that was unquestioned from the 1890s until the 1920s and, though contested, remained very powerful until the early 1970s.

In contrast to this approach, many current studies of Progressivism begin with the success of Progressivism as a political ideology in party-organized electoral contests from the early 1900s through 1915, chart its party-electoral collapse following World War I, and then reconstruct its past — and its future. This anachronistic way of proceeding has the corresponding tendency to encourage a flowering of nostalgic speculation about "alternative Americas" that "might have" been chosen — as if each generation of Americans can reinvent itself. Neither time nor topic warrants a close analysis of these readings, but a brief sketch of some prominent ones and their implications might provide an instructive contrast to my own.

One influential interpretation is that Progressivism never existed or, if it did, it took so many disparate forms that the term cannot stand for any coherent or unified view.[57] This interpretation makes sense only if the "Progressivism" one searches for is almost exclusively a political-electoral one. If no substantively coherent Progressive ideas are to be found in the legislative policies in this period, then the "Progressive movement" lacks coherent identity as a public philosophy. While this method may have made sense during the party-period of American politics, it is deeply ironic that Progressivism should be judged on this basis, since its chief aim was to break the grip of party-dominated institutions as the final arbiter of political ideas. Indeed, the success of Progressivism in national institutions and intellectual culture and the increasing power of that culture in our political life discredits this test because the very institutional and moral locus of effective governing power had changed. Moreover, as early as the 1890s, this test is especially irrelevant for understanding and explaining U.S. foreign policy and our emergence as a world power. Precisely because nongovernmental but national institutions and leaders, combined with an increasingly autonomous presidency, shaped foreign policy and foreign policy thinking, a party-electoral test of both coherence and saliency is misplaced.[58] The moral and material mobilization for World War I is the best example.

A variant of this same insular perspective reaches a complementary conclusion. It also starts by simply denying the coherence of Progressivism but, lacking confidence that the term marking an entire political era will simply disappear in our historical consciousness, takes the demotic route of including marginals and subalterns as constitutive actors in the formation and success of Progressivism. Whether it be the increasingly ethnic political machines of the North and Midwest or the one-party semifeudal Democratic South, these political forces are made an integral part of Progressive identity and meaning.[59] Richard Hofstadter's earlier incorporation of the Populist movement into "the age of reform" is the model for this mistake.[60] This incorporation of marginals is possible because Progressivism was assumed at the start by these historians to lack any philosophical or sociocultural soul—i.e., constitutive of a national identity—and was considered only a loosely connected series of ad hoc responses by decent Americans to perceived wrongs and social problems. Thus reduced to a wide array of innovative policy proposals or "reforms" to which various interests could and did variously attach themselves and from which they received direct and differential benefits, even the intentionally procedural and soulless soul of the Democratic Party as an institution could be incorporated into this understanding of Progressivism and therefore into the mainstream of American history.[61] Put directly, it is as if both the Civil War and the realigning and hegemonic election of 1896 never happened.[62] Put indirectly, it denies the brute facts of winners and losers and the intractable horizons that winning establishes for future conflicts.

Conclusion

Recent attempts to divide Progressives into "good" ones (i.e., pacifist, protosocialist, multicultural) and "bad" ones (i.e., technocratic, welfare-capitalist, WASP) represent a further retreat from or evasion of our history.[63] Reading back from the 1920s and taking its cue from the beautiful souls of the "Young Americans," this interpretation sees this confused and hopeless critique as a lost remnant of "good" Progressivism pointing to an alternative that might be reclaimed today. This understanding is not so much bad history as its denial—as if the truly free American can exist outside of history, and the larger world, and reclaim a lost freedom by mere assertion and will. Needless to say, this "idealism" is not only isolationist, it puts America in opposition to its national history and therefore to the history of the modern world that America has done so much to shape. One might call this reading of Progressivism a yearning for a new Jeffersonian moment when America did see itself as existing alone in endless space and not with others in historical time.[64] In the current discussion, Randolph Bourne is the hero, Walter Lippman the goat, and John Dewey the subject of interpretive struggle.

To deny the coherence of Progressivism as a public philosophy necessarily precludes a serious look at the international dimensions of Progressive ideas, for it is precisely on a world stage that the nation is the actor and must possess both articulate purposes and a unified will if it is to act effectively in the world as a single people. To see Progressivism as its intellectual founders articulated it — as a historically grounded public philosophy designed to create a democratic nation under new social and economic conditions — is also to see Progressivism as part of a world-wide endeavor to create the conditions in which a world of democratic nations can also come into being.

Notes

1. Eldon Eisenach, *The Lost Promise of Progressivism* (Lawrence: University Press of Kansas, 1994), 31–36, 42–44.

2. In the 1890s Bliss was founder of the Christian Socialist Society of the United States; secretary and national lecturer for the Christian Social Union in America; president of the National Social Reform Union; founding editor of *Dawn;* and editor of the *American Fabian*. After serving two years as an investigator for the U.S. Bureau of Labor, he worked with Josiah Strong's American Institute of Social Service, 1909–14, and compiled and edited writings from John Stuart Mill and John Ruskin.

3. Charles Foster, *Errand of Mercy: The Evangelical United Front, 1790–1837* (Chapel Hill: University of North Carolina Press, 1960), especially 274–80 for the list of missionary and reform societies in America and Great Britain. See, too, Daniel Walker Howe, "Religion and Politics in the Antebellum North," in *Religion and American Politics: From the Colonial Period to the 1980s,* ed. Mark A. Noll (New York: Oxford University Press, 1990).

4. On women and clergymen see Nancy F. Cott, *The Bonds of Womanhood: "Women's Sphere" in New England, 1780–1835* (New Haven: Yale University Press, 1977); and Ann Douglas, *The Feminization of American Culture* (New York: Doubleday, 1988).

5. Two studies that combine to clarify this relationship are Ronald Walters, *The Antislavery Appeal: American Abolitionism after 1830* (Baltimore: Johns Hopkins University Press, 1977); and William Gienapp, *The Origins of the Republican Party, 1852–1856* (New York: Oxford University Press, 1987).

6. For biographies of prominent Progressive intellectuals and reform leaders see Eisenach, *Lost Promise,* 31–36; and Robert M. Crunden, *Ministers of Reform: The Progressives' Achievement in American Civilization, 1889–1920* (Urbana: Uni-

versity of Illinois Press, 1984). The most prominent exception is the Columbia University economist Edwin R. A. Seligman, son of German-Jewish immigrants. On Seligman, see Eldon Eisenach, "Bookends: Seven Stories Excised from *The Lost Promise of Progressivism,"* in *Studies in American Political Development,* vol. 10, ed. Karen Orren (New York: Cambridge University Press, 1996), 172–74.

7. This transposition from churchman to philosopher is seen most vividly in scholarly journals and academic publication. Through the post–Civil War period, every distinguished intellectual journal in America was "theological" in that it was denominationally sponsored and edited by churchmen. Between 1888 and 1893, four of these journals ceased publication (*Princeton Review, Unitarian Review* at Harvard, the *New Englander* at Yale, and *Andover Review*). All but *Andover Review,* itself a leading vehicle for German theology and historicist philosophy, was edited by a German-trained scholar. The one survivor, *Bibliotheca Sacra,* relocated to Oberlin Seminary and added a journal-saving subtitle in 1894: *A Religious and Sociological Journal.* Without missing a beat, new academic professional associations and their journals immediately filled the void, including *Publications of the American Economics Association* (1886), *The Annals of the American Academy of Political and Social Science* (1890), *The American Journal of Sociology* (1895), and the *American Political Science Review* (1906). Bruce Kuklick, *Churchman and Philosopher: From Jonathan Edwards to John Dewey* (New Haven: Yale University Press, 1985), 191–229; Eisenach, *Lost Promise,* 97–103. See, too, Louise L. Stevenson, *Scholarly Means to Evangelical Ends: The New Haven Scholars and the Transformation of Higher Learning in America, 1830–1890* (Baltimore: Johns Hopkins University Press, 1986), 87–147 and Appendix 1; and George Marsden, *The Soul of the American University* (New York: Oxford University Press, 1994), Part 2.

8. See Eisenach, *Lost Promise,* 92–93; and Jurgen Herbst, *The German Historical School in American Scholarship* (Ithaca: Cornell University Press, 1965), 207–14, 230.

9. The best general discussion of localism, expenditures, and governmental growth during this period is Morton Keller, *Affairs of State: Public Life in Late Nineteenth-Century America* (Cambridge: Harvard University Press, 1977).

10. Leaders of the new professional associations regularly wrote for the new national magazines and, in turn, opened the pages of their professional journals to prominent reformers. For examples, especially of women reformers, see Eisenach, *Lost Promise,* 13–15, 149, 183.

11. Even in the new journalism, the religious press was the forerunner and provided the first models. Both the *Independent* and *Outlook,* for example, started as denominational publications and evolved into major mass circulation reform periodicals. See Frank Luther Mott, *A History of American Magazines,* vol. 3, *1865–1885* (Cambridge: Harvard University Press, 1957), 422–35, 292–94.

12. A good summary of these reforms is in Richard L. McCormick, *The Party Period and Public Policy: American Politics from the Age of Jackson to the Progressive Era* (New York: Oxford University Press, 1986), 332–48; and Michael McGerr,

The Decline of Popular Politics: The American North, 1865–1928 (New York: Oxford University Press, 1986). A good analysis of the institutional ramifications of these reforms is found in Martin Shefter, "Party, Bureaucracy, and Political Change in the United States," in *Political Parties: Development and Decay,* ed. L. Maisel and J. Cooper (Beverly Hills: Sage, 1978).

13. The most coherent and convincing case for this view is Sacvan Bercovitch, *Puritan Origins of the American Self* (New Haven: Yale University Press, 1977).

14. James Kloppenberg, *Uncertain Victory: Social Democracy and Progressivism in European and American Political Thought, 1870–1920* (New York: Oxford University Press, 1986). He is especially persuasive in showing that, between 1870 and 1920, "two generations of American and European thinkers created a transatlantic community of discourse in philosophy and political theory" (3).

15. The scale and reach of these internationally oriented organizations are difficult to comprehend today. The Student Volunteer Movement was founded by a Cornell undergraduate in 1888; shortly thereafter, six thousand college students pledged to become foreign missionaries in a one-year period. More than twenty thousand missionaries were eventually recruited by this group whose founder, John R. Mott, went on to work for the international YMCA and to head the World Student Christian Federation. Immediately after World War II, Mott was instrumental in the founding of the World Council of Churches. The "secular" and social service dimension of foreign missions is indicated in the fact that, of every one hundred American missionaries serving abroad, thirty were clergymen. See Eisenach, *Lost Promise,* 235–36; Marsden, *Soul of the American University,* 343–44; and Robert T. Handy, *Undermined Establishment: Church-State Relations in America, 1880–1920* (Princeton: Princeton University Press, 1991), 77–96.

16. Crunden, *Ministers of Reform.*

17. E. R. A. Seligman, *The Economic Interpretation of History* (New York: Columbia University Press, 1907), 132.

18. Quoted in Eisenach, *Lost Promise,* 89.

19. Henry Carter Adams, *Relation of the State to Industrial Action* and *Economics and Jurisprudence,* ed. J. Dorfman (New York: Columbia University Press, 1954), 159, 152–53. His immediate point was to restructure industrial relations so that workers have more weapons than strikes and managers have more legitimacy than as agents of owners enforcing property rights through force. With union recognition, subsidiary state law, and long-term collective bargaining agreements, wage-earners, he argues, will acquire a quasi–property right in their jobs.

20. Simon Patten, "The Reconstruction of Economic Theory" (1912) in *Essays in Economic Theory,* ed. R. Tugwell (New York: Knopf, 1924), 336. While Patten had formulated these ideas much earlier, this was the article that so deeply influenced Herbert Croly in his *Progressive Democracy* (1914) and Charles Beard's distinction between Jeffersonian "realty interests" and Hamiltonian "capitalist interests."

21. Charles Beard called this era of small-producer and agricultural capitalism "a type of economic society such as had never before appeared in the history of the world and can never exist again." *American Government and Politics* (New York: Macmillan, 1928), 132. See, too, Olivier Zunz, *Making America Corporate, 1870–1920* (Chicago: University of Chicago Press, 1990); and James Livingston, *Pragmatism and the Political Economy of Cultural Revolution, 1850–1940* (Chapel Hill: University of North Carolina Press, 1994).

22. Richard Ely, *Ground Under Our Feet* (New York: Macmillan, 1938), 136.

23. See William Cronon, *Nature's Metropolis: Chicago and the Great West* (New York: Norton, 1991) and Olivier Zunz, *Making America Corporate*. On the decline in southern agriculture, see Eisenach, *Lost Promise*, 151, 176, and 179–81.

24. On realigning elections and the "system of '96," see Walter Dean Burnham, *Critical Elections and the Mainsprings of American Politics* (New York: Norton, 1970).

25. McGerr, *Decline of Popular Politics,* 69–105; McCormick, *The Party Period and Public Policy,* 197–227; Joel Silbey, *The American Political Nation, 1838–1893* (Stanford: Stanford University Press, 1990), 224–41; and Eisenach, *Lost Promise,* 104–22.

26. See Bradford Perkins, *The Great Rapprochement: England and the United States, 1895–1914* (New York: Atheneum, 1968); Richard Collin, *Theodore Roosevelt, Culture, Diplomacy, and Expansion* (Baton Rouge: Louisiana State University Press, 1985); and Emily Rosenberg, *Spreading the American Dream: American Economic and Cultural Expansion, 1890–1945* (New York: Hill and Wang, 1982).

27. See Rosenberg, *Spreading the American Dream,* 24–27; and Martin Sklar, *The United States as a Developing Country* (New York: Cambridge University Press, 1992), 78–101. On the navy, see Peri E. Arnold, "Policy Leadership in the Progressive Presidency: The Case of Theodore Roosevelt's Naval Policy and His Search for Strategic Resources," in Orren, *Studies in American Political Development,* vol. 10, (1997), 333–59.

28. The term "parastate" refers to nationally oriented institutions and organizations (e.g., universities, professional and reform organizations, the new national journals, ecumenical church organizations) that came to shape both public and Republican Party opinion in this period. Those within the Republican Party who called for a purely national orientation and leadership by the "educated man" were voicing this same anti-party idea. See Eisenach, *Lost Promise,* 117–22, 135–36, and 161–63.

29. Richard Bensel, *Sectionalism and American Political Development, 1880–1980* (Madison: University of Wisconsin Press, 1984) is an excellent study of "core-periphery" politics in this period.

30. Quoted in Mott, *A History of American Magazines,* 657.

31. Estimates are that while the United States accounted for about 23 percent of world production in the 1870s and 35 percent in the period 1906–10, British shares fell from 32 percent to 15 percent in this same time period. In

roughly this time span, per capita income in America rose from $764 to $1,813 while Britain's grew from $972 to $1,491. See Alfred Chandler, *Scale and Scope: The Dynamics of Industrial Capitalism* (Cambridge: Harvard University Press, 1990), 52.

32. William Stead, *The Americanization of the World* (New York and London: H. Markley, 1902), 149, 440.

33. Matthew Arnold had earlier hailed Stead as the inventor of a new genre of journalism that combined human interest narrative with the cause of social reform. See Introduction by Harvey Wish to the reissue of *If Christ Came to Chicago* (1894; reprint, New York: Living Books, 1964).

34. Lyman Abbott, *The Rights of Man* (New York: Houghton Mifflin, 1901), 266. Abbott was the editor of *Outlook,* a leading Progressive weekly, and pastor of the leading Congregational Church in America.

35. See John E. McClymer, *War and Welfare: Social Engineering in America, 1890–1925* (Westport, Conn.: Greenwood Press, 1980), chaps. 5 and 6 on social workers; David M. Kennedy, *Over Here: The First World War and American Society* (New York: Oxford University Press, 1980), 33–44 on the universities; Neil A. Wynn, *From Progressivism to Prosperity: World War I and American Society* (New York: Holmes & Meier, 1986), 36–38, 43–44 on Progressive journalists, reformers, and women's rights activists; Ronald Schaffer, *America in the Great War: The Rise of the War Welfare State* (New York: Oxford University Press, 1991), 90–95 on women reformers and 127–48 on the universities; and Eldon G. Ernst, *Moment of Truth of Protestant America: Interchurch Campaigns Following World War I* (Missoula: Scholars' Press, 1974), 35–69 on liberal evangelical churches and ecumenical associations.

36. Quoted in Perry E. Giankos and Albert Karson, *American Diplomacy and the Sense of National Destiny,* 2 vols. (Belmont, Calif.: Wadsworth, 1966), vol. 1, 52–53.

37. Herbert Croly, *The Promise of American Life* (1909; reprint, Boston: Northeastern University Press, 1989), 266–67.

38. The counterpart of this image is that adult males embody liberal individualism and truncated ideas of citizen as voter. This argument is developed in Mark E. Kann, "Individualism, Civic Virtue, and Gender in America," in *Studies in American Political Development,* vol. 4, ed. Karen Orren and Stephen Skowronek (New Haven: Yale University Press, 1990).

39. Lyman Abbott, *The Twentieth Century Crusade* (New York: Macmillan, 1918), 52–54, 106, 103.

40. Quoted in Handy, *Protestant Hopes,* 160.

41. Quoted in Ernst, *Moment of Truth,* 59.

42. A more correct image might be that of a massive, nonsectarian Established Church that embraced the entire range of democratic institutions constituting American civil society, infusing them with shared purpose and value. This attempt is discussed in these terms in Eisenach, *Lost Promise,* 254; and Handy, *Undermined Establishment,* 184–88.

43. See Marsden, *Soul of the American University,* 343.

44. See Ernst, *Moment of Truth*, and George Marsden, *Fundamentalism and American Culture* (New York: Oxford University Press, 1980).

45. Indicative of the consciousness of this shift is Edward Scribner Ames, *The New Orthodoxy* (Chicago: University of Chicago Press, 1918).

46. "The American Intellectual Frontier," *The New Republic*, 10 May 1922, 303.

47. On the churches, see William McGuire King, "The Reform Establishment and the Ambiguities of Influence," in *Between the Times: the Travail of the Protestant Establishment in America, 1900–1960,* ed. William R. Hutchinson (New York: Cambridge University Press, 1989); on the federal bureaucracy, see Stephen Skowronek, *Building a New American State: The Expansion of National Administrative Capacities, 1877–1920* (New York: Cambridge University Press, 1982); and Brian Balogh, "Reorganizing the Organizational Synthesis: Federal-Professional Relations in Modern America," in *Studies in American Political Development,* vol. 5, ed. Karen Orren and Stephen Skowronek (New York: Cambridge University Press, 1991); on corporatism, the National Civic Federation, and welfare capitalism, see James Weinstein, *The Corporate Ideal and the Liberal State, 1900–1918* (Boston: Beacon Press, 1968).

48. See Eisenach, *Lost Promise*, 44, 77–87, 104–10, 122–29, 164–68, 185–91, 262–66 and David Rabban, "Free Speech in Progressive Social Thought," *Texas Law Review* 74 (April 1996): 951–1038.

49. See Paul Johnson, *A History of the Modern World, From 1917 to the 1980s* (London: Weidenfeld and Nicholson, 1983), 230–50.

50. David Plotke, *Building a New Democratic Political Order* (New York: Cambridge University Press, 1996), 293–335.

51. King, "The Reform Establishment," 122–40.

52. James MacGregor Burns, *Deadlock of Democracy: Four-Party Politics in America* (Englewood Cliffs, N.J.: Prentice-Hall, 1967). Burns also wrote a Progressive-style critique of congressional politics, *Congress on Trial: The Legislative Process and the Administrative State* (1949) and a later defense of a powerful presidency, *Presidential Government: The Crucible of Leadership* (1965).

53. The extreme restatement of Burns's position on bifurcation is Samuel Huntington's "Congressional Responses to the Twentieth Century," in *The Congress and America's Future,* ed. D. Truman (Englewood Cliffs, N.J.: Prentice-Hall, 1965), arguing that the two thousand new presidential appointments every four or eight years are a more nationally representative and therefore more "democratic" body than a locally elected — and endlessly reelected — Congress. Executive appointees come from dynamic national institutions and address issues from a national and cosmopolitan perspective; Congressmen represent local, provincial, and essentially stagnant interests.

54. A recent book that nicely captures some of the earlier Progressive nationalist perspective is Michael Lind, *The Next American Nation: The New Nationalism and the Fourth American Revolution* (New York: Free Press, 1995). See too Michael Sandel, *Democracy's Discontent: America in Search of a Public Philosophy* (Cambridge: Harvard University Press, 1996) that restates Progressive

arguments against rights-based individualism but, unfortunately, ignores the teachings of earlier Progressive political economy in favor of a nostalgic economic populism; and Richard Rorty, *Achieving Our Country* (Cambridge: Harvard University Press, 1998).

55. Some of these issues are discussed more fully in Eisenach, *Lost Promise,* 18–31, 205–24, and 259–66.

56. An excellent example of this kind of historical perspective is John Gerring, "Party Ideology in America: The National Republican Chapter, 1829–1924," in *Studies in American Political Development,* vol. 11, ed. Karen Orren and Stephen Skowronek (New York: Cambridge University Press, 1997).

57. Peter Filene, "An Obituary for the 'Progressive Movement,'" *American Quarterly* 22 (1970): 20–34; Daniel T. Rodgers, "In Search of Progressivism," *Reviews in American History* 10 (1982): 113–32.

58. An equivalent misreading is to explain national security policy, leadership, and practices, 1950–70, from the interest-group or "pluralist" reading of American domestic and electoral politics that dominated this period. Since this reading is false on its face, given the autonomous power of the executive establishment and its nongovernmental allies in foreign policy, those who insist that electoral/constitutional politics are everything must resort to capitalist "power elite" (left) or world government (right) conspiracy theory.

59. See John D. Buenker, *Urban Liberalism and Progressive Reform* (New York: Norton, 1978) on the North and Midwest; David Sarasohn, *The Party of Reform: Democrats in the Progressive Era* (Jackson: University Press of Mississippi, 1989) on the South.

60. Richard Hofstadter, *The Age of Reform: From Bryan to FDR* (New York: Alfred Knopf, 1955).

61. On the inconsistencies in these readings, see Eisenach, *Lost Promise,* 21–25, esp. notes 19 and 21. On the procedural ideal of the Democratic Party, see Douglas Jaenicke, "The Jacksonian Integration of Party into the Constitutional System," *Political Science Quarterly* 101 (1986): 85–107.

62. It also confuses Woodrow Wilson's sudden and necessary conversion to Progressive nationalist rhetoric with a sudden conversion of the Democratic Party rather than as the only viable rhetoric available in that presidential election campaign.

63. The best of these recent attempts is Alan Dawley, *Struggles for Justice: Social Responsibility and the Liberal State* (Cambridge: Harvard University Press, 1991); and see Rodgers Smith, *Civic Ideals* (New Haven: Yale University Press, 1996), 412–13.

64. Livingston, *Pragmatism and the Political Economy of Cultural Revolution,* is the most sophisticated but complex response to this position. Major Wilson, *Space, Time, and Freedom: The Quest for Nationality and the Irrepressible Conflict, 1815–1851* (Westport, Conn.: Greenwood Press, 1974) and David Greenstone, *The Lincoln Persuasion: Remaking American Liberalism* (Princeton: Princeton University Press, 1993), chap. 2, discuss the relationship between the development of American national identity and a historicist perspective.

The Legacy of Reform

Progressive Government, Regressive Politics

Jerome M. Mileur

The American democracy will not continue to need the two-party system to intermediate between the popular will and the governmental machinery. By means of executive leadership, expert administrative independence and direct legislation, it will gradually create a new governmental machinery which will be born with the impulse to destroy the two-party system, and will itself be thoroughly and flexibly representative of the underlying purposes and needs of a more social democracy.

—The New Republic, 14 November 1914

The Civil War ended slavery and restored the Union. It also marked the end of an older, culturally homogeneous, and simpler America — small-scale and localist in its political and economic organization, grounded in the habits and values of small towns and the countryside, parochial in its concerns, self-reliant and Protestant in its ethics. More and more, after the war, this America was displaced by a new, socially diverse and complex America — a boisterous, ambitious, energetic nation, grand in its scale; increasingly national in its industry, finance, and commerce; more professional and impersonal in style; urban and more secular in habit and value, with growing numbers of immigrants "foreign" in culture and religion to the older America.[1]

The final decades of the nineteenth century were pervaded by a growing discontent. Older elites in the East, long certain of their social position, grew restless, then discontented, as new men of great wealth — "tycoons" and "robber barons" — rose to prominence in their stead.[2] The West, meanwhile, rocked with agrarian and worker protest, sparked repeatedly by actions of the railroads and banks whose corporate managers were remote and well beyond the effective reach of local communities. This flood of unrest swirled around the two-party system, whose bosses in the East were beset by liberal Republican / Mugwump reforms of civil service and ballot law and in the west by a succession of populist protests and third party revolts that came together in the People's Party of the 1890s.[3] And through it all wafted the faint aroma of Socialism — an unease that some alien doctrine or force would triumph and radically transform the Founders' America.

The Civil War had, for the most part, settled the constitutional question of states' rights, though not the political one, which had indeed been complicated by the renewed sectionalism that emerged from the war. Both major parties embraced laissez-faire, though for different reasons: to Democrats, it meant the limited government of Jefferson; to Republicans, the free market of capitalism. With the end of Reconstruction, the party battle for national office became intensely competitive and regularly broke along sectional lines: the Republicans the party of the North, the Democrats the party of the South, the West a cauldron of discontent though more reliably Republican than Democrat.[4]

It was in this so-called gilded age — a time of great social transformation and economic dislocation — that the generation of Progressive reformers came of age and against which their efforts took shape. These were the children of Lincoln, to whom the martyred president, in the words of Merrill Peterson, "loomed as the Titanic expression of national genius in pursuit of the national ideal," whom they "not only saluted but sanctified."[5] For Progressives, Lincoln's virtues were obvious. He had saved the Union and freed the slaves, and was thus not only a nationalist but also a model of moral leadership grounded in the brotherhood of man. Moreover, Lincoln embodied the very ideal of American democracy and was a testament to its virtues: the common man, raised to greatness by his own wit and industry to save his nation. Indeed, for this "enthusiastically Protestant" generation of reformers, as Eldon

Eisenach depicts them, the Lincoln presidency was "the defining moment in American/biblical history and prophecy," "the rebirth of the American nation," and the "organizational and ancestral nidus" of their nationalism.

"Lincolniana," the term was coined in the late nineteenth century to describe all of the Lincoln materials and memorabilia being actively collected, infected the Progressive generation in all of its dimensions. The journalist Ida Tarbell came to prominence in the 1890s for her series in *McClure's* on the early Lincoln, followed soon by a second on the mature Lincoln; and the Lincoln ideal both informed and impassioned her subsequent "muckraking" career. Jane Addams in her settlement-house work urged immigrant children to follow the example of Lincoln, while the poet Vachel Lindsay, from Lincoln's hometown, painted the former president in heroic hues. Even Democrats William Jennings Bryan and Woodrow Wilson, as well as the Socialist Eugene Debs, invoked Lincoln to justify their calls for a more positive state to deal with the moral issues posed by the new social and economic conditions.

But it was the Republican Theodore Roosevelt whose torch for Lincoln burned brightest. TR took Lincoln as the model for his conception of the president as a strong, energetic, positive leader, representative of the national interest and, if need be, independent of the Congress. The image of the visionary, purposeful Lincoln, charitable and moderate in action, guided Roosevelt, who called Lincoln a "progressive" in his time and regularly asked, when faced with a decision, what Lincoln might do.[6] In the campaign of 1912 TR, Wilson, and William Howard Taft repeatedly called upon Lincoln in support of their respective candidacies for president, mirroring his symbolic importance for them and for the America of their time. To be sure, it was in large part a mythical Lincoln whom they embraced. The Lincoln who was a Whig, then Republican politician, a master of the political and patronage practices of his time and who made that politics work in the national (or at least northern) interest, was for the most part lost on the Progressives, who were of course hostile to the system of politics that schooled Lincoln and sustained his presidency.

For Progressives, the political legacy of the mythical Lincoln, Peterson writes, is twofold: "first the supremacy of the national government, and second, its responsibility to advance the freedom and equality of all citizens."[7] It was this Lincoln who gave sustenance to Progressive assaults upon the trusts and the party bosses and to their construction of a new democratic order in which government and politics served national purposes. In reality, of course, Lincoln, albeit a champion of Union, was no advocate of an expanded national state and had no evident interest in political reform. This empirical Lincoln, however, held no charm for the Progressives; it was the mythical Lincoln who served their purposes.

These purposes, as the essays in this volume attest, were bold; they transformed a localist regime of courts and parties into an at least rudimentary national state.[8] The Progressives, Carey McWilliams writes, "deserve much of the credit for building a government even remotely adequate to the problems of the twentieth century." Yet their achievements were mixed. As reformers, they were more successful, Eileen McDonagh argues, along the *institutional* axis of democracy ("arrangements defining the scope and centralization of the power of the state to act") than along the *participatory* axis ("access to political power in the exercise of governance"). In governance itself, Morton Keller concludes, the economic programs of the Progressives ("past-laden, incremental, and particularistic") were far less novel or dramatic than their social initiatives ("bold, sweeping, assertive"), though of the latter, he cautions, "the results hardly merit our unalloyed enthusiasm."

The Progressive program of political and social reform has also been, as Sidney Milkis writes, "an enduring feature of American political discourse and electoral struggle throughout the twentieth century." It was, however, as McDonagh suggests, in the Progressive reconstitution of the nation's politics — more precisely in the relationship of their idea of politics to their reconstitution of national governance — that the era had its most lasting but also its most dubious effects upon the American regime. Nationalists in their conception of government, Progressives were sentimentalists in their understanding of politics. Looking backward to an idealized time of citizen virtue associated with the Founders, now lost to bosses and machines, they reconstituted politics in a way not only alien to the party system of the nineteenth century but also deeply at odds with the national government they sought. The "great irony" of Progressivism, Philip Ethington concludes, is the damage these political reforms have done to democracy in America. The further irony is that much of this nettlesome legacy traces to differences between the empirical and the mythical Lincoln.

The Recasting of Lincoln

For Abraham Lincoln, the Union had a purpose, a telos, that could not be violated without making the Union something other than what the Founders intended. This purpose lay in the linkage of Union to liberty, the latter understood in positive as well as negative terms. Slavery, as J. David Greenstone argues, and especially its extension into the territories, framed this relationship squarely for Lincoln: Slavery was an evil that the national government should at all times deplore and against whose extension it should stand inflexible. At the same time, the Union, born of the Declaration of Independence, institutionalized in the Constitution, embodied the Framers' ideal of republican liberty and thus should be preserved at all costs, save that of slavery's expansion. To Lincoln, the Declaration's assertion that all men are created equal was the great object of the nation, but it was a goal to be pursued together with an equally important purpose — that of preserving republican liberty protected by the Constitution. These two great principles — the equality of all in a regime of republican liberty — came together in his conception of Union and, indeed, gave moral purpose and direction to that Union and through it to the nation.[9]

It was also within this frame that Lincoln understood politics: It was the public activity by which differences between legitimate interests could be resolved through reason and accommodation without violating the fundamental principles for which the Union stood. Politics was a way to maintain political order without the use of force, but other than securing order with freedom, there was no overarching purpose to the activity of politics in itself. There was no telos inherent in it. Yet, the practice of politics was not without moral purpose, but that purpose derived from the great object of the nation, i.e., the ideals of equality and republicanism as joined in the concept of Union upon which the American polity was founded. For Lincoln, politics should move the nation toward this goal, but do so without sacrificing any gains made in realizing either human equality or republican government. Politics thus functioned to moderate differences, isolating extremists in both the North and South as it sought accommodations that at once preserved the Union and moved the nation relentlessly, if incrementally, toward its larger purpose. Lincoln embraced the practice of politics in his time, seeking not to reform but to master it, as it was the means by which the larger ends of the nation could be peacefully sought and secured.[10]

For all their admiration of Lincoln — his moral leadership, his concern for national purpose in Union, and his positive use of the presidency — . Progressives, to a remarkable degree, stood his thought on its head. They retained his understanding of liberty as having both positive and negative dimensions but disconnected it from the idea of Union and the republican principles with which it was irrevocably associated in Lincoln's mind. To Progressives, the constitutional question of Union that had occupied Lincoln was settled by the Civil War; its place taken by that of the Nation. For them, the question was how to save the nation, as "founded" by Lincoln on the ideal of positive as well as negative liberty, when the threat was industrialism, not secession.[11]

In their understanding of positive liberty, Progressives followed Lincoln, who had illustrated the concept by arguing that public education, as a positive liberty, would increase literacy and thereby expand the rights of free inquiry and expression. Similarly, they argued that improvements in the social conditions resulting from the new industrialism and the political arrangements underlying it would expand liberty by providing Americans greater opportunity to realize the promise of the Declaration. Like Lincoln at Gettysburg, where he was said to have read "equality" into a Constitution in which the word never appears, Progressives set about making equality the measure of government and politics in America.[12] To realize their new goal of republican equality through positive liberty, Progressives largely ignored the constraining effects that the ideas of republicanism and Union had on Lincoln's thought, substituting the ideas of democracy and Nation for them. Their aim was to replace the laissez-faire constitutionalism of nineteenth-century America with an expanded role for national institutions in the nation's governance and to replace the party system of Jackson (and old guard Republicans) with a "new democracy" of direct linkages between the people and their government. Thus, for Progressives, *democracy* became the great object of the nation — a new telos. Unlike Lincoln's rich and textured understanding of the purpose of Union and the politics upon which it rested, the Progressive telos was reductionist, as they invested the ideas of republicanism, liberty, nation, and politics with a single ideal — democracy — which all were to serve.

The Challenge of National Democracy

The Progressives were nationalists and democrats, and for all the diversity in their interests and views, they had a coherent intellectual and political core: the belief in a positive national state and in the ideal of an informed and active citizenry directing that state. They also had a common diagnosis of the nation's ills and a prescription for their cure. The twin cancers on the body politic were the party bosses with their machines and the robber barons with their trusts, who were united by a mutuality of interests: the machines for money and patronage, the trusts for sympathetic legislatures and courts. This "interlocking directorate" of Jacksonian politics and laissez-faire economics was secured by a decentralized regime of limited national purpose that was resistant to popular control. The Progressive strategy, as Martha Derthick and John Dinan observe, was "to challenge the existing understanding of constitutionalism and to put forth a new interpretation," the principal objectives of which were twofold: (1) to restore democratic citizenship by returning power directly to the people and (2) to enlarge the role of national institutions, public and private, in the conduct of the nation's affairs. But for all their nationalist and democratic passion, the Progressives failed to devise an institutional structure for a national politics capable of sustaining the national government of their construction.

This failure, to be sure, is understandable. Many, if not most, Progressives were anti-party. Bosses and machines were, to their eyes, a principal corruptor of democracy in America, and their aim was to displace, not redesign, the party system as a democratic institution. The direct democracy, nonpartisan, and corrupt-practices reforms they championed, like the civil service and ballot law reforms of the Mugwump reformers who preceded them, altered the traditional practices and powers of the parties. At the same time, the new national associations welcomed by the Progressives — "parastates," as Eldon Eisenach calls them — became over time competitors with the parties, initially in governance, then in elections.

Of the Progressives none was more vocal in his opposition to political parties than Herbert Croly. Like others, Croly saw the parties as cornerstones of the political localism that nationalist reformers sought to dislodge. Through their control of both nominations for and appointments to office, the political parties at the grass roots, preoccupied with local concerns, dominated politics. Unlike others, Croly located the problem in the system of representative democracy, which was inevitably organized on a geographical basis that, by fragmenting politics, gave undue weight to local interests. His championship of direct democracy was thus an assault not just on parties, but on the whole system of representative democracy.[13]

Like other Progressives, Croly looked to the presidency — the one national office in the gift of the Constitution — as the institution through which to construct a national government. The president was to be assisted by a bureaucracy of experts who, guided by an educated public opinion and with training in the new social sciences, were to be "specialists" in discovering those programs that served the public good. Congressional deliberation on issues of national import posed by the chief executive would aid in educating public opinion. But for Croly, democracy was a social and not merely political ideal. Broad participation in politics and popular control of government were not ends in themselves, but rather means to a larger democratic purpose to which other social institutions contributed as well and as much. Thus, while Croly saw political parties as of some rudimentary and transitory value in the evolution to democracy, it was direct participation and individual responsibility that built the virtuous citizens required for this democratic state — and once this was achieved, there was no need for representative institutions like parties.

Among the Progressives, the principal champion of party government was of course Woodrow Wilson, whose thought was greatly influenced by his studies of and affection for the British parliamentary system. For Wilson, constitutional democracy was a representative system through which there was popular control of government. This meant that citizens should be able to remove from office those who *misgoverned* them, not that they be able to govern themselves in any immediate or direct sense.[14] Thus, while Wilson embraced many of the direct democracy reforms, such as the primary, he understood popular control of government as citizens having an effective check upon those who governed. His dilemma was that the U.S. Constitution, with its separation of powers, shattered sovereignty and left unclear where or with whom responsibility for the actions of government rested. In Britain the point of ultimate responsibility was clear: it was the House of Commons.

There was no counterpart in the American system, and Wilson set about trying to construct one.[15]

Political parties, for Wilson, were the most promising institution through which to build accountability into American government and politics, in part because they could provide collective leadership and in part because they had the potential for unified leadership in that they cut across the several branches of government. At the same time, American parties were ill prepared institutionally for this role, he argued, because they had grown up outside of government as private associations, not within the government itself as was the case in England. To make them effective as responsible agents for government required their being organizationally congruent with the government so that party leaders and public officials would be one and the same persons, thus establishing a clear connection between elections and government and making responsibility for the latter clear.

The question for Wilson was how to do this. In the late nineteenth century he looked to Congress, especially to the House of Representatives with its strong committee system, as the most promising location for an American "cabinet" that would be the point of ultimate responsibility within the government. In the twentieth century, and as president, he saw the chief executive as the most likely place to locate the ultimate responsibility for government, arguing, like Progressives generally, that it was the one office filled by election of all the people and thus best able to act in the interests and the name of the people and the nation. In the White House, especially in his first term, Wilson provided an example of a presidency-centered, "responsible" party government, that worked closely with his party's leaders in Congress to enact much of the New Freedom program on which he had run for the office.[16] But, the Wilson leadership was in fact personal, not institutional, more akin to that of Lincoln than to a British prime minister. Yet, his success as president gave credence to the Progressive conception of executive-centered government.

The presidency and the federal bureaucracy thus emerged from the Progressive Era as the institutional structure for a national politics to gird the new national democratic state. In the 1920s its prospects looked tenuous. But with the much expanded national state built in the thirties by the New Deal to combat the Great Depression, followed fast by World War II with yet greater expansion of the national government, and thereafter by Cold War that solidified the welfare/warfare state, political support for national government seemed secure in a strong presidency, now the leader of the free world.

In the heady nationalism of the postwar years, there were numerous attempts, both in and out of government, to build a stronger political/institutional structure to support the new state, all in one way or another looking toward a more national system of politics. Within Congress there were renewed efforts, on the one hand, to abolish the Electoral College so that elections for president might be truly national and, on the other, to establish a national primary with a runoff in the event no one achieved a majority vote. There were also initiatives to bring greater coherence and national oversight to the existing system of state presidential primaries.[17] Outside Congress, a committee on political parties of the American Political Science Association called for a "more responsible" national party system, while the National Municipal League presented a plan for a Model National Primary that would better integrate an already chaotic nominating process.[18] None of these efforts to design a more national system of party politics succeeded, and by the end of the 1950s, the moment and whatever opportunity it held had passed.

Reform of the nation's political institutions came in the late 1960s and 1970s. For Democrats it sprang from the social movements of the sixties. Fired by the flames of war in Vietnam and the Civil Rights Movement, it was anti-party in character, calling for a "participatory" democracy akin in spirit and practice to the direct democracy of the Progressives, not the nationalism of the fifties reformers. Party reforms transformed the politics of presidential selection, moving both parties toward a more candidate-centered system, the model for which was the 1960 campaign of John F. Kennedy. New Democratic Party rules, which sought greater grass-roots participation in the selection of delegates to the party's national convention so as to empower the rank-and-file at the expense of the "bosses," instead put the candidates themselves in control of party nominations for president.[19] The Republicans, in the minority since the 1930s, devised a new candidate-service party that with greatly expanded fundraising enabled the GOP to provide party candidates, all of whom had their own committees, with resources and expertise across the full spectrum of campaign activities. In both parties, more so perhaps for the Democrats, the effect of reform was to move, institutionally, away from a centralized system of politics and toward a more fractured and decentralized one that was in some ways more like that of the nineteenth century, which the Progressives had deplored, than the national system envisioned by postwar reformers.

Other reforms reinforced this outcome. The Federal Elections Campaign Act, passed in the aftermath of the Watergate scandal, established a regulatory system for campaign financing that centered on candidates and their campaign committees, thus institutionalizing the new, more decentralized system of candidate-centered politics. In addition the FECA gave statutory authorization to political action committees, which grew rapidly in number, and also limited direct party contributions to candidates. The result was that interest groups, not parties, became the principal source of campaign money, especially for Congress, eroding further the ability of the parties to provide institutional support for a national politics. Congressional reforms, in the name of democracy, also sought a more broadly participatory system of lawmaking. A reorganization of committees in the U.S. House of Representatives decentralized control of the legislative process, weakening a strong committee system and encouraging wider participation by giving greater authority to subcommittees and their chairs, thus fracturing further the process by which national legislation is made.[20] Together the party and congressional reforms released more centrifugal forces into American politics, all at the expense of a more national system.[21]

Beginning in the 1970s, in an ironic turn, the institutions on which the Progressives had counted to secure a national democracy seemed to turn on that objective. The initiative and referendum grew in popularity as an instrument through which to attack government. Broad-ranging tax-cutting referenda, beginning in California, won favor with voters in many states, advancing a conservative movement that sought ultimately to reduce the role of the national government in the lives of its citizens. In the 1980s an activist conservative, Ronald Reagan, won the presidency and used that bully pulpit to preach against both "big government" and the taxes that sustained it. At the same time, his administration's increased spending on defense produced large budget deficits that in turn increased pressure to cut federal spending on domestic programs (regulatory, as well as social and economic) and discouraged any new initiatives in these areas. In the 1990s the end of the Cold War removed international crisis as a buttress to the presidency, diminishing the aura of the office. Almost simultaneously, a new Republican majority arrived in the Congress, led by southern conservatives long nurtured in anti-Washington politics. This new Congress proved more aggressive and effective in setting a national agenda that was aimed clearly at diminishing further the scope and capacity of the federal government.[22] In a further irony the years since the 1960s have seen the federal courts, long the bulwark of conservatism and never a significant part of the Progressive plan for national governance, become in many ways the principal institutional guarantor of national power and, as a consequence, a primary target of conservative reformers.[23]

The failure of the Progressives to institutionalize a national politics adequate to sustain a national state seems at century's end to be undoing the state whose construction they began. Their idea of a direct democracy, of an immediate and positive link of citizens to the national government, has proven debilitating to deliberative institutions, contributing to changes in the character of both political representation and political rhetoric: the representative as "trustee" being displaced by the "delegate," instructed now by opinion polls and focus groups, and debate becoming more tactical than substantive with issues used as weapons. Whatever the momentary factors associated with the demise of deliberation — the rights revolution backed politically by single-interest groups with money and voter networks, professional campaigns designed negatively to demean the character of opponents, television's definition of "news" as picturable events that entail conflict — these changes trace ultimately to the Progressive recasting of Lincoln and, specifically, to their investing the activity of politics with a telos, "democracy." In their embrace of positive liberty, the Progressives remade the Constitution of American government. In their devotion to an anti-party direct democracy, they also reconstituted American politics. But as they expanded the institutional capacities of national governance, they fractured the political foundation upon which the new democratic state rested.

As constitutionalists the Progressives stand in contrast to the eighteenth-century framers of the Constitution, for whom republican government and politics were inextricably linked in their institutional design. The "science of politics" of which Hamilton speaks in Federalist 9 refers to the construction of a republican *government*. For the framers, politics was the "science of government."[24] It was the activity by which a free government of separated and competing powers into which legitimate and competing interests had been built could be made to work.

Their politics, while institutionalized extraconstitutionally in the political party, grew naturally from and gave coherence to their frame of government.[25] Progressives, however, in their construction of a new state, ruptured this coherence, and while they produced a more impressive national edifice, they failed to provide the solid political footings required to secure the structure. The incoherence in the design of the Progressive state has come increasingly to torment realization of the national democracy that was their dream.

The Torment of Politics

The Progressives did not like politics, especially the corrupt politics of the party bosses and their machines that they saw as denying citizens their democratic birthright. They embraced an expansive, activist, and positive view of democratic citizenship, not the limited, passive, and negative one they found in the Constitution. Popular government, the essence of political democracy, was *self*-government, and for the Progressives, this meant an engaged, interventionist, and national citizenship — not one limited to periodic votes for representatives to do the public's business, but a citizenship in which the people themselves had a direct role in the conduct of public affairs. It was an immediate citizenship, wherein individuals acted directly through primaries to influence nominations for office and through the initiative and referendum to effect public policy, as well as collectively through an enlightened public opinion to guide and sustain government. As members of a great community — a national community — the citizens envisioned by the Progressives had the duty to educate themselves on national issues through local forums or associations, as well as through an "educational" press, a bureaucracy of trained experts, and deliberations in Congress that followed the lead of the president. This was to be a full-throated citizenship, not one restricted to a vocabulary of "yes" and "no."

But their dislike for politics went deeper; they did not like the activity of politics itself — the endless bargaining, trading, and dealing. Politics did not charm the idealists, the reformers, the men of education, morals, and conviction. They saw no larger purpose in it, no higher good served by it, only a squalid enterprise, demeaning to intelligence, riddled with corruption, and culminating at best in the cheerful compromise of principle. Moreover, the politics they saw was not about the public purpose of the nation, but was instead consumed by local interests and private greed, indifferent alike to the idea of a great community and the idealism of grand purpose. Unlike the generation of Americans who framed the Constitution—or, for that matter, their hero, Abraham Lincoln—the Progressives were truly, as Robert Crunden labels them, "*ministers* of reform."[26]

The Progressive view of politics contrasts sharply with that of the American Framers. Indeed, the Federal Convention of 1787 is a case study in the art and science of politics in all its meanness and magnificence. Aptly described as a "reform caucus," the convention is a testament to the politics of deliberation—of calculation, negotiation, and compromise—and of bargains struck in the accommodation of differences for reasons at once principled and political.[27] For the Framers, politics was not merely an activity; it was the activity of free men by which and through which their liberty was to be secured. It was a principled activity precisely because it maintained political order while serving that higher purpose—"a scheme of ordered liberty," as Justice Benjamin Cardozo called it. With an understanding of politics from Aristotle, of republicanism from Rome, and of liberty from John Locke, they framed a government by the architecture of Montesquieu, setting power against power, interest against interest, ambition against ambition—a "machine that would go of itself" when oiled by the activity of politics.[28]

A century after its ratification, more and more social critics and reformers found problems in the Constitution, especially its system of negative liberties which had come to pose a formidable challenge to a positive governmental response to the social distresses that attended industrialization. Merely asserting positive liberty led only to a stalemate of principles with negative liberty. The Constitution in itself provided no guidance in choosing between or balancing these claims of liberty, though Supreme Court decisions tilted decisively toward restraints on action. A localist politics of mediation and accommodation provided no direction, though its institutional expression, the party machines, like the courts, served the status quo. To change this, the Progressives sought a national state and a national politics that together served a single purpose: democracy.

As an idea, democracy has a long history, yet it was only in the nineteenth century that it shed its association with mob rule and acquired the respectable garb of popular government.[29] In America, democracy could trace its lineage to the Puritans, but it was the admission of the western territories into the Union following the War of 1812 that gave the term both a common currency and positive connotation in describing the societies and constitutions of these new states.[30] The new "western" democracy — or "populism" — triumphed in the Jacksonian presidency, was central to the Lincoln-Douglas debates in 1858, and rankled the nation with protests and third parties in the final years of the nineteenth century. But for most Americans, Lincoln among them, democracy was, as it had been for Aristotle, a component of mixed government, and it was the latter, embodying the republican ideal, that had animated the Framers.[31] Popular control of government, in this frame, meant, as it did for Wilson, having a check upon government: the people could "throw the rascals out." Democracy was therefore not the *purpose* of republican government, but rather a component of a properly constructed mixed government — an *interest* in the polity, critical to the constitution of popular government, but one that must be checked so as to safeguard minority rights against any unwarranted intrusions of majority rule. In this frame, it was the moderate mediation of politics — the basis of political order — that protected the liberties of all.

In making democracy the purpose of both government and politics, the Progressives changed the nature of the American regime both conceptually and empirically. Where Lincoln's idea of Union drew purpose from a dialectic between republican principles and positive liberty as mediated through politics, the Progressive idea of Nation drew its purpose from the solitary ideal of democracy. Democracy was no longer to be one part of a mixed polity, but became instead the telos of the new American state to be served by a politics whose purpose was also democracy. Indeed, Progressives saw democracy as the true form of politics, and thus fettered, their politics was conceptually unlike that of Lincoln and the Framers. Moreover, by reducing politics to democracy, the Progressives built their new nation on a tautology: it was to be a political democracy governed by a democratic politics.

But this was not the only problem the Progressive idea of politics faced, for as the best may be the enemy of the good, so too a teleological politics can be the enemy of a free politics. Democracy may be a necessary element in mixed government, but it alone, as Bernard Crick argues, can be "destructive of the political community:" "Democracy is one element in politics; if it seeks to be everything, it destroys politics, turning 'harmony into mere unison,' reducing 'a theme to a single beat.'"[32] The reduction of politics to democracy meant that democracy now stood alone as the telos of the new nation, and for the Progressives, a truly democratic politics seemed sufficient to secure political freedom in the new polity, as had the politics of Lincoln and the Framers in the earlier republic. But the twentieth century has taught otherwise. Popular rule may require democracy, and democracy can stabilize free regimes, but democracy can also stabilize unfree regimes and has made totalitarianism possible. Again, Crick: "Totalitarian regimes, indeed, are a product of a democratic age. They depend upon mass support, and they have found a way of treating society as if it were, or were about to be, a single mass."[33] The Progressive formulation thus contained the seed of its own destruction, as the century-long struggle of political democracy with fascism and communism were to attest. The seed may not have germinated in American soil, perhaps because of the "looser genius" Milkis finds in American politics, but it remains an ominous presence, more so perhaps in the modern socially diverse, multicultural political community, where a teleological politics that seeks to bend all to a common purpose may make an ordered liberty more tenuous and less secure—especially when the national political institutions that mediate competition among these interests are themselves weakened.

Thus the torment of politics for Progressives was that, detached from the principle of democracy, the activity of politics enabled a free people to choose *not* to pursue the Progressive ideal of a great nation. But attached too intimately to politics, democracy might destroy the liberty upon which that nation had been founded originally. As a dialectic, the empirical question is who or what mediates the relationship between democracy and politics. The answer that emerged was: "power" within a regime of interest-group liberalism—though to be sure, this was not the answer given by the Progressives.

The Lost Cause of Progressivism

Progressives were not champions of interest-group liberalism.[34] They were indeed hostile to a politics of narrowly selfish interests, whether organized by groups or parties, and sought instead a national state that would govern in the public interest. But the Progressive reconstitution of government and politics provided all of the necessary preconditions for a regime of interest-group liberalism. On the one hand, their electoral reforms weakened the party system as an institutional buttress for a national state, thereby diminishing the capacity of the parties to organize politics on a broad popular base of generalized interests, creating a political vacuum that would be filled by interest groups.[35] On the other, their political infrastructure for a democratic government centered on the making of public policy by an expanded universe of experts, some in the public sector, others in the private, and many of whom moved regularly between the two. As experts became more narrowly specialists, this design of government leant itself increasingly to a politics of small-scale organization and private influence. This interest-group state began to take shape through the 1920s as professional and trade associations were regularly drawn into the design of public policy for the national government, brought there by no less a Progressive than Herbert Hoover.[36] In the end, the democratic theory that triumphed, as Ethington recognizes, was "group behavioral liberalism," and it is ironic, to be sure, as Hamby suggests, that a cause "hostile to special interests became an example of interest group politics."

As the Progressive idea of *a* national interest was displaced by the regime of interest-group liberalism, so too the democratic telos was eviscerated by the challenge of totalitarianism, where the telos of the new authoritarian state was also "democratic" in its mass appeal, based on the common good, and its devotion to the majoritarian principle. This new totalitarian state was, of course, not a *liberal* democracy. It was grounded in an aggregate conception of rights—those of mankind, not of individuals—and its governance was driven by historicist theories of a nationalist ideal that gave legitimacy to its actions, not by a free politics as Lincoln and the Framers understood that activity. The telos of the new totalitarian state came to be seen as an oppressive *ideology* that destroyed individual freedom, as positive liberties, in a sense, triumphed totally over negative liberties.

Communism and fascism as democratic ideologies thus became the enemy—indeed, the antithesis—of *political* democracy. The Progressive idea of democracy as telos suddenly smacked of ideology, which led to democracy being recast, not as the purpose of a liberal polity but as the *process* by which the liberal state was governed, one that promised fairness but was essentially neutral as to ends. In this reformulation, democratic governance was cast in the role of umpire, interpreting and enforcing the rules in a political game played by a multiplicity of self-interested teams, wherein "fairness" meant a kind of due process that assured all legitimate political claims would be treated the same under the rules. Moreover, the Progressive ideal of popular sovereignty — citizens participating directly in their own governance — was replaced by that of pluralist democracy: a polity filled with great numbers of diverse social and economic interests, each organized by more or less like-minded citizens, competing for influence through the democratic process.[37] Political democracy was thus transformed into a contest for power.

At the same time, the idea of political power itself was transformed. In drafting the Constitution, the American Framers were guided by an institutional conception of power that associated it with sovereignty and understood it as inhering in the organization of the state.[38] To secure liberty, the Framers fractured sovereignty in a constitutional design that divided political power against itself in a system of institutional negations — the separation of powers, federalism, and guarantees of individual rights. It was this system of negations that built *politics* into the Constitution and, through it, into the governance of the nation. Political power resided in these institutional negations as the capacity of one office to check another, thereby necessitating a political relationship if anything was to be accomplished. The activity of politics — of deliberation and compromise — that sprang from this institutional arrangement was the method by which the general interests of a polity could be identified and advanced by accommodating differences in an orderly and peaceful way that protected the rights of individuals. Having political power in this frame meant having a "voice" in the making of public policy — a place at the table — that derived from having an effective check upon the ambitions of another.[39] It did not mean the ability to control the outcome. Indeed, the whole design of the Constitution was intended to prevent the exercise of precisely that kind of power.

The new idea of political power changed this, moving it conceptually from political institutions to political actors. Empirically, this definitional shift in the location of political power focused attention on the behavior of individuals and groups acting politically, not on the institutional checks that disciplined their behavior. In this formulation, having political power no longer meant being able to force a political relationship or having a place at the table, but rather the ability to control outcomes: who got what, when, and how.[40] This conceptual move was due in part no doubt to the Progressive generation's rejection of the constitutional formalisms of the nineteenth century whose negative rights and powers frustrated national government attempts to deal with the social and economic ills of industrialism, but also in part to the Progressive embrace of the new behavioral social sciences of politics and psychology that Philip Ethington's essay explores. But whatever the sources of this change, the consequences of the new understanding of political power as control and not voice were twofold: (1) it erased any distinction between politics and the political, reducing the former to the latter and thereby making the idea of politics a *willful* activity, and (2) it made "good men" the key to good government and public opinion the key to educating citizens, not a well-designed constitution as the Framers believed. This new idea of political power was thus compatible with the Progressive theory of politics and democracy, divorcing the concept from the system of constitutional negations that they saw as impediments to reform and redefining it as a positive and purposeful act whereby having power meant empirically the ability of an individual to impose his will upon a political outcome.

The Progressive embrace of the presidency as the central institution in their new national state is a testament to the utility this new understanding of political power had for them. The power of the presidency was no longer seen as inhering in the institution itself, but rather in the will (and skill) of the person who occupied the office. Theodore Roosevelt embodied the Progressive ideal of the presidency: a bully pulpit filled by a steward of the people. Presidential *leadership* — the individual in the White House setting the national agenda, educating public opinion, directing policy making in Congress — was, for Progressives, critical to realizing their new democratic Nation. Embedded in this conception of the presidency is, of course, the idea of political power as the ability of the chief executive, through persuasion, to control the direction of public policy.[41] In this formulation, a president who asserts his will successfully is powerful, while one who must engage in a politics of give-and-take, of bargaining and compromise, appears weak.[42]

The new idea of political power had further, but less salutary, ramifications for the Progressive idea of citizenship. The location of political power in the actions of individuals transformed the Progressive ideal of the democratic citizen from one who had a direct voice in a deliberative politics of self-governance into a rights-bearer removed from a deliberative politics but with absolutist claims upon government.[43] Positive liberty, like negative liberty, restricts the realm of public decision open to politics and majoritarian democracy. While both forms of liberty stand in the same political relationship to government and the public, positive liberty presents different expectations of government. Where negative liberties can be protected with limited government intervention, applicable equally to all citizens, the securing of positive liberty requires an expanded and more invasive government intervening in social and economic relationships on behalf of particular classes of individuals, not the public in general.

As the courts discovered more and more constitutionally protected rights, like privacy in personal and family life, and Congress expanded individual entitlements in social and welfare programs, the realm of public decision subject to the control of popular majorities narrowed, which in turn gave a new political urgency and definition to the old tension between majority rule and minority rights. For the rights bearer, any incursion upon their positive liberty, like any on negative liberty, is an invasion of their freedom — and, with the new conception of political power, it is also a measure of their powerlessness in a regime of ostensible self-government. At the same time, for a public schooled in the idea of democracy as majority rule, the expansion of rights and entitlements diminishes popular control of government, erodes the idea of popular sovereignty, and encourages a sense of powerlessness in the public as well. In a regime that defines politics and democracy in terms of power, understood as the successful exercise of individual will, nothing is more debilitating for citizens and public alike than the sense of powerlessness, as the present cynicism of Americans about their government and politics would seem to attest.

Conclusion

The cause of Progressivism has thus been lost in a politics of special-interest groups and rights-bearing citizens that is framed by a zero-sum conception of political power. This is not the nation the Progressives promised, and it seems as if history has played a trick upon them. But it is a trick to which latter-day progressives were a party and one to which the conceptual reorderings in the thought of the original Progressives contributed, leaving one to puzzle over who tricked whom. The Progressives were nationalists, but they were not institutionalists. Indeed, their theory of governance was behavioral, not institutional — one in which, as Carey McWilliams argues, education (moral and scientific), not the frame of government, disciplined political actions. In this, they were quite unlike the founding generation of Constitution-makers. Nowhere is the Progressive refusal to build serviceable institutions of governance more evident than in the political structure they left to sustain an energetic national state.

The Progressive reconstruction of politics through direct democracy and nonpartisan reforms, individualist and anti-institutionalist in character, has provided a frail political structure in place of the virile, albeit corrupt, party politics of the late nineteenth century. "The drive to revitalize democracy," Hamby contends, "became an attack on a traditional party politics that, for all its shortcomings, had displayed considerable vitality and mobilized masses." The weaknesses of the Progressive constitution of politics was concealed for much of the twentieth century by the succession of crises from World War I through the Great Depression, World War II, and the Cold War that have dominated American public life since the second decade of the twentieth century. Crises, as Morton Keller observes, are the one thing in a free democracy that can focus public opinion. In the absence of crisis, the centrifugal forces of social pluralism are unleashed, unless harnessed by an institutional arrangement of politics — a mass-based party system — so constituted as to discipline these energies and concentrate them on the construction of political majorities. The radically individualistic politics of the Progressives has enervated national political institutions and left a system — with its candidate-centered campaigns dominated by narrow interests, money, celebrity, and the news media — that is, in its way, as fractured and antinational in character as its nineteenth-century counterpart, and no more democratic.[44]

Rather than a true citizen democracy, the Progressive reforms have produced a much more complex system of politics that places greater and often discouraging demands on voters. The direct primary, the initiative and referendum, and the temporal separation of elections for national, state, and local offices greatly complicate the electoral system, increasing the physical demands on the voter, while at the same time the Progressive insistence that the "good" voter is an *educated* voter, *fully informed* about all the candidates and issues, greatly increases the intellectual demands. Progressive reforms also complicate the voting decision by introducing nonpartisan forms of election that remove party labels, as a guide to voter choice, from the election ballot, and in addition radically change the incentives for voting through civil service and corrupt-practices reforms that sharply reduce patronage, through increased regulation of elections that routinize the organization and activities of political parties and make the formation of third parties more difficult, and through changes in electioneering that have abandoned "spectacular" popular displays in favor of "educational" campaigns whose appeals center on abstract and impersonal issues.[45] These reforms raised the costs and lowered the benefits of political participation for working- and lower-class voters, especially immigrants and minorities, and made a politics of mass organization more difficult. In many ways, the measure of Progressive "success" is to be found in the declining levels of voter turnout throughout the twentieth century and the changed pattern of turnout in which poorer, less educated, working class, minority, and immigrant populations are disproportionately missing from the voting booth.[46]

These reforms, however, were consistent with the executive-centered national state to which the Progressives aspired, one in which representative institutions — Congress and the parties — were to be less important than administrative ones. As the excerpt from *The New Republic* that introduces this essay suggests: the great constitutional objective of the Progressives was a "new governmental machinery" that would "destroy the two-party system" by eliminating the need for any "intermediaries" between the popular will and the government. The anti-party rhetoric of the Progressives emphasized the corruption of the bosses and their machines, but as Donald Weatherman points out, the party system the Progressives assaulted had grown from and strengthened the Constitution of the Founders. It was a party system consistent with the separation of powers that institutionalized the activity of politics the Framers built into the governance of the nation to secure republican liberty.[47] As the Progressives did not like politics, neither did they like the separation of powers. Thus, for them, political parties were not merely corrupt in their practices, they were more importantly a cornerstone of an older constitutional order — that of the Founders, and of Lincoln — that the Progressives sought to change in fundamental ways. They desired a more unitary system of government, which they tried to construct within a constitutional framework designed quite consciously to divide power. To this end, they weakened republican institutions by reducing the importance of deliberation in Congress and replacing leadership through an institutionalized party system with personal leadership by the executive guided by public opinion and aided by an expert bureaucracy.

It may be, as Sidney Milkis suggests, that the "looser genius" of American politics militates against the nationalization of party politics. But there was more to the Progressive refusal to reconstruct the party system than this. As Weatherman argues, the earliest party builders in America — James Madison and Martin Van Buren — demonstrated that a party system could be constructed within the Framers' design that would simultaneously strengthen the national government, secure the separation of powers, and enhance executive power, which leads him to attribute another motive to the Progressives: "The reason reformers were so eager to accuse parties and to attack them was that the progressive movement was, in the main, a movement of the educated upper-middle and upper classes. What these people disliked about political parties was their inability to control them."[48] Arthur Lipow shares this view, arguing that either the Progressives were "prisoners of their own foolish dogmas for ever having believed that a democratic system, requiring such sustained, direct participation, was possible in a modern industrial society" or they were knowingly serving their own interests — and he suggests that *both* may well have been the case.[49]

But whatever their motives, the Progressives clearly championed a populist, plebiscitary form of political participation. In associating these reforms with the direct democracy of the New England town meeting and packaging them accordingly as *true* democracy, the Progressives have privileged their idea of participatory democracy, in both concept and practice, against a politics of mass organization through political parties, though the latter is an equally legitimate form of democratic participation. Their success in "marketing" their idea of democracy has been truly remarkable, for it has gone substantially unchallenged since the 1920s by political practitioners, reformers, and scholars alike as *the* definition of democracy. As Lipow observes, the Progressive reforms and the assumptions underlying them have become the "natural political order" in America and been "remarkably free from serious ideological or organized political challenge."[50] It is the more remarkable in that their conception of democracy is at odds with how the American Founders and Lincoln understood the requirements of popular government, as well as with how other democratic nations have institutionalized their politics. Indeed, the United States is unique among the liberal democracies of the world in its embrace of the Progressive model.

The legacy of Progressivism, then, is one of institutional incoherence. On the one hand, the Progressives began construction of a national state that has been able to cope with the most severe challenges of the twentieth century, albeit better with those of international than those of domestic politics, but on the other hand have left a disorganized and decentralized politics grounded in a radical individualism and nonpartisan forms that seem increasingly incapable of sustaining the energetic national state of their design. In the end, what the Progressive political reforms achieved was not to make America a "true" democracy, or for that matter one more democratic than other liberal states, but rather to change the rules of the political game so that the Progressives and their conception of national purpose might triumph.[51] These new rules have produced, as the Progressives desired, a weakening of partisanship and political parties in the mass electorate, or what Walter Dean Burnham has described as the "disaggregation" of party politics.[52] They have also transformed American parties from mass to elite organizations and shifted the party battle away from the electorate and toward the bureaucracy and the courts, where it has become rhetorically less a reasoned discourse and more one of relentless negativism and personal attack.[53] Rather than giving the government back to the people, the Progressive reforms instead seem increasingly to have turned it over to policy specialists, campaign mechanics, lawyers, and lobbyists, none of whom has true political legitimacy in a popular regime.

The legacy of Progressivism, as Carey McWilliams rightly concludes, "deserves to be appreciated, but . . . is also an occasion for regret." This volume has been an occasion to reexamine that legacy. And as the political reforms of the Progressives, in practice, turn more and more against their great objective of an energetic national state, and as the incoherence of their political design becomes more evident, that reexamination inevitably begs the question their hero Abraham Lincoln asked about the incoherence of slavery in a regime of liberty: How long can this house divided against itself stand?

Notes

1. Histories of the era are many, but see especially Robert Wiebe, *The Search for Order* (New York: Hill & Wang, 1967).

2. On the role of social status in the era, see Richard Hofstadter, *The Age of Reform* (New York: Knopf, 1955).

3. On populism, see Lawrence Godwyn, *Democratic Promise* (New York: Oxford University Press, 1976).

4. See Paul Kleppner, *The Third Party System, 1853–1892* (Chapel Hill: University of North Carolina Press, 1979); H. Wayne Morgan, *From Hayes to McKinley* (Syracuse: Syracuse University Press, 1969); J. Rogers Hollingsworth, *The Whirligig of Politics* (Chicago: University of Chicago Press, 1963); Robert D. Marcus, *Grand Old Party* (New York: Oxford University Press, 1971); and John G. Sproat, *The Best Men* (New York: Oxford University Press, 1968).

5. Merrill D. Peterson, *Lincoln in American Memory* (New Deal: Oxford University Press, 1994), 141. See, too, Dwight G. Anderson, *Abraham Lincoln: The Quest for Immortality* (New York: Knopf, 1982), 211–15.

6. Peterson, *Lincoln,* 165.

7. Ibid., 156.

8. Stephen Skowronek, *Building a New American State* (New York: Cambridge University Press, 1982) and Martin Shefter, *Political Parties and the State* (Princeton: Princeton University Press, 1994), esp. chap. 3.

9. J. David Greenstone, *The Lincoln Persuasion* (Princeton: Princeton University Press, 1993), 16–21.

10. On Lincoln as politician, see Benjamin Thomas, *Abraham Lincoln* (New York: Knopf, 1952), 100–107, 152–70, 228–39; David Donald, *Lincoln Reconsidered* (New York: Vintage, 1961), chap. 4; Stephen B. Oates, *With Malice Toward None* (New York: Harper & Row, 1977), 78–89, 127–35, 161–79; and Philip Shaw Paludon, *The Presidency of Abraham Lincoln* (Lawrence: University Press of Kansas, 1994), 35–45.

11. Greenstone, *Lincoln,* chap. 9. See also James H. McPherson, *Abraham Lincoln and the Second American Revolution* (New York: Oxford University Press, 1990), 61–64.

12. Garry Wills, *Lincoln at Gettysburg* (New York: Simon & Schuster, 1992), prologue and chap. 4.

13. Herbert Croly, *The Promise of American Life* (New York: Macmillan, 1909), esp. chap. 7, and *Progressive Democracy* (New York: Macmillan, 1914). Croly's views on parties and democracy are, of course, spread throughout these two volumes. For a useful discussion of them, see Austin Ranney, *The Doctrine of Party Government* (Urbana: University of Illinois Press, 1962), chap. 8, and Edward Stettner, *Shaping Modern Liberalism* (Lawrence: University Press of Kansas, 1993), esp. chap. 5.

14. In this, Wilson follows the nineteenth-century English liberal John Stuart Mill, who argues, "Men, as well as women, do not need political rights in

order that they may govern, but in order that they may not be misgoverned." Mill, *Considerations on Representative Government* (New York: Bobbs-Merrill, 1958), 144.

15. Woodrow Wilson, *Congressional Government* (New York: Meridan, 1956), esp. chaps. 3 and 6, and *Constitutional Government* (New York: Columbia University Press, 1908), esp. chaps. 3 and 8. For a useful discussion, see Ranney, *Party Government,* chap. 3.

16. For a brief examination of Wilson as presidential party leader, see Arthur S. Link, *Woodrow Wilson and the Progressive Era* (New York: Harper & Brothers, 1954), esp. chaps. 2 and 3.

17. Manning J. Dauer, "Toward A Model State Presidential Primary Law," *American Political Science Review* 50 (March 1956), esp. 138–40. See also Clarence Berdahl, "Presidential Selection and Democratic Government," *American Political Science Review* 43 (February 1949): 14–41, and Paul T. David, Malcolm Moos, and Ralph Goldman, *Presidential Nominating Politics in 1952,* vol. 1 (Baltimore: Johns Hopkins University Press, 1954), chap. 6.

18. See "Toward A More Responsible Two-Party System," *American Political Science Review* 44 (September 1950), supplement, and "A Model Direct Primary Election System," Report of the Committee on Direct Primary, National Municipal League (New York City, 1951).

19. There is a large literature on Democratic Party reforms. For a sample of perspectives, see William J. Crotty, *Decision for Democrats* (Baltimore: Johns Hopkins University Press, 1978); David E. Price, *Bringing Back the Parties* (Washington: Congressional Quarterly, 1984); and Nelson W. Polsby, *Consequences of Party Reform* (New York: Oxford University Press, 1983). For historical perspective, see James W. Ceaser, *Presidential Selection* (Princeton: Princeton University Press, 1979).

20. See Lawrence C. Dodd and Richard L. Schott, *Congress and the Administrative State* (New York: John Wiley and Sons, 1979); Richard A. Harris and Sidney M. Milkis, eds., *Remaking American Politics* (Boulder, Colo.: Westview, 1989); and G. Calvin Mackenzie, *The Irony of Reform* (Boulder, Colo.: Westview, 1996). These reforms also strengthened the office of Speaker of the House, strengthening party leadership in the body, but a leadership nonetheless responsive to those interests most closely associated with the two parties.

21. Of nationalizing institutions in American politics, television news coverage has been perhaps the most important, but as competitors with the three established networks increase in number, its effect in this regard seems to be waning — and one can only speculate on the impact of the Internet, though for now it seems unpromising as a nationalizing force in American politics.

22. See Douglas B. Harris, "The Rise of the Public Speakership," *Political Science Quarterly* (forthcoming) and also Nicol C. Rae, *Conservative Reformers* (New York: Sharpe, 1998).

23. This new role of the Supreme Court traces, of course, to the 1920s. In what C. Herman Pritchett calls a "startling" constitutional development, the Court in *Gitlow v. New York* incorporated the First Amendment guarantees of

rights into the Fourteenth Amendment protection of liberty, thereby making them applicable to the states. This laid the foundation for the great expansion, especially in the 1950s, of federal court protections of guarantees in the Bill of Rights, which in many ways made the Supreme Court the national institution that best secured the national state. But the regime of rights it secured differed in many ways from that envisioned by the Progressives. C. Herman Pritchett, *The American Constitution* (New York: McGraw-Hill, 1959), 390, and *Gitlow v. New York,* 268 US 652 (1925). See also R. Shep Melnick, "The Courts, Congress, and Programmatic Rights," in *Remaking American Politics,* ed., Richard A. Harris and Sidney M. Milkis (Boulder, Colo.: Westview, 1989), 188–212.

24. This is not a play with words. E. E. Schattschneider notes that an early American dictionary, John Walker's *A Critical Pronouncing Dictionary and Expositor of the English Language,* published originally in 1804, defines "politics" as "the science of government." Schattschneider suggests that Walker's dictionary is "a fair record of the language used by the Founding Fathers." See Schattschneider, *Two Hundred Million Americans in Search of a Government* (New York: Holt, Rinehart and Winston, 1969), 101–2.

25. See Richard Hofstadter, *The Idea of a Party System* (Berkeley: University of California Press, 1969), and Joseph Charles, *The Origins of the American Party System* (New York: Harper & Row, 1956).

26. See Robert M. Crunden, *Ministers of Reform: The Progressives' Achievements in American Civilization, 1889–1920* (New York: Basic Books, 1982).

27. John P. Roche, "The Founding Fathers: A Reform Caucus in Action," *American Political Science Review* 55 (December 1961): 799–816.

28. See Michael Kammen, *A Machine That Would Go of Itself: The Constitution in American Culture* (New York: Knopf, 1986).

29. For a history of the democratic idea, see A. D. Lindsay, *The Modern Democratic State* (New York: Oxford University Press, 1943).

30. It was of course Alexis de Tocqueville's *Democracy in America,* published in 1835, that gave legitimacy to the term's new connotation.

31. Lincoln's great prepositional trilogy at Gettysburg defining democratic government as being "of, "by," and "for" the people is a textured and rich understanding of democracy. Not only do the prepositions refer to three distinct dimensions of the concept but, as others have noted, "government of the people" is genitive case with a dual meaning that democratic government draws its authority from the people and that it also governs them, similar in that regard to the biblical construction that Man is the son of God. See Mortimer J. Adler and William Gorman, "Reflections on the Gettysburg Address," *The New Yorker* (8 September 1975), 42ff. It may be noted that this was not Lincoln's first use of the phrase, nor was the construction original with him. See Garry Wills, *Lincoln at Gettysburg* (New York: Simon & Schuster, 1992).

32. Bernard Crick, *In Defence of Politics* (Chicago: University of Chicago Press, 1962), 59, 68. See, too, Kenneth Minogue, *Politics* (New York: Oxford University Press, 1995).

33. Crick, *In Defence of Politics,* 36. On the mass basis of totalitarianism, see

Hannah Arendt, *The Origins of Totalitarianism* (New York: Harcourt, Brace, Jovanovich, 1973). On different strands of democracy, see George Sabine, "The Two Democratic Traditions," *The Philosophical Review* 61 (October 1952): 451–74.

34. The term "interest-group liberalism" was coined by Theodore J. Lowi, *The End of Liberalism* (New York: Norton, 1969), 51 for a definition, chap. 3 for a general discussion. See, too, Grant McConnell, *Private Power and American Democracy* (New York: Harcourt, Brace, Jovanovich, 1973).

35. E. E. Schattschneider argues that politics takes two basic forms of organization: party politics, which is broadly based and socializes conflict, and pressure politics, which is narrowly drawn and privatizes conflict. See *The Semi-Sovereign People* (Hinsdale, N.J.: Dryden, 1960), chap. 2.

36. See Alan Dawley, *Struggles for Justice* (Cambridge, Mass.: Harvard University Press, 1991), esp. chaps. 8–9.

37. See Henry B. Mayo, *An Introduction to Democratic Theory* (New York: Oxford University Press, 1960). The idea of democracy as a process and the role of social forces therein was presented systematically by Arthur F. Bentley in the first decade of the twentieth century. See Bentley, *The Process of Government* (Chicago: University of Chicago Press, 1908). His "group theory" of politics was revived by David B. Truman, *The Governmental Process* (New York: Knopf, 1951), by which time pluralist theories of American government and politics had made democracy-as-process the dominant view among political and other social scientists, as well as some historians.

38. The concept of power has a long history in Western thought, especially among such philosophical "realists" as Machiavelli, Hobbes, and Montesquieu. For Machiavelli, power was unitary and inhered in the sovereign. Hobbes, however, drew a distinction between *will* power, which existed prior to civil society, and *political* power, which came into existence with civil society. See Thomas Hobbes, *Leviathan* (New York: Liberal Arts, 1958), esp. chaps. 10 and 14, part 1, and also John Plamenatz, *Man and Society,* vol. 1 (New York: McGraw-Hill, 1963), esp. 135–36. Montesquieu, of course, separated Hobbes's political power institutionally in his constitution of liberty. The American Framers followed in this tradition.

39. On political power as voice, see E. E. Schattschneider, *The Semi-Sovereign People.*

40. On political power as control, see Harold Lasswell, *Politics: Who Gets What, When, How* (New York: Meridon, 1958).

41. The best statement of this is, of course, Richard E. Neustadt, *Presidential Power* (New York: Wiley, 1960).

42. As president, for example, John F. Kennedy resolved the Cuban missile crisis with a political deal by trading U.S. missiles in Turkey for Soviet missiles in Cuba. But to avoid the appearance of weakness, he insisted that the public story be that he faced down Nikita Khrushchev and the Russian bear in an exercise of determined presidential will. See Ernest R. May and Philip D. Zelikow, eds., *The Kennedy Tapes* (Cambridge: Harvard University Press, 1997), 528ff and 675ff.

43. See Mary Ann Glendon, *Rights Talk* (New York: Free Press, 1991).

44. Barry D. Karl argues that the flaw in the American ideal of democracy is our commitment to the autonomous individual. See *The Uneasy State* (Chicago: University of Chicago Press, 1983).

45. See Michael McGerr, *The Decline of Popular Politics* (New York: Oxford University Press, 1986). On rational voting, see Anthony Downs, *An Economic Theory of Democracy* (New York: Harper & Brothers, 1957).

46. The literature on nonvoting in America is extensive, but see especially Paul Kleppner, "Who Voted?" in *The Dynamics of Electoral Turnout, 1870–1980,* ed. Gerald M. Pomper (New York: Praeger, 1982). See also Raymond E. Wolfinger and Stephen J. Rosenstone, *Who Votes?* (New Haven: Yale University Press, 1980).

47. Donald V. Weatherman, *Endangered Guardians* (Boston: Rowman & Littlefield, 1994), esp. introduction and chap. 1.

48. Ibid., 25.

49. Arthur Lipow, *Political Parties and Democracy* (Chicago: Pluto, 1996), 15.

50. Ibid., 13.

51. In this regard, the Progressive realignment in American politics might better be seen as James Q. Wilson has described the political changes of the 1960s: it was an elite realignment. James Q. Wilson, "Realignment at the Top, Dealignment at the Bottom," in *The American Election of 1984,* ed. Austin Ranney (Durham: Duke University Press, 1985), 297–310. As such, the era stands in contrast with the mass-level realignment of the New Deal in the 1930s.

52. See Walter Dean Burnham, *Critical Elections and the Mainsprings of American Politics* (New York: Norton, 1970).

53. See Benjamin Ginsberg and Martin Shefter, *Politics by Other Means: The Declining Importance of Elections in America* (New York: Basic Books, 1990).

Contributors

Martha Derthick is professor of political science at the University of Virginia. She is author of *Between State and Nation* and *Agency Under Stress: The Social Security Administration in American Government,* as well as of numerous articles and chapters in scholarly anthologies.

John J. Dinan is assistant professor of politics at Wake Forest University. He is author of *Keeping the People's Liberties: Legislators, Citizens, and Judges as Guardians of Rights.*

Eldon J. Eisenach is professor of political science at the University of Tulsa. He is author of *The Two Worlds of Liberalism: Religion and Politics in Hobbes, Locke, and Mill* and *The Lost Soul of Progressivism,* as well as numerous scholarly articles.

Philip J. Ethington is associate professor of history at the University of Southern California. He is author of *The Public City: The Construction of Urban Life in San Francisco, 1850–1900* and *The Metropolitan Crisis of Modernity in the United States, 1890s–1920s.*

Alonzo L. Hamby is distinguished professor of history at Ohio University. He is author of: *Man of the People: A Life of Harry Truman; Liberalism and Its Challengers: FDR to Reagan; Beyond the New Deal: Harry S.*

Truman and American Liberalism; and *The Imperial Years;* as well as other books and essays on American politics in the twentieth century.

Morton Keller is professor of history at Brandeis University. He is author of *Affairs of State: Public Life in Late Nineteenth-Century America; Regulating a New Economy: Public Policy and Economic Change in America, 1900–1933; Regulating a New Society: Public Policy and Social Change in America, 1900–1933;* and coeditor of *The Encyclopedia of the United States Congress.*

Eileen L. McDonagh is associate professor of political science at Northeastern University. She is author of *Breaking the Abortion Deadlock,* as well as of numerous articles and chapters in scholarly journals and anthologies.

Wilson Carey McWilliams is professor of political science at Rutgers University at New Brunswick. He is author of *The Idea of Fraternity in America; The Politics of Disappointment: American Elections, 1976–1994;* and editor of *The Federalists, the Antifederalists, and the American Political Tradition;* as well as essays in journals and anthologies.

Jerome M. Mileur is professor of political science at the University of Massachusetts at Amherst. He is editor of *Liberalism in Crisis: American Politics in the Sixties;* coeditor of *Challenges to Party Government* and *America's Choice: The Election of 1996;* and serves as coeditor of the University of Massachusetts Press series, Political Development of the American Nation.

Sidney M. Milkis is professor of politics at Brandeis University. He is author of *The President and the Parties: The Transformation of the American Party System since the New Deal;* coauthor of *The American Presidency: Origins and Development, 1776–1993* and *The Politics of Regulatory Change: A Tale of Two Agencies;* and coeditor of *Remaking American Politics.* He also serves as coeditor of the University of Massachusetts Press series, Political Development of the American Nation.

Index